Surrealism and Cinema

MICHAEL RICHARDSON

Oxford • New York

First published in 2006 by
Berg
Editorial offices:
1st Floor, Angel Court, 81 St Clements Street, Oxford, OX4 1AW, UK
175 Fifth Avenue, New York, NY 10010, USA

Berg is the imprint of Oxford International Publishers Ltd.

Library of Congress Cataloguing-in-Publication Data

Richardson, Michael, 1953-
    Surrealism and cinema / Michael Richardson.
        p. cm.
    Includes bibliographical references.
    ISBN-13: 978-1-84520-226-2 (pbk.)
    ISBN-10: 1-84520-226-0 (pbk.)
    ISBN-13: 978-1-84520-225-5 (cloth)
    ISBN-10: 1-84520-225-2 (cloth)
    1. Surrealism in motion pictures. I. Title.

    PN1995.9.S85R53 2006
    791.43'61163—dc22

                              2005033251

British Library Cataloguing-in-Publication Data

A catalogue record for this book is available from the British Library.

ISBN-13 978 1 84520 225 5 (Cloth)
ISBN-10 1 84520 225 2 (Cloth)

ISBN-13 978 1 84520 226 2 (Paper)
ISBN-10 1 84520 226 0 (Paper)

Typeset by JS Typesetting Ltd, Porthcawl, Mid Glamorgan
Printed in the United Kingdom by Biddles Ltd, King's Lynn

www.bergpublishers.com

Contents

Introduction: Surrealist Film Theory and Practice   1

1   Surrealism and Popular Culture   15

2   Luis Buñuel and the Snares of Desire   27

3   Jacques Prévert and the Poetry of the Eventual   45

4   Surrealism and Hollywood   61

5   Surrealism and the Documentary   77

6   Nelly Kaplan and Sexual Revenge   93

7   Walerian Borowczyk and the Touch of Desire   107

8   Jan Švankmajer and the Life of Objects   121

9   *Panique*: A Ceremony Beyond the Absurd   135

10   The Baroque Heresy of Raúl Ruiz   149

11   Surrealism and Contemporary Cinema   165

Notes   173

Selected Filmography   179

Bibliography   187

General Index   195

Film Index   199

Introduction

Surrealist Film Theory and Practice

1

The cinema is the operation of chance.

La Révolution Surréaliste no. 3

The conjunction 'surrealism and cinema' is a seductive one. It evokes an un-defined relation, a meeting point between the opposites of light and dark, presence and absence, actuality and imagination which suggests the actualisation of the supreme point which André Breton identified as the aim of surrealism. So evocative is this concurrence that it already seems present in the human imagination long before either 'cinema' or 'surrealism' actually existed. At least, the surrealist experience of cinema already seems to be familiar to the German romantic poet Novalis, to judge from some of his aphorisms:

> Dark memories hovering below the transparent screen of the present will present images of reality in sharp silhouette, to create the pleasurable effect of a double world.
> The outer world becomes so transparent and the inner world so diverse and full of meaning that one finds oneself in a state of nervous animation between the two.

> (Novalis, 1979: 25–6)

In these two statements, what drew the surrealists to the cinema is already suggested: it lies in its power to disclose what lies dormant within the collective consciousness, making manifest what is latent without destroying the mystery of its latency. In another aphorism we find Novalis writing that 'the viewer is the truly thoughtful man' (Novalis, 1979:26). This suggests a form of dialectic linking thought and sight to plays of light and dark which evokes a condition the surrealists believed the cinema was uniquely qualified to induce.[1]

In everyday parlance, misunderstandings about surrealism abound. This is especially so when it comes to discussing film. We frequently come across the epithet 'surreal' being used to refer to scenes or even whole films in a way that seems wholly arbitrary. At least, it is difficult to find any consistency in such usage. The notion of the 'surreal' is a curious one. Having assumed a vernacular ascription, can we say that it has a precise meaning, or is it simply a lazy synonym? Certainly, where people in the past might have said 'how bizarre!' they tend now to say 'how surreal!' Frequently the word seems to mean nothing, or simply denotes something that is slightly out of the ordinary. It might be tempting to say that such usage of the word represents nothing but a modern derision of language, but Julio Cortazár alerts us to the fact that something more is involved, that it is a characteristic of what he calls the 'realistic naïf':

> You have only to observe his behaviour before the extraordinary: he either reduces it to an aesthetic or poetic phenomenon ('it was really surreal, let me tell you') or rejects at once any attempt to discern in it a dream, a failed act, a verbal or causal association beyond the normal, a disquieting coincidence, any of the momentary disruptions of the continuous. If you ask him, he will say that he does not believe in everyday reality, that he only accepts it pragmatically. But you can bet he believes in it, it's all he believes in (1986: 18).

Any criticial examination of surrealism comes up against the evasion Cortazár identifies: the denial of the discontinuities of reality by reducing attempts to engage with them to the level of an aesthetic or stylist typology.

Thus, the 'surreal' assumes a specificity of usage, which advertising has not been slow to take advantage of: it often means 'strange' in a way that brings to mind the paintings of Dalí or Magritte. Through the visual imagery of these two painters more than any others of the couple of hundred painters to have participated in it, surrealism has been transformed, for many people, into an evanescent category denoting a strangeness, or incongruity, of juxtaposition. This category, reified as the 'surreal', has gained such currency that it is rarely questioned what it might actually mean. It is important, therefore, to emphasise the extent to which surrealism from its very origins has consistently refused to be identified as any sort of style. If both Dalí and Magritte were surrealists, it was to the extent that they embraced a shared moral sensibility; their painting is the result of this commitment rather than its aim. Surrealism has never been concerned with the production of works, even if this is what it is most noted for. The works of surrealism must rather be seen as a residue, a mark of the practice of surrealism. But they are not the essential element of that activity. As Alain Joubert makes clear, Buñuel's *Un Chien andalou*, for instance, 'cannot be considered as representative of some surrealist *form*; if we can witness the birth of a *personal* style in it, this does not represent the codification of a certain type of images according to a model destined to be indefinitely reproduced by others' (1999: 1).

We also need to take into account here the question of intention. Surrealists are not concerned with conjuring up some magic world that can be defined as 'surreal'. Their interest is almost exclusively in exploring the conjunctions, the points of contact, between different realms of existence. Surrealism is always about departures rather than arrivals. From this perspective, there can be no such thing as the 'surreal'. Or rather, if there is it has nothing to do with surrealism. In fact, when something is described as 'surreal' one can almost guarantee that it has no link with or even interest for surrealism.[2] Indeed, the art work of surrealism is so varied that no one would think to describe the work of the vast majority of surrealist painters as 'surreal'. This creates confusion which needs to be elucidated if we are to understand the relationship that surrealism has garnered with the cinema.

The notion of the 'surreal' is especially problematic because the word has gained such currency that it has marketable resonance – in today's parlance of wretchedness it could even, no doubt, assume 'brand-status'. For instance, while researching this book, I came across a web-site listing the thirty-four best-selling 'surrealist' videos. Trying to determine what criteria were being applied to define them as such would have been an exhausting task.[3] This is simply one example among many one could cite. Inconsequential it may seem, but it is symptomatic. Within popular conceptions, surrealism is misunderstood in many different ways, some of which contradict others, but all of these misunderstandings are founded in the fact that they seek to reduce surrealism to a style or a thing in itself rather than being prepared to see it as an activity with broadening horizons. Many critics fail to recognise the distinctive qualities that make up the surrealist attitude. They seek something – a theme, a particular type of imagery, certain concepts – they can identify as 'surrealist' in order to provide a criterion of judgement by which a film or art work can be appraised. The problem is that this goes against the very essence of surrealism, which refuses to be *here* but is always *elsewhere*. It is not a thing but a relation between things and therefore needs to be treated as a whole; the relevance of a particular film or film maker to surrealism depends upon how that film or individual is situated within a set of relations constituted by surrealist activity. Its relationship with film is one of intimacy and affection that has also been subject to jealous fits at times.

2

If surrealism is not a style, it is equally not a fixed set of principles or attitudes. Rather it is a shifting point of magnetism around which the collective activity of the surrealists revolves. It is, as Bruno Solarik expressed it, centred in 'a shared conviction that human integrity is neither based on isolated ideological action nor on isolated creative expression' (2004: 1). If 'surrealism' can be said to 'exist' at all it is in the tension that exists between the activities of the surrealists and the fundamental principles of surrealism as it has historically unfolded.

In order to appreciate the significance of this we need, I think, to explore the tension between 'historical' and 'eternal surrealism'. This distinction was drawn by Jean Schuster at the time of the dissolution of the French Surrealist Group in 1969 and, in making this distinction, Schuster was accused of 'liquidating' surrealism, making it a historically determined movement. The Czech surrealist Vratislav Effenberger made the objections clear in a letter he wrote to Schuster at the time:

> we should know that 'Swift was surrealist in his rage' only through the intermediary of surrealist ideology, which unveils and respects certain specific aspects of Swift's malice and rage. And it is precisely this ideology that is not 'eternal', but 'historic', because it evolves according to the evolution of systems of repression against which it turns. Thus, any state of mind can be surrealist only in so far as its surrealist authenticity can be perceived on the ideological or psycho-ideological plan (in Fijalkowski and Richardson, 2001: 82).

Effenberger's objections are acute, but Schuster's distinction still raises a crucial point in the very definition of surrealist activity. Indeed, the want of dialectical logic Effenberger perceived in Schuster's position could also be discerned in a contrary movement: without an 'eternal surrealism' against which to define itself, historical surrealism is inconceivable. The two concepts are linked through a dialectical tension: as historical surrealism requires an eternal surrealism against which to assess its current activity, so an 'eternal surrealism' is only possible because of the existence of a 'historical surrealism'. If the latter ceased to exist then so too, logically, would the former.

Breton recognised this point from the very beginning. In the *Manifesto of Surrealism*, in the section to which Effenberger is referring, he situated current surrealist activity in relation to its historical avatars. Yet if Swift became 'surrealist in his rage' through the intermediary of a historically situated surrealism which was taking shape in 1924, this did not change the nature of Swift's rage, but isolated an aspect of it that founded a historical continuity between the surrealism of the twentieth century and that of an earlier age which was not yet conscious of itself. These earlier figures were not always surrealists, he declared, because they 'naïvely clung to certain preconceived ideas and because *they had not heard the surrealist voice*, the one which continues to preach at the approach of death and above storms, because they were unwilling simply to devote themselves to orchestrating the marvellous score. Their pride as instruments was too great, and so they have not always conveyed a harmonious sound' (Breton, 1988: 329– 30). The 'surrealist voice' entailed recognition of a necessity, and Breton asserts that acts of *absolute* surrealism had been performed only by the participants of the Surrealist Group at that time.

Later, in *Surrealism and Painting*, Breton made it clear that he was seeking not to trace a 'surrealist art' but rather to situate surrealism within painting, whilst always retaining a clear sense of the separation made explicit by the title: surrealism *and* painting, not surrealist painting. In this work, he gives perhaps the only explicit statement of the qualities that make a work 'surrealist': it should, he asserted, strive to 'encompass the whole psychophysical field', constituted by 'unfathomable depths [in which] there reigns the absence of contradiction, the relaxation of emotional tensions due to repression, a lack of the sense of time, and the replacement of external reality by a psychic reality obeying the pleasure principle' (Breton, 1965: 70). Here we have a starting point for identifying the constituents of what might be considered the quality of a work of art that allows it to qualify under the rubric of surrealism. It is a more refined statement of the general surrealist exigency to seek that supreme point defined in the *Second Manifesto* as the place in which oppositions of real and imaginary, high and low, life and death, and so on, are no longer perceived as contradictions. More simply, the surrealist necessity is to make Marx's demand for 'the transformation of the world' and Rimbaud's demand to 'change life' one and the same thing. It is from this perspective that any consideration of the relation between surrealism and cinema must begin, not from any stylistic or aesthetic considerations.

Surrealism has always been in its very essence a collective movement. It was not simply, like most movements, a coming together of people for the development of their common interests. Nor was it ever an instrument to be used to advance common interests: surrealism made demands on those who approached it. This means that surrealism was and is a living thing. How then does one deal with it without reifying it? It cannot be understood simply through the work of those people who constituted it. Any individual work has to be considered by reference to the common activity of surrealism, by an appreciation of how individual surrealists contributed to it to found the point of convergence at which we can discern, although never definitively situate or articulate, the place at which surrealism can be found.

3

When it comes to the relation of surrealism to cinema, we have to take as a starting point Ado Kyrou's vast panorama, *Le Surréalisme au cinema* (1953, revised 1963), in which he sought to chart the various ways and by-ways of a surrealist response to cinema.

Kyrou's book was written in the early fifties, at the height of the surrealists' interest in cinema, and emerged from a maelstrom of discussions within surrealism but also touching on broader debates about film in France.[4] In it he argues that cinema is in essence surrealist. His whole analysis proceeds from this starting point, as he seeks to show the ways in which a wide range of films from a diversity of sources contain a surrealist charge. But what did he mean by saying that the cinema is essentially surrealist?

Kyrou does not justify his statement. Partly, one imagines, he may have been responding to André Bazin's contrary assertion that film was a fundamentally realist medium. Kyrou doesn't mention Bazin in his book, but we know that he was part of a movement that rejected Bazin's conception of cinema.[5] However, Kyrou was not necessarily completely disagreeing with Bazin, since he was making a different sort of claim: it is not film as such that is surrealist, but cinema: the experience of seeing a film in a darkened hall.

In making his statement, Kyrou was implicitly drawing upon a long history of surrealist responses to cinema. The claim that cinema is a fundamentally surrealist experience is founded upon several elements. The first is the obvious one of the analogy between film viewing and the dream state. However, it is more than this. It is significant that Kyrou entitled his book *Le Surréalisme au cinéma* (surrealism *in* the cinema); the significance being that surrealism is not necessarily embodied by particular films, but is a phenomenon established by the environment of the cinema, created by the relationship the audience creates with the screen. Virtually any film could thus be potentially surrealist, at least if viewed from a certain angle. Conversely, it might be argued that no film could be surrealist if seen on television, because television lacks the possibility of communion, which is the essence of cinema for the surrealists.

If a film could be viewed as surrealist under certain conditions, this did not make this or that film a 'surrealist' one. In fact there is no such thing as a 'surrealist film'. There are only films made by surrealists and films that have an affinity or correspondence with surrealism, as well as those that have no affinity with surrealism (top of the list for Kyrou would be the films of Griffith, Bresson, Cocteau and Disney).

Kyrou was attempting to do for cinema what Breton did in *Surrealism and Painting*: articulate an often intangible relation. Both books are, in their way, definitive in establishing criteria by which we judge the extent of surrealist sympathies and antipathies in respect to their different media, since they were accepted without challenge within the surrealist milieu.[6] If they are definitive *in their way*, however, they are also incomplete and subjective, since both Breton and Kyrou were establishing their criteria of judgement through their own experience. Even so, it must be said that Kyrou's book is not critically rigorous. It was written in a fervour that at times clouded his judgement and his analysis is often superficial, but he had a natural instinct for marking out the path that would reveal the riches a surrealist approach towards cinema might yield. It should not be thought that we can find benchmarks (here or elsewhere) for judging whether a particular art work or film is 'surrealist'. For Breton, this would simply be 'a task for grocers' assistants' (1965: 9). What these books reveal are the historically situated landmarks necessary to enable us to find our own way. In considering the relationship between surrealism and cinema today we need to take Kyrou's work as a starting point. At the same time, it is a work that needs to be held up to critical analysis, both in historical perspective and in view of subsequent developments.

In a famous statement, André Breton once asserted that criticism can exist only as a form of love. Yet Linda Williams, in her book *Figures of Desire*, berates critics who have approached surrealism with 'an overabundance of such love', which is really 'a defence against the possibility of falling out of love' (1981: xi). She may have had a point at the time, although I do not think it is correct to say that the 'love' Breton was evoking 'precludes careful and close analysis'. On the contrary, Williams's own book is a rare example of precisely what Breton meant, in which critical analysis not simply exalts, but extends and enriches an understanding of what is being analysed. I think, however, that she goes against her own precept in basing her whole analysis on the unanalysed assertion of *Un Chien andalou* and *L'Âge d'or* as 'the only unquestionably Surrealist films' (1981: xii). She later justifies this in relation to *Un Chien andalou* in the fact that it is 'the primary source for the spread of a Surrealist style in the commercial cinema, the first film to assault its spectator systematically, the classic example of cinematic poetry, and an important precursor of the current American avant-garde' (1981: 54). For surrealists, I would imagine, these consequences would be more likely to diminish the value of the film. While accepting that these two films have a special place within the history of the surrealist relation with cinema, they should still not be taken as vectors of a surrealist film practice. Williams criticises those critics who have seen surrealism in a broad perspective for failing 'to define adequately the true characteristics of this film movement' (1981: xii). However, surrealism was never in any sense a 'film movement', and to try to see it as though it was is to distort what is most vital about it. In the analysis of film in the context of surrealism we should not be asking whether a particular film or film maker is surrealist. The principal question to be considered ought rather to be: how does consideration of this particular film or film maker in relation to surrealism help us to illuminate either surrealism or the film?

Williams's criticism seems to have been taken to heart by those writing on surrealism and film in English, since virtually everything in the past two decades written on the subject has taken its analysis in a narrow focus, to the extent that a broad view has largely been lost: it is the narrowing of horizons this has given rise to that may risk 'impeding analysis'. In any event, the current work is an attempt to bring analysis to bear on the relation between surrealism and cinema precisely in a broad perspective.

4

Breton marked a certain surrealist 'cinema age' which for him was character-ised by his wanderings around Nantes as a young man in the company of Jacques Vaché, when they were in the habit of going to the cinema without taking any account of what was showing, entering 'at any point in the show, and leaving at the first hint of boredom – of surfeit – to rush off to another cinema where we behaved in the same way ... the important thing is that one came out 'charged' for a few days' (in Hammond, 2000: 73). This experience marks a fundamental surrealist attitude: a refusal to be dictated to by the given. It is why the surrealists are interested in *cinema* rather than in film: it is the environment within which films are shown that provides a place in which the marvellous may be encountered. Breton defined cinema in the *Manifesto*: 'Three cheers for darkened rooms!' If, therefore, film is a realist medium, then the arena in which it was screened effectively subverts this realism.

For the surrealists, going to the cinema was akin to an ancient ritual; it was the place where a modern mystery was enacted. This mystery was facilitated by the environment of the cinema in the early twentieth century. Being admitted to a darkened room, in which images made of light were projected on a screen in front of a group of physically passive spectators, was infinitely conducive to reverie even for the least imaginative of spectators. The fact that the storyline had to be sustained by the use of images and music, with only minimal support from words, made early film a unique medium for the exploration of universal themes. Early cinema equally functioned as a powerful democratising mechanism, since the darkened room abolished class distinctions among the audience, while the fact that speech could not be used meant that language barriers were also temporarily overcome.

This unique atmosphere did not last: each new technical innovation has served to break down the ritual atmosphere the surrealists cherished. In consequence, the surrealist experience of cinema has become increasingly remote with the passage of time. The introduction of sound shattered the cinema's claim to be a modern Tower of Babel, and with the coming of television, video and digital technology – each of which has served an alienating purpose – the ritual sense that once surrounded film screenings diminished. Cinema programming, especially the introduction of separate screenings rather than continuous programmes, has made it impossible to wander from one cinema to another without consulting the programme. The re-organisation of cinema, which seemingly responds to a will to make going to the cinema just another consumer outing (especially since the emergence of the multiplex), has at the same time destroyed any ritual quality going to the cinema once had. In addition, distribution processes have become so sophisticated that the film product has itself become increasingly homogenised: even if it were possible today to go from one cinema to another without consulting the programme, one imagines that the effect would be stultifying rather than energising. Antonin Artaud had already spoken in 1930 of the 'premature old age' of cinema, and one wonders if the sort of 'cinema age' Breton spoke about is still available to young people today. Cinema survives, but generally as a heightened and deliberated activity. Most film-goers would probably be hostile to any idea of treating it as a place of mystery or ritual in the way that was natural to it in the early part of the twentieth century. Nevertheless, the darkened hall remains: we are still alone with strangers experiencing an encounter with images of light which Paulo Antonio Paranagua evokes in this ideal scene:

Whenever the lights were extinguished the enlightened ones believed that the heroic epoch of mysteries had returned with an uninterrupted program of orgies and revels, continuing from week to week, transporting the unknown silhouettes in the theatre pit beyond the Marvellous. The adventurer who took the risk of an incursion into the darkened hall asked only that the ray of light dazzle the vision everyday life with the wonders of a new reality. The provocation felt by each viewer challenged him to let poetry burst into his whole being (1979a: 43).

5

The cinema experience is thus one which converges with the perception of the point of dissolution that is simultaneously also a point of origin, defined by Breton as the 'supreme point'. Cinema, rather than being a reality itself, lies on the edge of realities: there is no certainty in its setting. In this way it remains a place responsive to the perception of such a point of convergence, even if its responsiveness has diminished over the course of the past century.

It is for this reason, and not simply because its flickering images are experienced in a dark room, that the surrealists were able to equate the experience of cinema with that of the dream. Too often (asserted even by intelligent commentators like Adorno) the surrealist interest in dream has been characterised as being principally about bringing to the surface the detritus of the unconscious to provide the artist with new material. While it may be true that surrealist artists have used the dream in this way at times, to characterise this as a surrealist aim is to miss the point.

What the dream offered the surrealists more than anything was an experience of otherness. For them the unconscious did not simply contain the detritus of everyday life, nor was it principally the realm of repressed memory. For all their interest in Freud, they were not concerned to rationalise the dream or the unconscious in this way. Dream was also – and perhaps principally – an arena of unknown experience, one that was contained within the individual, but was also projected onto the collective. It was in this projective quality, as much as in providing an environment analogous with the dream state, that cinema could be equated with dream. Films were projected not simply in a literal but also in a communicative sense: the film was a point of convergence in which a collective myth, emanating from within the unconscious of society as a whole, could be enacted.

The fact that film was a visual medium, centred on the image, was also a key element. Octavio Paz defines the essential quality of the image in these terms as being not to 'explain; it invites one to re-create and, literally, to relive it' (1973: 97).

The power of the image was invoked in the first sentence of *Surrealism and Painting*, in what is perhaps the most hyperbolic statement in surrealism: 'The eye exists in a savage state' (1965:1). We know now without any doubt that this is not true, and Breton himself perhaps ought to have known it, since the findings of Gestalt psychology into the workings of the eye were available at the time. Nevertheless, the statement is significant and bears witness to a surrealist desire to clean the slate, to reach the essence of things. That the eye does not exist in a savage state, that it is in fact the most acculturated of all the senses, does not bring into question the surrealist demand, but gives it a further dimension. What Breton perhaps ought to have written was: 'We need to learn to place the eye in such a state of receptivity that it becomes able to see in a savage way'. At least this is one of the starting points of surrealist cinema, as is underlined by the famous first scene of Buñuel and Dalí's *Un Chien andalou*.

6

If surrealism cannot be seen as a style or a mechanism, equally it is not a mode of existence. Surrealism can never be tied down to a thing; it is a relation between things. We have seen that Kyrou argued that any film could be perceived under a surrealist angle. In considering the phenomenology of the cinema experience, we have demonstrated the ways in which this is the case (and see Petr Král's *Private Screening* [1985] for an example of what this might mean in practice). It would, however, be an exhausting and a hardly rewarding task to discern the surrealist element in a purely arbitrary selection of films. It only makes sense to consider a film within the context of surrealism if it responds in one way or another to fundamental imperatives, either by means of a direct link with surrealist activity or through a convergence of themes or an affinity of intention. This is not always an easy task, however. Since surrealism cannot be fixed and because, in terms of film, it is a relation between viewer and film object, surrealist elements cannot by their very nature be positively identified; and even among participants in surrealism there has never been a clear consensus about which films contain a surrealist charge, even if one could draw up a list of films that may be 'privileged' in one way or another from a surrealist point of view.

At the same time, surrealism has not developed in a vacuum. It demands some active form of involvement. This may be direct (through involvement in collect-ive surrealist activity), indirect (through an active involvement, at a distance, with surrealist ideas) or involuntary (a surrealist intention may be discerned in the film unbeknownst to the film maker). In this book we will engage with each of these aspects, although most of the film makers we will consider in detail belong to the second category.

Little needs to be said to introduce Luis Buñuel, undoubtedly the most well-known film maker to emerge from surrealism, and who always insisted upon the surrealist provenance of his films, even if his active involvement in the Surrealist Group came to an end in 1932. Jacques Prévert's direct involvement in the

Surrealist Group ended even earlier than Buñuel's, but, like the latter, he never compromised surrealist principles, and a continuity of surrealist intent is apparent throughout his work. Nelly Kaplan has never really participated in surrealist collective activity, but has always defined her work in relation to surrealism in general, maintained by numerous friendships within the surrealist milieu. The same thing is true for Walerian Borowczyk. Alejandro Jodorowsky, Fernando Arrabal and Roland Topor participated directly in surrealism for a while, but not in a fully committed way. Raúl Ruiz has never had any direct involvement with surrealism, but his work raises important issues about the relation of film and surrealism that this justifies extended discussion of him as a significant example of a film maker who belongs to the third category enumerated above. In strict terms, Jan Švankmajer is the only major film maker whose work fully belongs to surrealism, in so far as he has conceived and realised the majority of his films in the heart of the Czechoslovak Surrealist Group.

7

These film makers have been chosen as significant illustrations of the range of surrealist involvement with cinema. The not inconsiderable number of other films made by participants in surrealism or on its margins will not be considered in detail because most of them, while certainly not insignificant, are ephemeral. The films made – or, more often, not made – within the surrealist milieu during the twenties and thirties have in any event been subject to an overload of critical attention hardly justified by the importance of the films themselves. Man Ray's films are little more than home movies, as he admitted, now having only a historical interest. The same thing is largely true for the films of Joseph Cornell, although *Rose Hobart* (1936) has a genuinely oneiric and unsettling quality and some of his unfinished films (especially the splendid *Jack's Dream* [1939], which anticipates Švankmajer) suggest a genuine, unfulfilled, cinematic imagination. *The Seashell and the Clergyman* (Germaine Dulac, 1927), drawn from Artaud's script, is an interesting film, but entirely belongs to the avant garde, not surrealism. With the coming of the Second World War and the migration of a significant number of surrealists to the United States, surrealism became an attraction for American avant garde film directors, who appear to have completely misunderstood it (see Benayoun, 1964a, for a compelling critique of these films). The one exception to this miscomprehension among avant garde directors is undoubtedly Maya Deren, whose unfinished film, *Witch's Cradle*, was made in collaboration with Marcel Duchamp, but her films nevertheless cannot really be considered part of surrealism.

Other films, such as *Entr'acte* (René Clair, 1924), those of Hans Richter or Marcel Duchamp's *Anemic Cinéma*, belong to Dada, not surrealism, even if the former has its place within any consideration of the crossover between Dada and surrealist humour. I don't propose to discuss here the relationship between Dada and surrealism. In a broad sense whether there is a continuity or a disjunction between Dada and surrealist concerns is a complex question. In terms of cinema, however, the disjunction seems fairly clear-cut. Thomas Elsaesser points out that what:

> made cinema so powerful a social institution – its ability to simulate in its *textual* effects the psychic apparatus as a desiring machine (the cinema as the most efficient simulacrum of the psychic apparatus when mapped onto the perceptual system, as has consistently happened since Freud) – by and large ran counter to Dada: it was the Surrealists who saw in filmic processes a way of representing the relation of psychoanalysis to matter, mediated through rhetoric and figuration (1987: 26).

Dadaist 'cinema' was anti-film, a negation of film practice, that sought in cinema a kind of utopian space in which the processes of film production would be annulled. This was in conformity with the Dadaist opposition to all values: film, as a form inseparable from the modern progress they denounced, was of value only to the extent that it could contribute to this generalised demoralisation.

The same thing can be said of the later Situationist films, even if the films of Debord have a great deal of substance to them. They were circumstantial, intended to be experienced as part of an environment that could not easily be re-created, and certainly not to contribute to any form of film culture. As such it doesn't seem appropriate to discuss them in the current context (see Agamben, 2002, and Levin, 2002, for accounts of Situationist cinema).

There are a vast number of scenarios imagined by surrealists such as Antonin Artaud, Robert Desnos, Benjamin Fondane and Philippe Soupault which help us to define a certain surrealist relation to cinema, but, being unfilmed or even often deliberately unfilmable, it is one that is static, and has already been subject to a lot of critical comment (see, for instance, Williams, 1981; Kuenzli, 1987).

There are also a number of short films emerging from out of day-to-day surrealism in the fifties and sixties by Michel Zimbacca, Georges Goldfayn, Wilhelm Freddie, Marcel Mariën and Raymond Borde that are of great interest but are difficult to access and, taken as a whole, they are hardly less ephemeral.[7] J. H. Matthews (1971) has adequately described these films, which could be subject to a deeper and more critical analysis, but this would not divulge a greater sense of surrealist involvement with cinema since all of these films were made on a largely amateur basis and as such do not confront the tension between conception, realisation and reception that makes the surrealist engagement with cinema so resonant. Furthermore, analysing films that few of the readers of this book will be likely to have an opportunity to see seems rather self-indulgent.

Other feature films emerging from the surrealists' critical engagement with cinema are equally obscure. Ado Kyrou's *Bloko* (1963) is an interesting, if minor, war film that wears its surrealism so thinly it is difficult to detect. His version of *The Monk* (1973), despite being taken from Buñuel's screenplay, is, from any point of view, a dreadful film: as complete a disaster as one could imagine. The two feature films made by Robert Benayoun, *Paris n'existe pas* (1969) and *Sérieux comme le plaisir* (1971), were both well reviewed at the time but seem since to have entirely vanished from view.[8]

8

The existing literature on surrealism and cinema in English is sadly incomplete, since none of the key books written by surrealists, especially the two works by Ado Kyrou, have been translated. Critical considerations of surrealism frequently show little awareness of the issues they raise, and this has tended to distort the nature of the debates that have been generated in the literature. The major exception and undoubtedly the most important work in English is Paul Hammond's anthology, *The Shadow and its Shadow*. Now in its third edition, each of which have added further material, and accompanied by an indispensable and authoritative introduction, it nevertheless only covers part of the surrealists' engagement with cinema. Two books by J. H. Matthews (1971, 1979) are informative but uncritical, even hagiographic. Matthews was largely concerned to explain surrealist intentions rather than engage with them critically. Both of his books also suffer from the author's lack of real feeling for film (one has the impression that he hasn't actually seen all of the films he writes about, many of which are admittedly, even today, infuriatingly inaccessible). Other books on surrealism and the cinema tend to focus on narrow issues, usually historically limited to the period of the twenties (Kovacs, 1980; Kuenzli, 1987), or to specific films. Linda Williams's incisive *Figures of Desire* (1981) and Robert Short's more recent *The Age of Gold: Surrealist Cinema* (2003) are both excellent, but equally largely limit themselves to discussion of films by Buñuel. A book by Michael Gould published in 1976 with the title *Surrealism and the Cinema* is so stupid that any other comment on it would be redundant – the only value of this work is to reveal the extent to which it is possible to misunderstand surrealism.

9

The history of surrealism cannot be dissociated from the encounter of friends evoked in Max Ernst's famous painting *Au rendezvous des amis* from 1922. It can only be understood, as František Dryje says, as a 'history of formative meetings' (in Švankmajer and Švankmajerová, 1998: 10). It is an activity that emerges from a collective engagement with a set of ideas that have taken a particular historical shape. In terms of film, if we are to understand the significance of surrealist activity, we need to approach it in terms of how particular films and film makers can be situated in relation to this collective activity.

As an idea, surrealism is dynamic or it is nothing; in order to study it, therefore, a degree of ethnographic involvement is necessary, and surrealists are rightly suspicious of scholars who think they can understand surrealism from outside the eddies of its day-to-day activity. In this respect the current work owes an incalculable debt to discussions and conversations with a range of participants within surrealism over the course of many years, most especially with the late Robert Benayoun, Johannes Bergmark, Roger Cardinal, Stephen Clark, Kenneth Cox, Krzysztof Fijałkowski, Mattias Forshage, Kathy Fox, Joël Gayraud, Guy Girard, Allan Grabaud, Paul Hammond, Bruno Jacobs, Alain Joubert, Nelly Kaplan, Rik Lina, Michaël Löwy, Floriano Martins, Marie-Dominique Massoni, Sarah Metcalf, Bertrand Schmitt, Gerald Stack, the late Ludvik Šváb and Gabriela Trujillo. Thanks are also due for their help in innumerable other ways to Satoshi Arai, Ian Christie, Yosuke Dobashi, Tomoko Hosaka, Isabelle Marinone, Elizabeth Williams and Ayako Yoshida.

CHAPTER I

Surrealism and Popular Culture

An interest in popular culture was apparent in surrealism from the beginnings of the movement. Partly this was a provocation against bourgeois notions of excellence, an aspect of the surrealists' revolt against what they perceived as a decadent culture. But it also responded to a deeper need that had drawn intellectuals during the nineteenth century, well represented by Rimbaud's celebration of 'stupid paintings, door panels, stage sets, back-drops for acrobats, signs, popular engravings, old-fashioned literature, church Latin, erotic books with bad spelling, novels of our grandfathers, fairy tales, little books from childhood, old operas, ridiculous refrains, naïve rhythms' (1966: 193).

This attitude had its roots in German romanticism and its revolt against the classicism and elitism of the Enlightenment. Seeking the genius of the *Volk* in the culture of ordinary people, the romantics sought out the traces of folk traditions in their legends, myths and fairy stories. Of course, the surrealists shared none of the latent, and sometimes manifest, nationalism behind the German romantics' valorisation of folk culture. Nevertheless, like the romantics, the surrealists were concerned with the reconsideration of tradition. Their interest, however, assumed a much broader extent: in their internationalism, they were concerned with a universal sense of cultural tradition and what this could mean. The approach was also very different. Where the folk culture that interested the romantics was invisible and had to be actively sought out by individuals like Achim von Arnim and the Grimm brothers, the popular culture that interested the surrealists was only too visible, but was despised by the cognoscenti. Where the folk culture that attracted the romantics belonged entirely to the people who made it, part of an oral tradition passing from person to person in a direct way, the popular culture at the time of the surrealists was irrevocably part of the commercial apparatus of modern society, what Adorno was later to call 'The Culture Industry'. Unlike the romantics, therefore, the surrealists did not have to recover what had been lost or hidden. Their concern was to explore the unconscious motivations of what surrounded them and generally passed unnoticed. Aside from the very significant changes in the productive and distributive processes of society at the beginning of the twentieth century, the intellectual environment was also different. Freud had revealed the way in which the repressions of modern society were unconsciously enacted in often expected ways in collective as well as individual activity. It was this that underlay the surrealists' interest in manifestations of popular culture. At the same time, however, there remains a definite continuity with the motivations that impelled the romantics to be interested in the folk culture of their time.

The world in which surrealism was formed was also very different to the one in which the surrealists had been brought up as children. The First World War destroyed any belief they had in the 'civilising mission' of Western culture, and this caused them to look outside of it for inspiration. From the beginning, the surrealists recognised that what they had been brought up to respect and see as the pinnacle of civilisation was nothing of the sort but rather was deeply implicated in the 'crisis of consciousness' they experienced. Whatever else it may have been, popular culture was largely excluded – at least in terms of its content – from the culture the surrealists opposed, and this made it a potential area for surrealist exploration. We should not infer from this that the surrealists accepted popular culture in its totality: they were well aware of the cretinising impact which the mass media were already having on the circulation of popular culture. In fact, it is probably more accurate to describe what they were interested in as 'oppositional culture' irrespective of whether it was designated as 'high' or 'popular'. They recognised that such phenomena as cinema, comics, penny dreadfuls, dime novels, naïve art, and so on, represented a detritus, what was usually excluded from bourgeois art and yet often contained its cultural contradiction, which meant that it provided fertile ground in which myths capable of motivating a new sensibility could be sown. The surrealists' principal aim was to find means to disrupt the complacency of the dominant cultural traditions and establish the basis for a new way of thinking about cultural tradition.

In this sense surrealism has nothing in common with the more recent re-valorisation of popular culture that has tended to be effected under the rubric of postmodernism. Far from wishing to collapse the distinction between popular culture and high culture, the surrealists emphasised it not so much to valorise the former as to hone it as a tool against the cultural fabric of contemporary society. Popular culture was of interest to the surrealists only to the extent that it had established an insolent and oppositional grounding: in this respect, they did not seek to appropriate it, but saw it as acting in parallel with their own activity. What surrealism found within it was not an amorphous category that can simply be labelled 'popular culture' but rather certain 'popular accomplices' who were pursuing a certain surrealism 'without knowing it' (see Rosemont, 1979).

For the surrealists, such accomplices placed in evidence the genius of ordinary people. This foregrounded a key definition of surrealism, presaging the 'communism of genius' they saw as being one of the directions to be followed in order to create the basis for a new society. At the same time, like Adorno, they recognised that the relationship between high culture and low culture was a dynamic one subject to manipulation by the culture industry. Unlike Adorno, however, the surrealists saw the sites of resistance to this process as lying less within high culture than within popular culture. At times they may even have regarded popular culture as having a greater possibility for subversion than was open to themselves as bourgeois intellectuals confined against their will to a narrow context of endeavour. The work of comic strip artists like George Herriman and Windsor McKay or popular film makers like Louis Feuillade (discussed below) may from a certain perspective be considered more 'surrealist' than the work of the surrealists; that this is a 'surrealism' unconscious of itself was part of its power and allowed it to work its way through the popular consciousness in a way that was not open to the surrealists themselves.

In addition, surrealism took as one of its starting points Ducasse's injunction that 'poetry must be made by all, not by one'. In so far as popular culture was generally collective rather than individual, it offered a greater possibility for the realisation of a contagious modern mythology, something that could be accomplished particularly effectively in film. Of course, this was not a simple matter. Well aware though the surrealists were of the commercial pressures that had in many ways already overwhelmed popular culture, undermining any independent impulse it contained at one level, at another level those very pressures created a tension that encouraged opposition and allowed for a flowering of a popular consciousness of revolt that could not be suppressed by the dominant ideology, which indeed was often oblivious to it. In a broad sense, it seems unlikely that the surrealists would fundamentally have disagreed with anything in Adorno's critique of the Culture Industry (even if they could not have articulated it in such a rigorous way). Yet, while they would no doubt also have agreed with the distinction he made between 'mass culture' and 'popular culture', they did not accept that the former subsumed the latter. Recognition that the primary tension existing between the mass functioning modes of the Culture Industry and the aspirations of creators did not always have negative consequences is a characteristic of surrealists' understandings of modern culture. This is due to their recognition of the potential of the unconscious aspects of the collective mind to overflow into consciousness, in a latent if not a manifest form. In distinction to Adorno, for whom resistance was individual and conscious, the surrealists perceived that it took a more significant form when it was collective and often unconscious. Of course, a belief in the power of the unconscious, both at an individual and a collective level, is one of the determining elements of surrealism.

In so far as surrealists were interested in manifestations of popular culture, then, it was only to the extent that it eluded the massification of culture that was the focus of Adorno's critique of the Culture Industry. As such, they implicitly denied that the Culture Industry was as all-encompassing as Adorno believed. Adorno's theory, of course, is limited by its theoretical presumptions, and his attempts to give it an empirical basis were often disastrous, as in his notoriously unperceptive critique of jazz. This does not necessarily damage the theory: there is always a gap between a theory and the data forming its basis because practice always exceeds the limits of what can be theorised. A surrealist disagreement with

Adorno (this is hypothetical since the surrealists have never directly engaged with his theories, although the surrealist work we have available on popular culture allows such a conjecture) would appear to find its locus in Adorno's view that 'mass culture' is neither of the mass, nor is it culture. This may be true, but it does not then follow that all popular manifestations of culture can be subsumed by such massification, at least not unless one accepts that people are brainwashed by the processes issuing from the Culture Industry.

Adorno's own tastes led him to valorise high culture, the defence of whose purity had become necessary to combat the generalised vulgarisation that mass culture brings in its wake, something he seemed to see as a kind of tidal wave that would, if adequate defences were not prepared, inundate modern culture. While largely accepting that the Culture Industry does function as Adorno describes, the surrealists see the very process of massification as opening up new avenues for exploration that allow for revolt as much within 'popular' as within 'high' culture. Revolt was not, for the surrealists, a privileged state, but a quality of being. For this reason popular revolt and fervour could not be contained by the massification of culture.

In this respect, the surrealists' approach to media may appear, if one wishes to place it in the context of one of the most famous disputes of twentieth-century theory, closer to Benjamin than to Adorno. It is not certain, however, that this is the case, since for the surrealists the 'popular culture' they celebrated was only tangentially linked to technological development; its realisation lay not centrally in those processes, but in their interstices. The expression of popular culture they valorised is a by-product of the Culture Industry, something it paradoxically – although at the same time dialectically – throws up in its will for control and power. It is this very will of domination as it galvanises opposition, if only at an unconscious level, that allows the deeper aspirations of the human spirit to become manifest. This understanding of popular culture as a return of the repressed explains the interest the surrealists had in what were conventionally regarded as bad films. They did not, however, like films because they were bad, and they had nothing in common with connoisseurs of the badly made film. The surrealists always took film seriously, and even when praising technically badly made films they did so to bring attention to the ways in which content could often triumph over form. They never had the condescending attitude of those who praise films as being 'so bad they are good', or who extol the 'camp' or 'kitsch' qualities of this or that film. As Kyrou makes clear, they recognised that production difficulties could often give rise to an involuntary poetry, that the material could impose itself through the intervention of chance. This was not simply a peculiarity of film production. The surrealists recognised the same possibilities in their own work, as when Marcel Duchamp's *Large Glass* was 'completed' by being accidentally smashed in the process of transportation. It was for this reason that Kyrou urged: 'learn to go and see the "worst" films; they are often sublime' (1985: 276).

The relation between surrealism and popular culture has been little studied, but we do have a recently published book by Robin Walz which claims to be a study of it. Although enthusiastically written, it is unfortunately not very enlightening, at least when it comes to its analysis of surrealism. What is curious is that the author appears to have no great interest either in surrealism or popular culture as such; at least the book is only tangentially concerned with either.

It starts promisingly when Walz argues that the surrealists 'drew inspiration from currents of psychological anxiety and social rebellion that ran through certain expressions of mass culture' (2000: 3). Unfortunately, however, he never follows through this insight, and his phraseology already seems inadequate, reflecting a certain attitude that undermines his analysis throughout the book. By saying that the surrealists merely 'drew inspiration' from these currents, he implies that they did not share this psychological anxiety and social rebellion, but simply used it to develop their own ideological position. This seems to reflect the fact that the author, despite himself, is loath to admit popular culture unless it is 'legitimated' by what he sees as a higher authority, in this case as represented by the surrealists. It would surely be more accurate to say that the surrealists recognised their own psychological anxiety and social rebellion within popular culture.

Throughout the book one has the impression that the author is using surrealism as a pretext to explore topics that have a personal interest for him, without having any real understanding of surrealism itself. More serious than the selective and tendentious focus is Walz's conclusion, which in effect dismisses further consideration, asserting that the surrealists lost interest in popular culture after 1930. This claim is no doubt intended to serve as a cover for the fact that Walz's work deals adequately with the surrealists' interest in popular culture neither before nor after 1930.

It was in film (largely ignored by Walz), perhaps more than in any other cultural form (although the early comic strip might run it close), that the surrealist 'affinity' with popular culture is most clearly apparent. We have already considered the arguments that the cinema experience was essentially 'surrealist'. It used to be a commonplace to say that the beginnings of film were marked by a double movement that acted in concert – or opposition – to define the contrary pulls to which film makers were subject. If Lumière opened the cinema with a move towards realism, Méliès made a counter-move to introduce the fantastic and pro-vide cinema with contradictory temptations. This over-schematic characterisa-tion was never very satisfactory and today seems woefully naïve. Nevertheless, it is the case that the surrealist interest in cinema really begins with Méliès, and in their 'advice' of 1951, the surrealists specifically set Méliès against Lumière (Hammond, 2000: 51). Even so, Kyrou recognised that Lumière still 'understood that the cinema is something *other*. In 1895 he projected *Demolition of a Wall* upside down, thus giving the impression that the wall was reconstituting itself on its own, thanks to a reversal of time' (1985: 19). In chapter 5, we will problematise whether it is ultimately possible to oppose Méliès to Lumière when we look at surrealist uses of documentary. For the moment, however, let us consider the significance of Méliès as the initiator of a cinema of the marvellous.

Méliès was important to a surrealist understanding of cinema less for his subject matter than for his attitude. Emerging from the burlesque tradition of popular entertainment, he represented not so much the 'fantastic' aspect of film as its continuity with popular culture. His opposition to Lumière – if one wishes to view it as such – lies not in an opposition between realism and the fantastic but in one between a view of film as a replication of the world that serves scientific classification of it (which was Lumière's starting point) and one that sees film as having its own reality founded in a materiality of form serving its own purposes (which is where Méliès was coming from). This may represent a certain opposition between positivism and magic: for Lumière the camera was essentially a recording instrument; for Méliès, it was a magic apparatus for playing with the marvellous. Rather than assuming one or the other side of these different conceptions of cinema, we ought to see surrealism as collapsing such distinctions.

The quality the surrealists nevertheless especially valued in Méliès was the marvellous. The marvellous is something to be sought – 'the marvellous is always beautiful, anything marvellous is beautiful, in fact only the marvellous is beautiful' (Breton, 1988: 319) – but it is not a state; it is certainly not something outside of or opposed to reality. Nor is it a privileged realm of marvels. If anything, it is a methodological principle, or a tool by which reality can be judged. It is in this that it is opposed to realism, but, being such, does not imply that it stands for a transcendence of realism. This is something critics have always found difficult to follow in surrealism: the marvellous is as much opposed to the fantastic, or any kind of fantasy, as it is to realism. Kyrou emphasises that the characteristic of the marvellous, 'instead of reducing man to the level of a kneeling domesticated animal, lifts him up, makes him aware of the power of revolt and puts him in touch with the treasures he refused to see surrounding him' (Kyrou, 1985: 64; translated in Hammond, 2000: 159).

The distinction between the fantastic and the marvellous, although at times tenuous and difficult to grasp, is important to an understanding of surrealism. The fantastic may be defined as that which accepts the conventions of realism while bringing them into question or going beyond them, so that we are unsure of the ground of reality on which we are standing. In contrast, the marvellous refuses the realist demand for verisimilitude, and reconciles – or holds in tension – the contradiction between real and imaginary, making it propitious to the determining of the supreme point that was surrealism's aim. This does not mean that there is a clear line of demarcation between the fantastic and the marvellous, any more than there is a clear line of demarcation between the marvellous and a realist representation. It is to Adorno, in fact, that we can look for a fine illustration of this distinction. Arguing against the conventional interpretation of Kafka's work, he insists upon the fact that his texts are designed not to sustain a constant distance between themselves and their victim but rather to agitate his feelings to a point where he feels that the narrative will shoot towards him like a locomotive in a three-dimensional film. Such aggressive proximity undermines the reader's habit of identifying himself with the figures in the novel. It is by reason of this principle that surrealism can rightfully claim him . . . fate serves not to deter but to entice (1981: 246).

Here we have a – purely surrealist – explication of the marvellous: it is precisely this quality of enticement, linked to fate, which reveals the working of objective chance and provides the thread of the marvellous that Méliès introduces into the technical miracle of cinema. As Kyrou writes:

> Méliès didn't believe in the solidity of a solid body, in the humidity of waters, in sadness or in boredom, in the immobility of the spirit, in rational logic . . . from an avalanche of gratuitous acts, an intense, salutary poetry is born and as in the most beautiful paintings of the douanier Rousseau an infinite tenderness, a love of the human blossoms in the midst of stylised plants and ghostly apparitions. *Everyone is happy in the films of Méliès* . . . (1985: 68).

As we can discern from Kyrou's comments, what the surrealists particularly admired in the films of Méliès was a communicative quality: he brings us into contact with different worlds. Méliès was less a film *maker* than a conjurer and illusionist who used the moving picture to extend the showmanship and inventiveness of his magical stage performances, in which respect he had already extensively used the magic lantern show, which he described as 'visual sorcery'. In the way he was able to play with appearance and reality, showing the relative rather than absolute nature of time and space, Méliès opened up the possibilities of cinema and set the stage for its later developments.

In Méliès we can see the intimations of a surrealist way of thinking about cinema, but they are as yet only intimations. He reveals its roots in popular entertainment and leads the way for cinema to become a medium of popular communication. The intimations contained in Méliès's films had to wait for their full realisation, however, in the films of Louis Feuillade. Nowhere can one see the unconscious working through of popular receptivity to subversion better than in the films Feuillade made at the time of the First World War.

In his films, Feuillade established many of the conventions that instigate the genres of film that most interested the surrealists: crime and humour were his staples, with an anticipation of the horror film thrown in for good measure.

Louis Feuillade is an unlikely surrealist hero. A politically conservative Catholic royalist, he became a force in French cinema around 1908, when appointed head of production at Gaumont. Incredibly prolific, Feuillade is thought by some estimates to have made around 700 films between 1906 and 1925, as well as writing many screenplays for other directors. Most were short one-reelers, but some were very long (each of his serials ran between five and seven hours).

In 1916 alone, he made one whole serial (*Judex*, five hours in length) as well as completing *Les Vampires* and making sixteen shorter films (whose length varied between fifteen minutes and one hour). At the time he had a considerable reputation as a director of comedies, and his influence on American and burlesque cinema was not negligible. Today, however, his comedies have largely been forgotten (although one can see in his serials that he was a master of comic timing) and his reputation lies in five serials: *Fantômas* (1913-14); *Les Vampires* (1915-16); *Judex* (1916); *Tih Minh* (1918); and *Barrabas* (1919). In many ways, we might see Feuillade as the compleat surrealist director *avant la lettre*, even if such an idea would no doubt have appalled him. This designation calls for some elaboration.

In Feuillade's five serials, anti-social crime is celebrated in ways that have rarely if ever been seen since in film. If we may, in contemporary film, especially since *The Godfather* (1971), have become used to seeing criminals justified, if not glorified, Feuillade shows us something quite different. He does not glorify criminals but the act of crime itself as a motiveless, joyous, exuberant action performed against society, any society, and having its own justification as such. Feuillade's films might be taken up to illustrate Mandeville's *Fable of the Bees* as interpreted by Marx in *Critique of Political Economy*:

> The criminal produces an impression now moral, now tragic, and renders a 'service' by arousing the moral and aesthetic sentiments of the public. He produces not only text-books on criminal justice, not only law books and thus the legislators, but also art, literature, novels, and even the tragic drama, as *Oedipus* and *Richard III*, as well as Mullner's *Schuld* and Schiller's *Räuber* testify. The criminal interrupts the monotony and day to day security of bourgeois life. Thus he protects it from stagnation and brings forth that restless tension, that immobility of the spirit, without which the stimulus of competition would itself become blunted ... (quoted in Green, 1989: 36).

This ambivalence is one of the keys to the world filmed by Feuillade in these serials. Fantômas is the prototype of all of the anti-social criminals to be found in Feuillade's films. The first of Feuillade's serials (although unlike the others it is not strictly a serial, but a series of linked films), it was adapted from the popular novels written by Pierre Souvestre and Marcel Alain from 1911, inspired without much doubt by the activities of the Bonnot Gang, an anarchist group which had terrorised France between 1909 and 1911.

Fantômas is the perfect representative of the contradiction that Marx saw the figure of the criminal embodying. The surrealists found in him a personage sufficiently rich in associations to act as an emblem for the total revolt they advocated, as well as representing the revenge of the repressed within capitalist society. Fantômas, in their eyes, was both the logical outcome of the capitalist attitude (his only motive seems to be to make money by whatever means necessary, especially the most nefarious) and its negation (Fantômas seems to want money in order to dissipate or waste it, not to accumulate it). He represents the sleeping evil residing in our subconscious, likely to come to the surface and strike at any time. If he is the embodiment of evil, it is a disinterested evil, an evil that surges up as a necessary response to the self-interested evils underlying capitalist society.

Fantômas lies at the heart of any crime that is committed. His attacks on society are devastating because they come from within and they are all-encompassing: no one is exempt from being his victim, but at the same time anyone may become – wittingly or unwittingly, it hardly matters – his accomplice. In fact, the distinction between victim and accomplice sometimes vanishes altogether: what Fantômas really steals is people's souls (though without being in the service of the Devil – as with money, his concern is to dissipate souls, not make them subject to him). His is a secret existence: he is everywhere and nowhere all at once, an endlessly mutable personage able to blend in with his environment and to choose his character to correspond to it. At war with society, Fantômas is more a spirit, existing wherever society has a weak point, than a man. He induces fear not because of what he does, but simply because he exists. Fantômas figures only in the first of Feuillade's films but his character provides the template from which he developed the shadowy beings who populate his later films, most memorably the female outlaw Irma Vep, incarnated by the surrealists' heroine, Musidora.

The surrealists liked Feuillade precisely because he was able to address a popular audience without being patronising but also without being trivial. They had in fact grown up with his films. His working methods, too, were what the surrealists approved: working quickly, being unafraid to improvise and being largely unconcerned with logic in his storylines were all qualities that the surrealists saw as being akin to automatic writing, which may also partly explain why the films could have contained a subversive message unbeknownst to the film maker.

Even more significant, Feuillade's films are redolent with a sense of the marvellous, much more so than in Méliès. They evoke a world in which fantastical events surge forth in the most everyday situations. Filmed on location, often in Paris locales the surrealists knew well, the films assume a dream atmosphere that is uniquely material and matter of fact. This especially emphasises the strangeness of some of the imagery, which attains a poetic delirium that has rarely been equalled in the cinema.

Feuillade was a director who had a powerful sense of the tangibility of the physical world: one does not so much watch his films as enter them. In this world, the characters seem to be engaging in dreamlike conspiracies that are without motivation (or if they have a motivation, it is one that goes beyond their own consciousness), which suggests the workings of some landscape that is both of this world but at the same time elsewhere: anything may happen at any time. Fuillade creates a mood of uncertainty in which characters and situations are strangely mutable. Nothing is stable: one thing may assume another aspect without notice. And it is so compelling that we, as spectators, always feel part of this mystery. Feuillade never allows us the luxury of either distance or familiarity. Our fascination comes from the fact that we are at once within the frame of the picture and outside of it.

We are faced with the enigma of Feuillade's work: how do we reconcile the fact that these films were made by a man who apparently harboured conservative, not to say reactionary, sentiments? Feuillade thought of himself as a popular film maker. He was simply, as Hollywood producers later liked to claim, 'giving the public what they wanted'. He seems to have been as suspicious of 'intellectuals' as any of the later Hollywood moguls. Was he, then, devoid of any moral consciousness when making his films, but simply went with the flow of whatever the box office demanded? Even if this were so, it would beg questions as to why such films were so much in demand during the period surrounding the First World War.

There is a sense, however, in which we might recognise that Feuillade's reactionary sentiments converged with a public mood disillusioned with the modernity that had underwritten the First World War, and that, far from there being a contradiction between what appears to us as an almost anarchist sensibility in many of the films and Feuillade's political views, the two may not have been so far apart. In *Judex*, the film he made to satisfy those who had condemned the apparent anarchism of *Les Vampires*, the underlying sentiments appear to be the same as in the film that was criticised by the authorities. While the hero, unlike Fantômas or the apache gang in *Les Vampires*, appears to be upholding natural justice, it is a justice that is contrary to bourgeois law. Kyrou was doubtless right to insist that 'the eternal censors did not understand that for Feuillade, good and evil were not contradictory, that these notions did not even exist in his films and that Fantômas and Feuillade belonged to the great family of liberty' (1985: 56). Thus we can say that if Feuillade was a 'reactionary', it was in the best sense of the word, since it imbued his work with a refusal of the given. At a manifest level he and the surrealists would hardly have seen eye to eye had they discussed their respective politics; below the surface, however, there is a point at which their attitudes, especially towards the modern world, conjoined and flowed into one another.

To argue this is not to deny that, for the most part, the motivations of Feuillade's films are unconscious and come from his method of working. In this respect, he was doubtless not so different from his contemporaries, but he appears to have grasped the material process of making film more effectively than any other director of his time. Of course, film was already an industry, perhaps more strongly so than it became later. Directors did not think of themselves as artists, Feuillade least of all: they were artisans making a product. Yet this industry did not yet have the cynicism that came to dominate it with the development of Hollywood. Producers did not so much try to form or manipulate public taste as to merge with it.

One should also not underestimate the effect of the technical limits of early film making. The limitations of early cinema were not simply restrictions; they also imposed a discipline which would be lost as the technique of film became more sophisticated. This was especially so in respect of the relationship between film maker and audience. Early cinema was popular because it was essentially a collaboration between the film maker and audience. For the film to work, the director had to take the audience into his confidence. This pact between film maker and audience was fundamentally ruptured by the revolution in editing techniques that D. W. Griffith effected with *The Birth of a Nation,* made as Feuillade was filming *Les Vampires.* As Griffith established the principles of modern film language as being based upon fast cutting and the movement of the camera, so he was giving to directors a power over the film which meant they could lead the audience into the film, giving or withholding information as they saw fit. The room open for the viewer to enter into the film on terms other than those established by the director was diminished; instead of a relationship between film maker and audience, the audience were encouraged to foster a sense of identification with the characters on the screen, *as though they were real characters* (the basis of the 'suspension of disbelief' catechism which realism insists we need in order to appreciate films).

Feuillade's characters, which rely on an extension of the imagination, could have no place in such a world. Furthermore, after Griffith, film making became a matter of editing and montage, something alien to Feuillade's way of making films, and which immediately made them seem dated. However, it might be argued that Griffith's cinema did not represent an advance over the way Feuillade made films, but rather established different principles. It did not so much represent a step forward in the process of film making as prioritise certain techniques while disqualifying others. In this sense, it might rather be seen as effecting a paradigm shift, in the Kuhnian sense. For what is amazing when looking at Feuillade's films today is how fresh they are. Indeed, once one has got used to the different conventions being used, Feuillade's films hold the attention more easily than most films made now (it is difficult to imagine any modern director being capable of making a seven-hour film that is as enjoyable to watch as *Les Vampires*). Early cinema in fact appears to offer a different model of how a film should be made, one that was abandoned after Griffith. What is important in Feuillade's films is not editing but staging. Each image is conceived in terms of its composition, so that drama is created not through the juxtaposition of images but through movement *within* the image. This is allied with a careful use of location to heighten the action. The effect is to leave the viewer less subject to manipulation and freer to imagine the film in multiple ways, which seems to result in the compulsive quality that Feuillade's films have. Only a very few modern directors are able to construct the image with anything like the skill Feuillade brought to the task. Equally important from a surrealist point of view was the fact that Feuillade's way of making films showed how responsive cinema potentially was to the sort of spontaneous creation the surrealists sought through techniques of automatism (an automatism, too, that was centred in collective rather than individual activity).

Surrealist disillusion with cinema lies in the fact that the possibilities opened up by Feuillade's films were almost immediately closed down again.

Feuillade's films thus point to a direction in which film making might have developed but didn't. In Feuillade one might say that a popular 'surrealist' cinema was born and died before surrealism as such came into existence. Even for directors like Buñuel and Resnais, who were greatly influenced by Feuillade, changes in production standards meant that any return to his way of making films was impossible. The ultimate consequence was that films were divided into two categories, later theorised by Third Cinema advocates as a First Cinema characterised by the high production values of the Hollywood 'factory' and an 'art' cinema divorced from a mass audience, a distinction reinforced at every level of the production and distribution network. This did not occur all at once of course, and even today is possible to bridge the gap between them, but one can never escape the paradigm that had been established, as those film makers who sought to create a Third Cinema discovered: one either capitulates to them or remains marginalized. A genuinely 'popular' cinema, one which makes direct contact with the audience in the way that was natural in early cinema, is impossible: everything is mediated in one way or another by the demands and processes of the film industry.

Although we have today become accustomed to taking popular culture seriously, the surrealists' understanding of popular culture pre-dates and is of a quite different nature from this current interest. They were not interested in the mechanics of popular culture for sociological reasons but in the ways in which revolt came to be inscribed within it. What we think of as 'popular culture' now in any event doubtless bears no relation with that which existed a century ago. The atomisation of today's world – its mediated nature – makes the very concept of a genuinely 'popular' culture unlikely, if not impossible. It would no longer, I suspect, be appropriate to speak of surrealism's 'popular' accomplices because it is not possible to evade the mediating controls of the mass market. Adorno may have been empirically mistaken in his discussion of the mass culture of his time, but he was alarmingly prescient about the massification process that constituted it and which now seems irresistible. In cinema history, this did not happen all at once, and Griffith was not a simple villain. The innovations he introduced had positive as well as negative aspects. A surrealist understanding of the history of cinema, however, alerts us to the fact that the type of cinema that Griffith made possible served as the first stepping stone (having a similar significance for cinema to Brunelleschi's discovery of perspective for art history) onto a path that cinema became ideologically obliged to take (because it served the requirement of the capitalist system that underwrote the way films could be produced and distributed). As inevitable as this development may now seem, we shall see in chapter 4 how it occurred only over a very long period of time, and that even in Hollywood films have often been notable for the extent of their resistance to incorporation into this process.

CHAPTER 2

Luis Buñuel and the Snares of Desire

For many people, including most of the surrealists who have written on cinema, Luis Buñuel is *the* surrealist film maker. For Octavio Paz, Buñuel 'shows us that a man with his hands tied can, by simply shutting his eyes, make the world jump. Those films are something more than a fierce attack on so-called reality; they are the revelation of another reality which contemporary civilization has humiliated' (1986: 52). For surrealist film critics Ado Kyrou and Robert Benayoun, likewise, Buñuel could do no wrong. In drawing up his ideal surrealist programme of films, Alain Joubert included a Buñuel film in every category, which he explains as indicating 'how much the strong points of surrealism profoundly impregnated the mind of this free man, throughout his life as a film maker and a poet' (1999: 2). André Breton and Benjamin Péret also emphasised the continuity of surrealist themes in his work, Breton speaking of 'Buñuel's spirit which, like it or not, is a constituent part of surrealism' (1993: 164), while Péret observed 'a remarkable continuity, because Buñuel's fixed idea in all of his films is the denunciation of a world of ignorance and poverty' (1992: 278). Despite his 'resignation' from the Surrealist Group in 1932, Buñuel later asserted his fundamental surrealist credentials, and the case for him to be regarded as *the* surrealist film maker would seem to be open and shut.

If the surrealists themselves seem largely agreed that Buñuel is the quint-essential surrealist film maker, so too do critics, a few dissenting or sceptical voices notwithstanding. The main point of contention has been whether his whole body of work should be considered within the context of surrealism, or only his first two or three films. If the latter is the case, then what relation exists between his early surrealism and the concerns of his later films?

Certainly throughout Buñuel's films there is a discernible thematic continuity that essentially seems in harmony with a surrealist world view. Buñuel is also probably unique as a film director in the fact that, more or less, as Robert Benayoun remarked, each of his films went beyond the previous one, in the sense that each new film, without demonstrating any 'advance', deepened and made more incisive the central themes of the others (1974: 23). Most critics would probably agree with this. The question is therefore raised as to whether this unfolding is something that can be said to have transpired *through* surrealism or whether surrealism was simply something that nourished Buñuel's evolution as an artist. Did it even occur *despite* surrealism?

In researching Buñuel's involvement in the murky world of French and Spanish communism in the thirties, for instance, Paul Hammond (1999, 2004) has introduced a note of caution about Buñuel's commitment to surrealism. He locates a certain cynicism in Buñuel's attitude and argues that his 'resignation' from the Surrealist Group in 1932 was more significant than it has been generally regarded.

The question of authorship is of some significance here because, more than most major directors, Buñuel always relied upon collaborators to realise his vision. We know, of course, that *Un Chien andalou* was as much Dalí's work as it was Buñuel's. Petr Král (1981b) has also clearly shown how Dalí's influence remained pervasive in *L'Âge d'or,* even if he was not directly involved in the film making. Paul Hammond (1997) has gone further, arguing that the latter film was essentially a collaboration of the Surrealist Group, no doubt made coherent by Buñuel, but in the ensemble of which he was but one voice among many. There equally seems little doubt about the collaborative nature of *Las Hurdes*, the third of Buñuel's early films, in which Pierre Unik's contribution was probably as important as Buñuel's own.

In so far as *Un Chien andalou* was a realisation of Dalí's and Buñuel's ideas (although one feels that Pierre Batcheff's contribution must also have been of some significance), we can see in it the genesis of Buñuel's own approach only indistinctly. As both Dalí and Buñuel made clear, *Un Chien andalou* represented a miraculous meeting of minds. Although it is quite possible to extract from it elements that belong to one or the other, it seems vain to do so since the power of the film comes precisely from the convergence of two sensibilities. And if we can see images and ideas that recur later in the work of one or the other of them, this may not mark their own contribution to the film, but represent a fascination triggered by what the other man had suggested: a contagion of possibilities was clearly at work here. Furthermore, *Un Chien andalou* is probably the most over-analysed film in cinema history and one is reluctant to add still more critical exegesis to it. In fact, in order to see it with fresh eyes, it is probably more necessary to remove some of the critical grime that has adhered to it. Petr Král reminds us that its conventions (as well as those of *L'Âge d'or*) are largely drawn from Hollywood burlesque comedy (1981b: 47). More extreme, more self-aware and conscious of a broader cultural context though they may have been, one has to agree with Král that both of Buñuel and Dalí's films reveal a continuity of intention with Keaton, Chaplin, Harry Langdon, and so on, in their plays with narrative logic and lack of respect for social codes and correct behaviour. Like silent comedies, too, the films are held together not by the editing (as impressive as it may be) but by timing: *Un Chien andalou* is probably the most well-paced film in the history of cinema. It is important to remember that these conventions would have been far more familiar to a contemporary audience than they are to us today, and our unfamiliarity today with them may mask from us the essential playfulness of the two films. As Král emphasises, they take their power not from symbols but, again like burlesque comedy, from gestures, which often assume an insolent form.

A passport into surrealism rather than a surrealist work in itself, *Un Chien andalou* became part of surrealist mythology. As is well known, however, the surrealists – and Buñuel himself – were ambivalent about the reception accorded to the film, seen as part of the avant-garde they despised; a 'passionate call to murder' had been domesticated.

The remarkable convergence of two minds that *Un Chien andalou* represented was carried over into *L'Âge d'or* but extended to reveal a collective accomplishment. Here I see no reason to dissent from Hammond's view that *L'Âge d'or* has to be seen as a collective effort of the Surrealist Group, in which Buñuel's voice is probably dominant, but not determining. Buñuel asserted as much himself. Speaking of *L'Âge d'or* he said, in conversation with Max Aub: 'My ideas are clearly visible. Not mine, the ideas of the Surrealist Group are clearly visible' (quoted in Hammond, 1997: 42).

While there can be no doubt that *L'Âge d'or* is the key film of surrealism, it does not follow that it provides a model by which the work in film of other surrealists can be judged. On the contrary, in fact: *L'Âge d'or* was the result of a unique set of circumstances unlikely ever to have been repeated. The fortunate configuration that made the film possible was that a young ambitious film maker appeared in surrealism at a time when a wealthy sponsor associated with the surrealists, the Vicomte de Noailles, wished to support film as a vanity project. The role of Marie Laure de Noailles was crucial for acting as a mediator between her husband and the surrealists. Buñuel's first three films were the result of such objective chance: *Un Chien andalou* having been financed by his mother, *Las Hurdes* by an anarchist friend who happened to win the lottery. Few, if any, film makers have started with such generous and indulgent producers. None, I would venture, have ever used their patrons' generosity in so devastating a way.

This was especially significant in respect of *L'Âge d'or*. The generous terms of its sponsorship not only offered Buñuel the opportunity to make an ambitious film on his own terms; they also allowed the Surrealist Group, for the first and only time, to make a collective contribution to the making of a film. Paul Hammond (1997) asserts that Max Ernst, Gaston Modot, Jacques Prévert and Jean Aurenche (Prévert and Aurenche would in fact later become two of the most important writers in French cinema) all had a hand in the script, which probably was also passed around the members of the Surrealist Group for comment and amendment. It is this that makes it not only the most surrealist film but also the most surrealist work *tout court*: the fact that it went beyond individual authorship to express a collective vision. Although all films are collaborative and although, like the vast majority, the overall shape must be credited to its director, *L'Âge d'or* is probably also unique in film in that the collaboration took place at the thematic rather than organisational level; it was not, that is, a matter of people sharing ideas in order to make an effective film, but of their using the film medium to explore their ideas in common.

We can glean the extent to which *L'Âge d'or* was a surrealist project from the manifesto the surrealists wrote to accompany the film's first screening. This is not a document written as a comment or commentary. It does not appear to be a reaction to the film, but something coterminous with it; it is a programmatic extension of the themes the film treated.

This text, written by Breton, Crevel, Éluard, Aragon and Thirion, bears witness to debates taking place in the Surrealist Group at the time. This is not to say that the film is simply an application of surrealist principles to the cinema. Far from it: the fascination of the film comes from the extent to which surrealist concerns were transfigured onto film, via the intermediary of Buñuel, of course, but still in a way that emerged from the collaborative effort of the surrealists as a group.

Despite its prestige, *L'Âge d'or* is a difficult film to analyse, precisely perhaps because of the number of different voices it contains. This marks it as very different from its predecessor. *Un Chien andalou* is a critic's delight, since it leaves itself wide open to interpretation; *L'Âge d'or*, in contrast, is opaque, making critical interpretation extremely difficult. Indeed, it almost seems to have been designed to set traps for critics, traps into which many of those who have written about the film have fallen. Where *Un Chien andalou* directly assaults the spectator, but does so in such a way as to flatter the spectator's masochism, *L'Âge d'or* is a smouldering pit of sulphur, the approach to which is dangerous and has to be negotiated with caution. It cannot be denied that *L'Âge d'or* is a film of uncompromising revolt that illuminates central surrealist attitudes towards society and human relationships. Beyond this, we can say that what the film is not is precisely what many critics have taken for granted as its starting point: an assault on bourgeois hypocrisy. If bourgeois hypocrisy is represented in the film, this is tangential to, or a minor aspect of, its central theme, which Linda Williams, in an exemplary analysis, has identified as nothing less than the founding and dissolution of civilisation. Her statement that '*L'Âge d'or* is a questioning of society and of the illusory unity of the social body, once more through the disruptive force of erotic desire' (1981: 131) is as concise a summation of the film's central theme as it is possible to give. Beyond this, critical exegesis runs the risk of distortion. It is a film of infinite richness and all of the themes of the film will be explored further by Buñuel in his later work. In fact one could see *L'Âge d'or* as the embryonic form of all of his films. It might even be said that they are expositions of it, to the extent that one might wonder if Buñuel wasn't himself disturbed by the film and spent the rest of his career seeking to explicate its implications.

In this respect it is difficult entirely to accept Petr Král's (1981b) assertion that there is no essential difference between the two early films, that *L'Âge d'or* is simply a continuation of *Un Chien andalou*. Král is undoubtedly right to insist on the fact that the thematic of the earlier film was carried over into *L'Âge d'or*, and that the two films are equally brilliant. However, it is surely the case that they provide a counterpoint to one another rather being than two halves of a single assignment. Linda Williams (1981) sees *Un Chien andalou* as 'psychological', while *L'Âge d'or* is 'anthropological', which is a useful, if provisional, starting point. But *L'Âge d'or* is still a thematically richer and more disturbing film than *Un Chien andalou*.

The prestige of *L'Âge d'or* has tended to be taken for granted. This has its dangers, and we need to be wary of the fact that, even as we assert it as *the* surrealist film, we may be recuperating it. In so far as it makes visible a surrealist collective vision, it seems to provide us with a vector by which to judge surrealism as a practice. In doing so, however, it sets up a snare. The fact that its prestige is effectively guaranteed by the scandal it created and its subsequent notoriety tends to imbue it with a myth-like status and so eclipses the surrealists' other efforts in film. Furthermore, its very visibility now also makes it subject to processes of recuperation, in so far as it offers a pretext by which surrealism may be 'explained'. Yet surrealism was never concerned to scale some ladder of achievement, as Americans may strive to write the 'Great American Novel'. On the contrary, for surrealism 'perfection is *laziness*', as Breton and Éluard emphasised in their *Notes on Poetry*.

L'Âge d'or was made at a key moment in surrealist history. The period of the surrealists' most direct political involvement, which caused wide dissention within the group and provided the backdrop to the 'crisis' of 1929, it was also the time that they most intensely confronted questions of personal morality and explored the intricate webs of sexuality and love (indicated by the 'Recherches sur la sexualité' and the 'Enquête sur l'amour' which appeared in the final issue of *La Révolution surréaliste* that same year). *L'Âge d'or* has to be seen against the background of these explorations.

The film has often been seen as a love story founded in rage (although Linda Williams [1981] reminds us that the love story is only present in two of the film's five distinct sections). And it is in this rage that it presents us with the exemplary surrealist text. As the accompanying surrealist manifesto has it, the film brings us the 'gift of violence': the lead characters struggle to overcome the obstacles placed in the way of the realisation of their love. Yet, at the same time, as Petr Král points out, 'the film is less about love and desire as about their frustration and the obstacles they encounter' (1981b: 47). And this frustration is not simply social; it is also contained within the lovers themselves. 'Love', indeed, is even revealed through separation, if one accepts the proposition of the surrealists' manifesto: 'one of the culminating points of this film's *purity* seems to us crystallised by the image of the heroine in her room, when the power of the mind succeeds in sublimating a particularly baroque situation into a poetic element of the purest nobility and solitariness' (in Hammond, 2000: 200).

This statement alerts us to the fact that these characters do not represent the exemplary surrealist couple: as febrile as their love is, it is also as if detached from them. Passionately drawn to one another, to an extent that causes them to tear at the restraints society places on love, they are still only able to relate *beyond* one another. We see this most clearly in the scene when they appear to reach some orgasmic climax in the garden. Occurring under the sign of Thanatos as it does, the scene is still more disturbing in that, far from conjoining the lovers, it seems to emphasise their distance from one another. Král, for instance, points out how, when we see the woman transformed into an old lady, the man remains as he is; this is thus not a representation of her aged self (and thus a sign that their love has transcended temporal limits) but signals the fact that she has been transformed into the man's mother. The tragedy for the man and the woman is that, as much as they tear at the immediate restraints of society, it is their own oedipal subjugation they are really fighting, which they appear unable even to begin to confront.

The couple are thus not simply suffused with the power of love; they are also victims of it. We should here remember, too, that they remain bound by their class background. Even as their love induces their revolt, the mores of their class remain entrenched within them. The man is, after all, a politician, and his behaviour may at times even bring to mind the arrogance we see frequently in politicians who think they are above the law (as a class, we might reflect, few people have less respect for the law than politicians). His attitude may even remind us of numerous politicians whose careers have been destroyed through their inability to control their sexual appetites. In fact, while his behaviour may provoke an immediately scandalous reaction, this is soon forgotten and in the end is largely tolerated it in much the same way as the lies and indiscretions of politicians today scandalise us while generally being indulged. In *L'Âge d'or* the man, having been arrested, is released purely on the basis of his political authority, and, although he is reproved for slapping the hostess at the party, the police are not called and he is not even actually thrown out, merely 'disowned' by polite society, to the extent that when he surreptitiously returns to the salon, the initially disapproving looks he receives almost immediately turn to indifference.

We will return to look in greater detail at the themes of *L'Âge d'or* in the context of Buñuel's later films. For now it is enough to signal its thematic complexity and how difficult it is to impel it to divulge its meaning. Many of the implications of the film were even concealed from the surrealists (including Buñuel) themselves, something which, far from being a weakness, is the indication of the film's authenticity: it uniquely gave expression to a collective surrealist unconscious. It may even be the case that the broadness of its canvas and the fact that it is the expression of multiple voices, which may at times be in conflict with one another, make any definitive interpretation of the film impossible. It is this that seems to mark its fundamental difference from *Un Chien andalou*, since here the convergence of voices plays beyond a harmony of approach towards a dissonance of affect.

Yet, if we are right in seeing *L'Âge d'or* as a uniquely collective effort, how do we situate Buñuel the film maker in relation to it and – by extension – to surrealism?

In strict terms, the film represents Buñuel's only substantial contribution to surrealism. Aside from a few largely inconsequential writings, he produced nothing else during the period in which he was directly associated with the surrealists. We might question the extent to which Buñuel saw even *L'Âge d'or* as more than a stepping stone in his career as a film maker. When the scandal of the film broke, he was not in Paris but in Hollywood and seems to have been more embarrassed than thrilled by the commotion it had generated. In fact he appears to have shown greater solidarity with the plight of his sponsor, the Vicomte de Noailles, than with the surrealists' efforts in support of the film. Ironically, given his latter disavowal of the film, it was actually Dalí who was most active in defending it at the time. Even in his autobiography, Buñuel tells us virtually nothing about the film itself, confining himself to recounting details about its filming. In fact he claims that he has never seen the film again and 'I am incapable today of saying what I think about it' (1982: 141). A curious reticence, given the resonance the film had, in terms both of Buñuel's career, and of the history of surrealism.

In any event, the ideas Buñuel was considering for future productions were not continuations of the incendiary cinema *L'Âge d'or* represented but attempts to integrate his own vision within a commercial framework. They were, in fact, projects much like the sort of films he was later to make in Mexico: *The Duchess of Alba and Goya* and his (or rather Pierre Unik's) adaptation of *Wuthering Heights* (which he actually did later make, although using a different script). It appears that Buñuel re-worked *L'Âge d'or* into a more acceptable form. Completed in 1934 as *In the Icy Waters of Egotistical Calculation*, this new version apparently pleased the Vicomte de Noailles, but it was still banned by the censors and virtually no one else ever saw it. It is difficult to see how any re-working of the film could have been anything but a betrayal but, since it no longer exists, we cannot know this for certain. However, that Buñuel was prepared even to consider re-editing the film tends to indicate that he did not regard it as sacrosanct (although it should be said that Buñuel himself claimed to have done no more than change the title in a futile attempt to elude the censors [see Colina and Perez-Turrent, 1981: 14]).

This might cause us to question the extent of Buñuel's commitment to surrealism, even at the time he was actively involved with it. Paul Hammond (1999, 2004), at least, has cast doubt on it. Despite his later avowal of fundamental, if not total, adherence to surrealist principles, Hammond argues that Buñuel had in reality abandoned surrealism by 1932 for Stalinism for the same opportunist reasons as his friend Aragon and only subsequently re-made himself as a surrealist, dissembling the extent of his break with surrealism in order to legitimate his later career.

Some of Hammond's evidence is circumstantial and his conclusions are debatable, but he does show that Buñuel was less than frank about the extent of his involvement with communism, arguing that he remained sympathetic to Stalinism even into the sixties. In this respect, Hammond finds Buñuel's 'resignation letter' from surrealism, sent to Breton on 6 May 1932, 'epochal'. Personally I don't find it so. It seems on the contrary to be an honest exposition of a dilemma. Buñuel recognises an incompatibility between membership of the Communist Party and participation in surrealist activities. There is no dissembling here, no attempt to play both ends against the middle, as Aragon and later Éluard tried to do. Defining his priorities, Buñuel decided that communism was more important to him than surrealism. Yet, he seems unequivocal that this does not mean a rejection of surrealism:

> My separation from your activity does not imply the complete abandonment of ALL your conceptions, but only those that TODAY are opposed to the acceptance of surrealism by the PC, and which, I emphasise, are of a formal and passing nature. For instance, in the matter of poetics, there can be no question of my having any other conceptions than yours even as it is impossible for me today to maintain a 'closed' conception of poetry standing above the class struggle (Thirard, 2000: 64).

The evidence we currently have is insufficient to determine the extent to which Buñuel retained a commitment to surrealism during the thirties and forties. For myself, I do not see him as a man of strong commitments, but rather as someone who allowed himself to be carried along by the currents that seemed most immediately present to him. Whatever the case, however, when his career as a film maker resumed in the fifties it is clear that he had retained empathy with surrealist ideas, as his important essay of 1953, 'Cinema, Instrument of Poetry', reveals (in Buñuel, 1995: 136-41; also in Hammond, 2000: 117-21). What Buñuel always seems to have emphasised when speaking of his relation to surrealism was its moral sensibility and its communal sense. In his autobiography, for instance, he reasserts that: 'For the first time in my life I'd come into contact with a coherent moral system that had no flaws. It was an aggressive morality based on the complete rejection of all existing values' (1982: 107).[1]

Whatever doubts we may have about his commitment, in this respect there was certainly something elemental about Buñuel's involvement with surrealism. Those three years Buñuel spent in the Surrealist Group appear to have been determining for him, providing him with a framework within which he could think through issues that were of concern to him and realise himself as a film maker. It should therefore not be a matter of evaluating whether or not this or that film provides evidence of Buñuel's surrealism, but of being aware of how the contagious atmosphere which surrealism generated (which problematises any clear assigning of individual authorship) underlies and provides us with a greater understanding of the films. Buñuel's career was a process of maturation, and we ought arguably to see the early films not as statements of surrealist intent made by Buñuel as a young man to which he remained (or did not remain) true, but rather as a prelude to a film career which engaged, often in a problematic way, with ideas as he experienced them at the time of his active involvement in the Surrealist Group. Rather than Buñuel's contribution to surrealism being confined to his first two or three films, it is only when he finds his own voice, in the films from the fifties, starting with *Los Olvidados*, that Buñuel really engages with surrealism. In *L'Âge d'or*, I think, what we see is Buñuel articulating ideas that were collectively present within the environment of surrealism.

From this perspective *L'Âge d'or* is interesting in being both like and unlike Buñuel's later work. He drew upon the ideas contained in it in ways that suggest that he was as much inspired by the film as the inspirer of it.

In considering Buñuel's contribution, Paul Hammond comes to a somewhat perplexing conclusion: 'Surrealism's sinuous sublations over half a century frequently got the best out of those who were drawn to the movement, but it also consumed them, drove them away, and what they subsequently achieved was an extramural "sort of" surrealism adulterated by alien influences' (2004: 24). Presumably Hammond sees Buñuel's later films as part of this ersatz 'sort of' surrealism. But what does this mean? Can surrealism really be isolated in this way from what surrounds it? Is there a pure surrealism and then various degrees of its adulteration? How is one to make such a distinction?

Buñuel's films do not represent an unproblematic surrealist continuity. If this continuity nevertheless does exist, it unfolds in a way that is often problematic. Far from this being a weakness, however, it may be a strength. Rather than being a 'surrealism adulterated by alien influences', it reflects the way surrealism was expanded through an encounter with 'external' elements. In this respect, whether Buñuel's dilemma in the thirties concerning his commitment to surrealism or to communism represented a genuine crisis of consciousness or opportunism seems to me less important than the way in which the dilemma itself continues to be present in Buñuel's later work, given expression in multiple ways when dealing with the relation between order and freedom and the reconciling of desire with the need to function within society. One of the central concerns of Buñuel's work, in fact, is with the *establishment* of authority: how it functions not simply to maintain itself through society, but also how it replicates itself within the individual and collective psyche. Buñuel was certainly not an anarchist. Everything in his work suggests that he considered the problems of human society to lie within the human psyche and not to be an accretion that has accrued to it through the repressiveness of the institutions imposed by society. His revolutionary sympathies were always tempered by his distrust of the perversities of human nature. If he was not a Stalinist, he was certainly concerned to examine the human problematic that had given rise to Stalinism and allowed it to flourish. As Buñuel once said, in a phrase which offers a key to his thinking: 'I like all people; I don't like the society that certain of them have created!' (quote by Kyrou, 1985: 247). They have created it, however; it is not something imposed from above. This is, I believe, a starting point for consideration of his work: he is asking, throughout his work, how basically decent people can create such a perverse society. How does this square with his surrealism?

Buñuel's involvement with the Surrealist Group coincided with the most turbulent period of its history. He entered the group just as the crisis of 1929 was breaking and left it at the culmination of the Aragon affair which had convulsed the group during the previous two years. Although he found a sense of fellowship, he also experienced the tensions at the heart of even the closest of friendships which can easily erupt to tear them apart. This was also the time of the surrealists' intense interest in Hegel's philosophy. All of these things appear to have made their mark on Buñuel's films. We cannot, I think, appreciate his work fully without taking its Hegelian element in it into account, especially in terms of how he understands human relationships. This is most immediately apparent in *The Exterminating Angel*, which is essentially a meditation on Hegel's dialectic of master and slave.

The guests trapped in the mansion in *The Exterminating Angel* belong to a world in which they, like Hegel's masters, retain mastery, but from whose living sources they are detached and who are thereby made listless. Left to themselves, the servants having abandoned them to their fate, their lack of spiritual resources is cruelly exposed. All they retain are rules of etiquette that define their position in society but which dominate them to such an extent that they have neither the will nor the spontaneity to respond to a situation that is out of the ordinary. Their lives are determined by rules which estrange them from their human needs. Instead of living as they would like, they are constrained to perform meaningless rituals which they impose upon themselves in order to maintain their privileged status in their own eyes. Their acquaintances are established not on the basis of friendship but through the need to be seen in the right company; in modern parlance, they need to 'network'. They are therefore respectful when necessary, gossipy when they get the chance, but always within a framework imposed upon them by the social circle they cultivate. At the same time they are oblivious to all that is going on around them and incapable of making deep friendships: everything exists for them at a superficial level.

By passively accepting the comfort of their social status as something natural, the guests are caught within a trap of their own making. In *The Exterminating Angel,* even as their situation deteriorates, becoming more extreme as the food runs out, the irritation of the guests with one another comes to the surface but remains constrained as they try to maintain proper behaviour rather than think through the reasons for their confinement. Inhibited by their social upbringing, their inability to adapt leaves them in thrall to a situation that threatens to spiral out of control. They have become ensnared by some invisible presence, but it is one that emanates from themselves, perhaps from their own proximity to one another: it is as though they have kidnapped themselves (or, more precisely, have shipwrecked themselves; Buñuel's initial inspiration was apparently Géricault's painting *The Raft of the Medusa*) in the midst of plenty. It is because they are victims of themselves that no one can help them; they have placed themselves outside society so that neither law nor religion can come to their aid: just as those inside cannot leave, so those outside are unable to enter the house.

The theme of the shipwreck is central to Buñuel's work as something people impose upon themselves in their inability to communicate effectively with others.

The characters in *The Exterminating Angel*, like those in *The Discreet Charm of the Bourgeoisie*, are ultimately as alone as Simon on top of his pillar or Robinson on his island.

As a kind of companion piece to *The Exterminating Angel, The Discreet Charm of the Bourgeoisie* was seen by many critics as a sign of Buñuel mellowing in old age and revealing him as having become tolerant of bourgeois mores. Dig just a little below the surface, however, and we find something altogether more disturbing, a sugar-coated pill laced with poison. Where in *The Exterminating Angel*, the company were trapped by their own lack of imagination, in *The Discreet Charm* they are condemned to a form of eternal return in which, as Robert Benayoun said, they are under 'a curse worthy of their ridiculous small-mindedness: they never manage to sit down around a table together without something annoying happening to discomfort, irritate or abuse them' (1973: 20).

The communal meal represents, we know, a primal form of collective consecration. In *The Exterminating Angel* the guests do at least have their meal before submitting to panic. In *The Discreet Charm* their inability to eat together signifies an even greater lack of social cohesion. Like the characters in the British horror film *Dead of Night* (1945), a film which must, if only sub-consciously, have inspired Buñuel, we are in a world of eternal return where each person is living the other's nightmare. We might even see them as an example of what Giorgio Agamben (1998) calls 'bare life': a living form that functions without knowing why it functions. Benayoun puts this in stark terms: 'Perhaps they are dead like their class, embalmed and re-animated for a timeless dinner date'. A death that is not a death but a 'twilight state, pleasant and comfortable' (1973: 21).

The real barb in *The Discreet Charm* is the way Buñuel lulls us into an acceptance of death as a state of existence (Benayoun points out that there are seventeen corpses in the film). The 'discreet charm' of the bourgeoisie lies not in any critique the film may offer of the characters in the film but in our identification with them: their hypocrisies are ours, as are their 'deaths'.

We know of course that eating is a feature of many of Buñuel's films and the sharing of food is often imbued with meaning. The most famous 'meal' in Buñuel's films – the scene in *The Phantom of Liberty* when the company excrete together, but eat alone – is not so much a reversal of social norms as a failure of social congress, a collective return, one might think, to the anal stage. This reflects a persistent theme throughout Buñuel's work: an inability (on the part of the bourgeoisie in particular, but this extends to all parts of capitalist society) to consecrate anything.

There is one question that almost all of Buñuel's characters seem unable to ask themselves, which is: where are we going? Like the protagonists in *The Discreet Charm* they are all embarked on an endless, empty route to nowhere founded in a capitalist attitude. Despite the claims it makes, capitalism is unable to advance; it only *accumulates* one thing or another. But as it adds more and more to every sphere of life, it does nothing to address the problems of human existence and so leaves life in a profoundly unsatisfactory state. Words like 'progress' and 'freedom' are used to camouflage this lack, which is covered over by empty promises of a good life of comfort and ease such as that lived by the six protagonists of *The Discreet Charm*. Completely 'free' as masters in the Hegelian sense, able even to flout the law, in reality they are as abandoned to themselves, unable genuinely to experience anything. The only check on their behaviour comes not from the law but from their constant fear of retribution, something which nevertheless conditions their every action.

The theme of an abandoned freedom is taken further in *The Phantom of Liberty*, a profound meditation on the elusiveness of freedom, which can be grasped only, as the title alerts us, in 'phantom' form. Given the extent to which the rhetoric of 'freedom' has been abused in recent political discourse, this perhaps has even greater resonance now than it did in the seventies. The 'phantom' is announced by the opening scenes of the film set against the backdrop of the revolutionary wars in Spain, in which the 'freedom' the French claim to be bringing to Spain can only be imposed with the gun, to which the Spanish prefer their own constraints. 'Long live chains', the cry of the Spanish loyalists at the time, would be echoed a century later by 'Long Live Death', the banner under which Franco would define his revolt and rally his troops against the Republican government. The denial of freedom – or at least the ambivalence of its claims – contained in these catchphrases is a theme present throughout Buñuel's work.

For the surrealists, the great guarantor of freedom is love, a love nevertheless laden with trip-wires. In 1929, Buñuel's response to the question 'Do you believe in the victory of admirable love over sordid life, or of sordid life over admirable love?' was an emphatic, 'I don't know' (*La Révolution surréaliste*, issue 12: 71). This response is explored in Buñuel's films. Love serves as a disruptive force, but his lovers rarely achieve consummation; when they do (in *Un Chien andalou* and *Wuthering Heights*), it is only in death. Buñuel's version of *Wuthering Heights* is interesting for the fact that Buñuel ignores the *amour fou* detailed in the early part of Emily Brontë's novel to concentrate on the section in which she denies her love for Heathcliff. In Buñuel's film it is only when Catalina is dying that she admits (or perhaps even recognises) her love for Alejandro, and only in the scene upon which the film ends, when Alejandro desecrates Catalina's tomb to find death at the hands of Ricardo (whom he perceives in a vision to be Catalina), are they finally united. This ending, with its echoes of the final scene of *Un Chien andalou*, is as ambivalent as it is sublime, the filmic equivalent of the 'I don't know' with which Buñuel answered the surrealist enquiry about the triumph of love. These two examples aside, love is decidedly elusive throughout Buñuel's films. Even if it may be given powerful expression in *L'Âge d'or*, it is a love that, as already noted, overwhelms rather than allows the lovers to realise themselves.

Linda Williams (1981: 133) emphasises the extent of the lovers' 'impotence' in *L'Âge d'or*, even as she recognises that in the scene in the garden the lovers do seem finally to consummate their love, at least in so far as they bring themselves physically to a point of ecstasy. But even this ecstasy is disconnected: there is little suggestion of a unity of sensations. Their love is rather experienced tangentially to one another. They may come together in desire but, as Linda Williams insight-fully argues, the realisation of their passion achieves only a narcissistic satisfaction. The woman's retreat into the arms of the orchestra conductor thus seems to be less a rejection of love than recognition of the incapacity of the man to satisfy her desire. The impotence here is less a physical disability than an inability to rise above societal authority, which is inscribed within the lovers themselves. Williams is here right to question Kyrou's contention that 'the lovers are revealed to themselves through love and desperately defend this love by their indifference, scorn and hate of society'(1985: 213). It is surely one of the themes of the film that society does destroy love, or at least makes it impossible. For all of its fever, the love of the man and woman is shallow and they are easily distracted from it. Their revolt is surrealist only in its violence: febrile, it is soon dissipated, leaving an impotent rage which can be satisfied only through unmotivated violence. Thus the woman returns to the security of the father's authority, as represented by the orchestra conductor, while the man, afflicted, it seems, by the same headache as the father figure, gives vent to his frustration in a scene that even Kyrou admits is extremely troubling as it conveys us to the murderous setting at the castle of Selliny which ends the film.

It is, I think, virtually impossible to 'read' this ending. This is probably where the collaborative aspect of the film is most strongly in evidence. It is, however, precisely in its over-determination that this ending contains its scorpion's sting.

Rather than trying to 'explain' this scene, I think we need to take it as a starting point for considering the nature of desire as the red thread that runs through Buñuel's work as a whole, where it is treated with an almost anthropological precision. For Buñuel, it seems, it was a thread that was attached to a cask of dynamite. Few if any of his characters succeed in detaching this cord from its deadly accessory; the most they can do is to prevent it from combusting. Almost all of Buñuel's characters are condemned to solitude. They may experience the ferment of mad love, but it – and this is where Buñuel probably differs from most other surrealists – never takes them out of their solitary state, even momentarily. Those characters who have a sense of purpose or self-certainty (Nazarin, Viridiana, Simon) are revealed as deluded precisely because they have denied desire and the possibility of love, but their 'liberation' does not promise them a better life as such; it merely enables them to live in society.

In Buñuel – and here again we see a Hegelian element – recognition of human society is elemental to human becoming. Innocence exists, but it is perverse, since it involves a denial of desire and the need for others, and therefore needs to be overcome. But society itself is equally perverse, so that Nazarin in accepting the pineapple offered by the woman at the end of the film, Viridiana when she enters the card game, and Simon in his beatnik hang-out each undergo a bemused transformation which initiates them into society, but it remains an initiation without comfort. This is a reversal of Christian original sin. It follows from Breton's assertion that 'there has never been a forbidden fruit: only temptation is divine'. Divine it may be, but for Buñuel temptation does not offer any solutions.

The culmination of Buñuel's career, and the film in which he most profoundly addressed the problematic of solitude and desire, is *That Obscure Object of Desire*. If Buñuel's last film is an almost perfect summation of his work, bringing the themes that concerned him full circle (I see no reason to dissent from the oft-made point that the final image of the film acts as a dialectical counterpoint to the opening image of *Un Chien andalou*), it is also the film that elucidates his attitude towards love and the inevitability of human solitude, against which it is at once a protest and a verification.

One of the strangest moments in the film occurs when Conchita and Mathieu are discussing their future, and she wants to know whether he will still love her when she is old. Given the difference in their ages, we know that there is no likelihood of Mathieu even being alive when Conchita reaches old age, yet this is presented as a perfectly reasonable demand. This brings attention to the fantastic nature of their relationship: is Conchita being ironic, an irony that Mathieu, in his self-absorption, fails to pick up? Or is it further evidence that Conchita in fact does not exist but is solely a projection of Mathieu's desire, a desire that functions in disregard for the objective conditions of his life?

In this story, which we only hear from Mathieu's point of view, Conchita appears to be the ultimate tease, leading on her poor victim, intent upon exploiting him and having no intention of satisfying his desire for her. Buñuel, however, barbs his discourse, so that what we actually see as the tale unfolds undercuts, when it doesn't contradict, the assumptions made by Mathieu's narrative. Unlike the passengers on the train who have only Mathieu's words to guide them, as an audience we are able to see that what Mathieu tells his listeners is at best an outrageously slanted view of what actually happened (especially via the suggestion in the opening scene that he may have raped her), although we are still excluded from Conchita's own perspective.

What is apparent is that reciprocity – central to Hegel's phenomenology of human becoming – is absent from this relationship. Mathieu can respond to Conchita only as prize or a commodity, to be bought or won, but she can never be accepted for what she is, so that, instead of a processes of becoming, what we witness is essentially a play of mirrors in which any resolution is impossible: the object of desire must remain always elusive because it has no tangible existence, even if it is even physically present. The master and slave dialectic is once more not far away: Mathieu is an absolute master, having the means to do whatever he wants, but what he really wants is still denied to him; in fact, he wants it precisely because it is denied to him.

Mathieu's fixation is a desire based upon lack. It actually requires non-reciprocity (if Conchita surrendered to him, it seems apparent that he would soon tire of her). Linda Williams says that 'The one thing this story is not is a realistic depiction of a man and woman in love' (1981: 200). Well, yes and no. The question here is begged of what 'love' might be. In so far as love is an energy force that passes through people rather than being, as in its sentimental designation, a simple mutual attraction, then the film is indeed a love story, albeit a phantom one in which no resolution is possible. In this respect, we have further confirmation – something that is almost a constant in Buñuel's work – that *amour fou* is an impossible force which, rather than bringing two people together, forces them to confront their essential solitude without allowing them to resolve the lack it entails.[2] This lack is as much social as it is sexual, and lies in the fact that people are divided within themselves as well as from one another. Mathieu, in a sense, is a man *in love* but unable *to love*. Or perhaps that he *needs* to love, but is not able to see the object of love, which remains a mirage. Conchita is neither here nor there; she is everywhere and nowhere.

If Conchita is only a phantom for Mathieu, she has a real existence for Buñuel and is found elsewhere in his films under the names of Susana, Viridiana, Célestine, Séverine or Tristana. At least, we might say that each of these characters fills the empty space that surrounds Conchita. None of these women attain fulfilment in their relationships. All of them are trapped by different forms of male oppression, and even the most self-possessed, Célestine in *Diary of a Chambermaid*, fails in her attempts to challenge male authority, ending up married to a bigoted, retired captain. Taking into account the experiences of these women as a whole, we can appreciate the reasons for Conchita's elusiveness. Of all of them, only Tristana gains a glimpse of a better life in her love for Horacio, but Buñuel allows us to see little of their life together and their relationship ends in tragedy. Conchita, in contrast, recognises the phantom nature of love and prevents herself from becoming a victim of it by becoming herself a phantom. This enables her to withhold the recognition Mathieu demands of her while taking advantage of the possibilities for experience his need of her opens up. When she plays with this need, however, going so far as to humiliate Mathieu, she has offered him a provisional recognition which fatally brings her into complicity with him (and so they both die in the explosion that closes the film as well as Buñuel's film career).

The tragic sense of life this implies is an important, and generally unremarked upon, aspect of surrealism (we shall encounter it again, if differently configured, in the work of Prévert, Borowczyk and Švankmajer). In his films, Buñuel portrays a troubling world of conflict and disassociation, yet there is no evil in this world, or if there is it lies within the textures of people's relations with one another rather than inhering in anything or anyone. His surrealism is anthropological: he observes but he does not condemn. People are alone, and to surmount their loneliness they sometimes do terrible things, to themselves as well as to others. Their spite or malice is always, however, reactive: there is no originating malevolence. What is most troubling is that there seems to be no remedy for this condition. Buñuel offers no comfort but, more than this, his characters rarely if ever experience any resolution of their conflicts. Being at the mercy of their phantoms is a fact of human existence.

In this respect, we might take as symptomatic the regretful look of Robinson Crusoe in Buñuel's 1954 film as he takes leave of his island home for the last time. Although he feels immense relief at finally being able to re-enter human society, his look conveys a sense of loss at leaving his lonely sanctuary and recognition that the desired return to society will be insufficient to satisfy him.

Buñuel's 'communism' is thus not political but anthropological: it is tied to a dialectic of solitude and the human need for others, in the recognition that this dialectic is at the heart of the existential problem of living in society. Throughout his work, as much as authority may be challenged, Buñuel does not appear to recognise any alternative it. To this extent and the fact that he considered industrialised capitalism to be such a perverse form of social organisation that an alternative to it needed to be found, one might give credence to Paul Hammond's assertion of a certain 'Stalinism' in his thought. Far from seeing this as a something for denunciation, or as evidence of an abandonment of surrealism, however, it would surely be more fruitful to see it as an engagement with a fundamentally surrealist problematic: how to reconcile human freedom with the need to function within society, how to forge personal identity in harmony with others, how, in a word, to engage with 'love' (as the realisation of the surrealist supreme point) in a society in which love is outlawed.

This returns us to the most troubling scene in *L'Âge d'or*: the transition between the hero's frustration and the murderous crimes of the Blangis/Christ figure. Clearly we are intended to correlate the two events, although I do not see how, as some critics have argued, Blangis is simply the hero later in his life (Durgnat, for instance, absurdly asks whether the young murdered girl may be 'Lya Lys whom he once loved?' [1967: 45]). The intertitle expressly excludes this, since it tells us explicitly that the two events of the hero throwing feathers out of the window and the emergence of the reprobates from the castle occur 'at the exact moment ... but very far away'.

In denying temporal logic, since the reprobates are dressed in clothes of an earlier age, the scene confirms the collapsing of time apparent elsewhere in the film (again, the mutability of time is a theme Buñuel will often return to in his later work), but it does not entitle us to disregard what it manifestly states. We must therefore see the two events as independent of one another but correlated. They are linked principally by a sense of transgression of social norms, but also by the fact that the characters are representatives of the class that maintains these norms. Is not what we see revealed here the contradiction inherent within social organisation? The hero and heroine of *L'Âge d'or*, like Sade's reprobates, are ultimately trapped within their social class. As we have seen, love overcomes them, impels their rebellion, but ultimately does not transform them: it merely leaves them unfulfilled.

Buñuel's work can be seen as an exploration of the tension raised by the contradiction between desire and social order. His surrealism lies in the way in which his encounter with the surrealists opened his eyes to this problematic and determined how he would confront it in his films. Surrealism thus nourished his entire career, but it is a surrealism that was contained by the moment of his involvement with it. There is little indication that Buñuel took any interest in surrealist activity after he departed from the group. For this reason, no doubt, Swedish surrealist Mattias Forshage posits that

> Buñuel's late movies show at the same time the triumph and the limits of traditional surrealist cinema. Fundamentally built upon the element of surprise, they proceed through industrious gags and absurdities (actually rather close to popular 'misconceptions' of surrealism); drawing on dreams, simplistic anti-bourgeois sentiments, more or less outdated anticlerical reflexes and murky banal eroticism. They are beautiful, marvellous, instigative, but they also represent an obvious cul-de-sac (personal communication, 2004).

Although the examination of the bourgeoisie in these films seems to me far from simplistic, the anti-clericalism is not outdated and the eroticism far from banal, what perhaps is outdated is that by centring the films on these themes as he did, Buñuel showed himself to be constrained by personal interests founded in the period of his youth. Having become an internationally renowned auteur, he fell prey to the lures of the 'art cinema' circuit, creating this cul-de-sac Forshage speaks of, not so much in terms of the films themselves as in the fact that they have come to be subsumed, in a reified way, by surrealism.

Forshage's comments alert us to the fact that Buñuel's surrealism begins and ends in the early 1930s. As rich as it was, his sensibility was set in time, and Buñuel himself may have been commenting on this fact in the scene of *The Phantom of Liberty* which appears to relate not so much to what Breton invoked as the 'simplest surrealist act' as to the impermeability of society to it. Having randomly killed several people in the street, a man is brought to trial and found guilty and sentenced to death. Following the verdict, his handcuffs are removed, everyone shakes his hand and he walks into the street a free man. The 'death' society deals out for committing this act is recuperation: it congratulates the perpetrator and incorporates his actions into the structure of society. This scene might even be his final comment on the reception accorded *Un Chien andalou*, that 'impassioned call for murder' which the 'imbecilic crowd' found beautiful, but one that implicates his later films as well.

In considering Buñuel's films in relation to surrealism, therefore, we should be careful not identify them too casually with a general surrealist attitude or as the sole or principal examples of 'surrealist' film making. They belong to a specific historical moment of surrealism constituted by the experience of Buñuel's own life. In order to be fully appreciated, they need also be seen in terms of how they went beyond their immediate context to enter the 'eternal' surrealism constituted by what preceded them and what came after them.

CHAPTER 3

Jacques Prévert and the Poetry of the Eventual

The significance of surrealism for cinema lies less in the fact that a handful of films were made directly under its rubric than in the way in which it often imperceptibly seeped into a broader film discourse. The view often promulgated that the surrealists' attraction to cinema after 1930 was principally that of spectators disillusioned with the actual practice of making films appears to a peculiarly myopic one if one looks at the history of French cinema. The involvement of surrealists in French cinema has been intense, at the level of both production and criticism. We need only cite a few of the names of those participants in surrealism who made substantial contributions to the cinematic life of France: Jacques and Pierre Prévert, Jacques Viot, Jacques Brunius, Jean Ferry, Roland and Denise Tual, Georges Goldfayn, Michel Zimbacca, Robert Benayoun, Ado Kyrou, Gérard Legrand.[1] This list does not include Jean Vigo, never a member of the Surrealist Group but whose films are thoroughly imbued with its sensibility. That many of these names may be obscure (especially to an Anglo-Saxon audience) should not blind us to their importance. Of these, none made a greater contribution than Jacques Prévert, the premier screenwriter in the history of French film.

Born in 1900, Jacques Prévert participated in the Surrealist Group between 1925 and 1929. He was a poet, a dramatist, a collagist, a scriptwriter, or more accurately he was none of these things but rather he was able to give expression to his life through poetry, drama, collage and film. His poems are among the most popular of the twentieth century, having been transformed into song and rendered by singers like Juliette Gréco, Serge Reggiani and Yves Montand, and the films he wrote are some of the most memorable of French cinema. It is widely asserted that Prévert's contribution is what gives them their characteristic flavour, perhaps the only instance in which a writer's involvement in films is considered to be more significant than the director's, especially in relation to the films he made with Marcel Carné. Prévert also wrote for other directors, among the greatest of the era: Jean Renoir, Jean Grémillon, Christian-Jaque, André Cayatte, Jean Delannoy and Joris Ivens, as well as for his brother, Pierre. A clear thematic continuity runs through all of these films, no matter whom they were written for, and this is also a continuity that is maintained with Prévert's other activities. As with other surrealists, it is not possible to separate his different modes of expression from one another.

Despite this, he has only intermittently been subject to critical consideration for his contribution to film. His writing for the cinema is generally seen as one facet of his activity as a poet, if it is not relegated to a sideline, something he did for a living. The most substantial study of Prévert as a film *maker* is a chapter in Dudley Andrew's *Mists of Regret*, which gives us an evocative account of his position within French film making of the time (see Andrew, 1995: 74–86).[2]

Doubtless this reflects the dominance that the idea of the film director as auteur retains, and it remains true that the director is ultimately the person who determines the overall sense of any film. It is also complicated by the fact that, despite their distinctiveness, few of Prévert's scripts came from his own conception. Many were adaptations of novels, and he frequently worked on them with other people (at first he was simply regarded as a 'gag man', brought in to spice up otherwise pedestrian scripts). In fact, very few of the many original scripts Prévert wrote were ever made into films. We can see the range of these projects in a posthumously published volume (Prévert, 1995). Nevertheless it seems widely accepted that Prévert had a kind of magic touch that imbued most of the films he made with unique qualities, of which those he wrote for Marcel Carné are the most celebrated, but not necessarily the most significant. His reliance on his scriptwriters was a pretext for the critics of *Cahiers de cinema* to dismiss Carné as a significant director. From a surrealist perspective, of course, the question of authorship is irrelevant: that Carné's films came from a collaborative project is in fact one of their virtues. The fact that he allowed Prévert to explore surrealist themes within them is another. In this respect, we can compare Carné with Buñuel, with one important proviso: where Buñuel established his own vision by working through the ideas of others, Carné's virtue as a director was his readiness to appreciate and accede to other people's ideas rather than to impose his own vision on them. This is a rare quality among film directors. It was probably because Carné did not interfere with what he recognised as high-quality writing that Prévert was able to establish such a distinctive screenwriting presence.

It was still a curious partnership, forged between two temperamentally very different characters. Carné was a humanist and a socialist with a liberal perspective. As a moderate, he appears to have shared little of Prévert's rebellious temperament and will of transformation. Both men were at ease among the working classes and the marginals of Parisian life but Carné's sensibility appears to have been fundamentally reformist: one has a sense that for Carné the surrealist will to 'change life' and 'transform the world' was meaningless. Nevertheless, he seems to have been drawn to surrealism to the extent at least that he recognised its creative energy (after his partnership with Prévert broke up, he turned to Jacques Viot, another former member of the Surrealist Group, as his scriptwriter), an energy that perhaps he acknowledged his somewhat prosaic personality required in order to impassion – or give poetry to – his films.

Prévert's initiation into film making came in 1928 when he worked with his brother Pierre on *Souvenirs de Paris ou Paris-Express*, a short documentary imbued with the surrealist spirit and an interesting companion piece to texts like Aragon's *Paris Peasant*, Breton's *Nadja*, Soupault's *Last Nights of Paris* or Desnos's *Liberty or Love?* Having participated in the making of *L'Âge d'or*, he became disillusioned with film making (not for the last time) following the suicide of Pierre Batcheff (the 'star' of *Un Chien andalou*), with whom he had been working on a film called *Emile-Emile*. It was not until 1934 that Prévert really entered the world of commercial film making when he worked on the screenplays of two films by Richard Pottier, *Si j'étais le patron* in 1934 and *Un oiseau rare* in 1935. At this time, however, his main work was in the theatre, as writer for the October Group, an agit-prop workers' troupe established in 1932 and emerging from the proletarian theatre movement of the twenties which was putting into practice Piscator's ideas and seeking to advance the idea of class struggle by directly addressing a working-class audience. It was in this context, as the main writer in a collaborative group and having to improvise scripts and sketches at short notice, that Prévert honed his skills as a writer with a gift for telling observation and dazzling dialogue. No doubt these were the qualities that caused Jean Renoir to engage him to write the dialogue for *Le Crime de Monsieur Lange* (1935), the film that really established him as a screenwriter.

Prior to this he had collaborated again with his brother on *L'Affaire est dans le sac* (1932), a short film that represents, along with the three Buñuel films, a highpoint of surrealist film making in this era (far more significant than any of the Man Ray films). *L'Affaire est dans le sac* is an anarchic comedy that tells the story of a bored millionaire who is kidnapped in error. The kidnap is organised by a hatter, and the gang have problems when the millionaire begins to enjoy his position – he is no longer bored. Meanwhile, life goes on all around them – people are too busy exploiting one another to care about a kidnap.

Paying homage to the American comics the surrealists admired (one could even imagine the film as a Marx Brothers vehicle), *L'Affaire est dans le sac* is also very much an agit-prop drama that emerged from the environment of the October Group. In its way, it belongs to the surrealist milieu as much as does *L'Age d'or*, which begs the question of why it has failed to achieve the prestige of Buñuel's films.

Jacques Brunius may be right to assert that 'the Préverts disconcerted spectators rather than making them laugh'. He does not see this as a weakness of the films, however, and his explanation seems problematic. He claims that the spectators 'undoubtedly recognised themselves too clearly in the detestable and ridiculous characters on the screen' (1954: 160). There is a curious paradox here: although the surrealists claimed an affinity with a popular audience, they tended to ascribe the popularity of some of their own films (like *Un Chien andalou*) to the inability of the audience to recognise themselves in film's mordancy, while here Brunius sees the failure of *L'Affaire* to lie in the fact that they recognised themselves only too well. What does this signify? That the Préverts' film is more successful, from a surrealist perspective, than *Un Chien andalou*? And how does one account for the popularity of the similarly mordant comedies of the Marx Brothers or W. C. Fields? How does one know what an audience is? Who is to say that those who liked *Un Chien andalou* were not the same people who were flocking to see Harry Langdon and Buster Keaton films? Do we assume that the surrealists were unable to reach a popular audience and consigned to making films for the bourgeoisie, even with a film like *L'Affaire*, which came out of the workers' movement? Clearly other factors are at work that caused Pierre Prévert's films to find favour with neither audiences nor critics.

Brunius is on firmer ground in his further diagnosis: 'Prévert's cruelty needed the covering provided by Carné in a cinema technique as impeccable as it was dazzling; his most bitter retorts had to pass through the mouths of the best actors before finally being accepted' (1954: 160–1). Pierre Prévert's films are too whimsical, too spontaneous to be really popular or to appeal to critics. One has to be attuned, perhaps, to their sensibility to appreciate them. Brunius is probably right to say that they disconcerted – and probably still disconcert – spectators, less, however, because they recognise themselves in the characters than because they do not know how to take them. The length of the *L'Affaire est dans le sac* (35 minutes) didn't help: it was neither a short nor a feature film. But Pierre's films are too abrasive: too serious to be treated as comedies, not serious enough to be regarded as dramas. They do not do full justice to the poetry of Jacques's scripts, which, Brunius may have been right to say, required a higher level of acting than he was able to command. This may have represented a failure of communication. Or maybe it was just that Pierre was never given the sort of budget that would have enabled him to reach a wider public. Whatever the case, it was the films Jacques wrote for other directors that became celebrated.

The influence of Prévert's work for the October Group is still clearly discernible in the first major film he was associated with: Jean Renoir's *Le Crime de Monsieur Lange*. There is even a certain continuity of mood and theme with *L'Affaire est dans le sac*, but here the humour and the seriousness are fully integrated into the film. It tells a story set in a publishing house run by unscrupulous capitalist Monsieur Batala. When Batala is reported dead in a train crash, the workers take over the business and run it as a co-operative, turning a loss-making concern into a great success. But Batala did not die in the train crash, and he returns and tries to reclaim the business, taunting mild-mannered M. Lange (whose western stories are one of the successes of the press); the latter, his passion raised, kills him. Lange flees with his girlfriend, Valentine, and the story is told by the latter in flashback to a group of workers at the border who have recognised Lange as a wanted man and are undecided whether or not to turn him in.

Le Crime de Monsieur Lange may seem to be a surprising film to consider in the context of surrealism since André Bazin held it up as a characteristic example of realist cinema. Yet, the 'realism' of the film is not incompatible with its 'surrealism'. Even as it was founded as an anti-realist movement, surrealism was not so much opposed to realism as it was to its exclusive claim to be able to represent reality, especially when it became monolithic, asserting that realism alone was able to engage with reality. Surrealism, as needs perhaps to be emphasised again, is not a style, and was not opposed to the use of realism as a mode of representation. In Renoir's film, we need to look beyond the surface realism to its themes – of communal solidarity, faith in love as a redemptive force, and opposition to an oppressive order – to see how it conjoins with surrealism through Prévert's contribution to it.

Renoir testified to the importance of Jacques Prévert in the making of the film. This was not so much as scriptwriter: the script had in fact been written before Prévert became involved with the picture and Prévert did no more than re-write the dialogue. The way he did this, however, served to transform the film. He was present on the set and improvised the dialogue as the film developed. This film was, as Renoir said, 'a bantering collaboration'. Here we can see how *Le Crime de Monsieur Lange* is an example of the way surrealism 'infected' certain films through the presence of participants in surrealism in its making. This 'contagious' quality of surrealism requires further examination and can be seen more clearly in Prévert's collaboration with Marcel Carné.

Prévert first worked with Carné on *Jenny* (1936), a moderately successful film that cemented Carné's reputation as a young director of promise. It was with a film of the following year, *Drôle de drame*, that their collaboration was really initiated. Coming after the modest success of *Jenny*, the film was not, however, well received by the public or the press. Despite this, Carné liked working with Prévert, and all of his films over the next decade, with the exception of *Hôtel du Nord* (1938), were forged in collaboration with him.

In his discussion of the film, Dudley Andrew advances what seem rather contradictory theories for *Drôle de drame*'s lack of success. On the one hand he suggests it was simply misunderstood at the time in much the same way as Renoir's *La Règle du jeu*, and found its audience only after the war. This was because, as he paraphrases Edward Turk, the film is 'so darkly pessimistic in its humour that it could please only the small band of leftists who managed to preserve their cynicism' (Andrew, 1995: 83). On the other hand, he discusses how the film's weakness stems from an incompatibility between Prévert's script and Carné's direction.

It is certainly the case that *Drôle de drame* stands apart from the other films Prévert and Carné made together and has a kinship more with those Prévert made with his brother. Does it fail, then, for the same reasons? Personally, I think Pierre Prévert's films are better than *Drôle de drame*. Andrew seems to be spot on when he says 'Carné's sober camera rather deadens the effect of Prévert's language run wild' (1995: 84). *Drôle de drame* doesn't really work as a film, although there is nothing wrong with the script; Carné was simply unable to bring out its comic aspects. He treats the characters as though they were real people, rather than people taken to an extreme of their personalities through satire. The result is that we are distanced from the absurdity of the action and are rather discountenanced by the fact that these people would not act in the manner depicted. Paradoxically this makes it the most 'surreal' film Carné made, but the least surrealist. *Drôle de drame* ought perhaps to have been directed by Pierre Prévert, or by Renoir (in comparing it to *La Règle du jeu*, Andrew wonders if this might be 'blasphemous', but one feels it would have made a fine companion piece to it). One might also ponder what might have happened had it been directed by Buñuel.

It is intriguing at this point to ponder what the result might have been had Prévert and Buñuel collaborated on a project. In some ways it might be thought that Prévert's 'sentimentality' would clash with Buñuel's sensibility. *Drôle de drame*, however, seems to be a perfect script for Buñuel, and one can conceive of a resulting film that would perhaps have formed a trilogy of films of bourgeois manners along with *The Exterminating Angel* and *The Discreet Charm of the Bourgeoisie*. In any event, one can imagine what Buñuel would have made of a story of a bourgeois couple who supplement their income by pseudonymously writing scandalous detective stories (which in fact are plagiarised from stories their orphaned maid tells them) and whose sense of social propriety is such that, when one of their relatives arrives, they would prefer to cook the dinner themselves than admit that their servants had resigned, and then, when it became believed that the husband had murdered the wife, they would continue the pretence than admit the truth. Carné, however, treats all this absurdity as simply a manifestation of bizarre behaviour, giving the film a lack of conviction which the fine script and acting can never rise above.

In their next two films, however, Prévert and Carné found the magic formula that tied their worlds together to fashion a cohesive creative partnership. *Quai des Brumes* (1938) and *Le Jour se lève* (1939) were both on the surface deeply pessimistic films, far darker than *Drôle de drame* and unrelieved by humour, which tends to give the lie to the suggestion that *Drôle de drame* failed because of its pessimism, for these two films were quite popular, despite attacks from both the right and the left (Jean Renoir notoriously, apparently on orders from the Communist Party, denounced *Quai des Brumes* as 'fascist').

Quai des brumes was based on a novel by Mac Orlan and it retained this author's bleak vision, although changing its characters and plot details. It is set in Le Havre, to which Jean (played by Jean Gabin), who has deserted from the army because 'it isn't much fun to kill', has made his way, intending to seek passage to South America. In a bar, Jean becomes immediate friends with a suicidal painter, Jacques. He also meets Nelly, with whom he falls in love. But Nelly is coveted as a girlfriend by a small-time gangster, Lucien, who is humiliated by Jean when he tries to assert his right to Nelly. She is also lasciviously watched over by her nasty guardian, Zabel. Having decided to kill himself, Jacques leaves his clothes and passport to enable Jean to assume a new identity. The next day Jean is able to obtain passage on a ship bound for to Venezuela. After spending the night with Nelly, Jean tells her he is leaving. He goes to the ship, but returns to shore to see Nelly once more, where he finds Zabel trying to rape her and, in the confrontation, he kills him. As he is leaving, Lucien arrives and shoots him down. Dying, he asks Nelly to kiss him, quickly. This kiss, as so often in Prévert, signifies a definitive rejection of this world, in which, as he said to her earlier in the film, people 'don't have the time to love'.

Quai des brumes is an affecting and haunting films of human loneliness. Le Havre itself assumes an isolated feel in the film, attaining a mythical quality as a place where the world ends, a space in which time and space are, if not stopped, held in abeyance. This is accentuated at night time, as a new day is awaited that will offer the possibility of something new, whether it be escape, love or death. As so often in Prévert's film work, happiness is briefly attained, only to be cruelly broken by circumstances.

If in *Quai des brumes* life seems to be held under a kind of postponed, if indistinct, malediction, in *Le Jour se lève* the curse is all too present. Time is truly held in suspension for a night as François, a worker holed up in his apartment under siege by the police after having killed a man, reflects on the events leading to his desperate situation. It happened as a result of his falling in love with Françoise, a young flower vendor. She, however, was seduced by the sinister Valentin, a music hall artist who, like Batala, has the power to twist words to his own advantage. The devaluation of language in the service of corruption is a key theme in Prévert: we can usually tell the villains by the fact that they abuse either language or animals (Valentin is an animal trainer who also mistreats his dogs). But their twisting of words in the end is also often their undoing. Here François, like Lange before him, is unable to bear the taunts of his oppressor, and kills him in a rage, which brings an end to François's story as dawn approaches.

Le Jour se lève was in fact conceived by Jacques Viot, and Prévert was responsible only for the dialogue, but again the film very much bears his imprint (although his sensibility and that of Viot were remarkably similar). In this film, the very title announces the significance of the coming of dawn, this time without any possibility of escape.

Both of these are 'film noirs' (they were actually called this at the time in France and it was from them that the term came to be applied to the later Hollywood films of similar mood). They could also be considered in conjunction with another film Prévert wrote at this time, *Remorques* (1941), directed by Jean Grémillon. This also stars Jean Gabin and Michèle Morgan, who played the lovers in *Quai des brumes*, and shares their mood of fateful melancholy. In this film, Gabin plays a tug-boat captain married to Yvonne, a woman who, unknown to him, is suffering from a fatal illness. After rescuing a ship in distress, he falls in love with Catherine, the wife of the ship's captain. The idyll is interrupted when a messenger brings him the news that his wife has fallen seriously ill. He returns home to find her dying as he is called out on another rescue mission on the sea. The untranslatable title of this film alerts us to a central Prévertian theme (it literally means 'tug-boats' but is used to question what is it that ties people to one another and how they recognise their situation within the scheme of things).

Concern with questions of destiny and freedom are central to surrealism generally, and this is no more clearly seen than in Prévert's work. Destiny assumes a place in virtually all of his films as a character in its own right (this is literally the case when we come to *Les Portes de la nuit*), but in these three films it assumes a particularly sombre and heartbreaking tone which reflects the period in which they were made. Not the least of Prévert's qualities was his unforced empathy with working-class aspirations. His characters may face inevitable defeat, but they are always in tune with this destiny and never victims of it.

Les Visiteurs du soir (1942), Prévert's next film with Carné, was very different in tone but in many ways was just as ill-fated. Drawing on an old legend, it tells a story of a world in which the Devil sends his envoys to Earth to sow discord. When one of his messengers is overcome by the power of human love, the Devil is forced to assume human form and intervene to maintain the rule of evil. Despite all his efforts his attempts to change the course of true love fail and he is forced to turn the lovers to stone for having defied him. Even turned to stone, however, their hearts continue to beat in tune with one another.

As portrayed by Jules Berry (who played the villains in both *Monsieur Lange* and *Le Jour se lève*), the Devil is so subtly evoked that his resemblance, as the master of deception, to Hitler seems to have passed unnoticed by the authorities, as does the fact that the film appears to be transparently an allegory of France under Nazi oppression. Audiences, it seems, were more aware: the film was one of the great box-office successes during the Occupation. The film's message ('Those who love do not suffer. They are marvellously alone') has to be seen in this light. In the context of the Occupation, *Les Visiteurs du soir* was a film of hope: the heart of France would continue to beat no matter what the Nazis did. In the context of the broader themes of Prévert's work, however, it assumes a darker tone as a continuation of the working through of themes of destiny and fateful coincidence.

Prévert's and Carné's next film together was *Les Enfants du Paradis* (1945). If *Les Visiteurs du soir* had been the most successful French film made under the Occupation and embodied a sense of resistance to Nazism, its popularity pales in comparison with *Les Enfants du Paradis*, which is identified with the re-assertion and renaissance of French culture after the humiliation of conquest. Perhaps the most famous film in French film history, *Les Enfants du Paradis* also effects a remarkable convergence of surrealist themes with the popular mood.

As representing something of a patriotic myth, there may appear to be something curiously paradoxical about considering *Les Enfants du Paradis* in the light of surrealism. After all, the surrealists had made it an article of faith to oppose any form of nationalism and had declared that 'for us France no longer exists'. The war did not temper this hostility and nothing would reconcile them to calls for patriotism, not even opposition to Nazism. In 1945, Benjamin Péret would publish a notorious pamphlet, *Le Déshonneur des poètes*, attacking those writers – notably former surrealists Aragon and Éluard – who had sung patriotic anthems during the war, summing up a position that would remain constant among the surrealists. Nevertheless, there is a sense in which *Les Enfants du paradis* represents a moment when the French national spirit conjoined with a surrealist sense of the marvellous in a way that recalls the short-lived state of grace the lovers attain in so many of Prévert's films: for a moment surrealist themes and the destiny of the whole society subtly converged. In this sense its surrealist elements are striking precisely because they cannot be reduced to surrealism. One cannot say of it 'this is a surrealist film' because the surrealism is layered into it and inseparable from its overall impact, but it represents a surrealism extended and contagiously present within something that is at the same time *other than surrealism*. Those people who are oblivious to the surrealist aspects of *Les Enfants du Paradis* are still exposed to them. From this perspective, it contrasts with *L'Age d'or*, which outrages or enchants in equal proportions but never achieves a reconciliation between divergent positions. *Les Enfants du Paradis* is protean in its impact, affecting spectators in very different ways. It may, of course, be enjoyed by people who have no knowledge, familiarity with or interest in surrealism. It may even be a favourite film of those who are out of sympathy or even actively hostile to it. This, however, involves no contradiction; in fact it is something that emphasises its surrealist provenance, since it achieves a transcendence of origins that points towards the supreme point of surrealist endeavour in which contradictions are no longer perceived as oppositions.

In effecting a kind of reconciliation between surrealism and the national mood, *Les Enfants du Paradis* is also significant for its approach to history. It represents history *à rebours*, history not as it was but as it 'should have been': as a myth. Taking place in legendary time, it assumes what Walter Benjamin called for, a history that recognises 'not only the flow of thoughts, but their arrest as well' (1970: 264). As we can also see in some of Buñuel's films (*Viridiana*, *Simon of the Desert, Phantom of Liberty*, for instance), history is treated not as a procession of past events but as a lateral process in which the past remains eternally present.

If *Les Enfants du Paradis* represents a convergence of surrealism with the public mood, the next film Prévert and Carné made marked its dissociation. This may reveal the fragile, even mistaken, grounds upon which such an accord was based, or the inability of the surrealist imagination to allow itself to be fettered by public taste. Probably it is both. In the wake of the liberation, surrealism became part of the euphoric air people breathed. For the first and only time, surrealism became 'French', since for a brief moment the French spirit merged with a universal epiphany. It represented a momentary glimpse of the 'supreme point' of reconciliation, realising universal aspiration in a local setting. Such a moment could not last. Liberation soon turned to retribution, euphoria to spite.

Les Portes de la nuit (1946) reflects this shift. It acts as a negative complement to *Les Enfants du Paradis*. An underrated film, it is in its way as significant as *Les Enfants du Paradis*, even if it lacks that film's grandeur. It provides us with some of the keys of Prévert's work. Like Sternberg's *The Shanghai Gesture* (1941), it is about the end of all things, set on an evening when debts must be repaid. Few films are so filled with sadness – it is in this that it doubtless captures perfectly the vengeful, despondent mood that followed the joy of liberation; its overall atmosphere recalls nothing so much as post-coital disgust. Its melancholy is not of the same nature as the films from just before the war. Equally it is not, as in *Les Visiteurs du soir*, a matter of the Devil interfering in the affairs of humans; it is the humans who are incapable of being anything other than 'human, too human'. It is a film that rather takes us back to the early surrealism of the 'Enquiry into Suicide': watched over by a baleful – if regretful – Destiny, the characters play out the game of death over the course of a single night. Destiny announces: 'The world is as it is. Don't expect me to give you the key. I am not a warden or a jailer. I am Destiny; I come and go ... nothing more'.

The film takes place in the period immediately after the Liberation and centres on the fate of Diego, a former member of the Resistance, who travels to Paris to tell Claire that her husband Raymond died at the hands of the Nazis. He discovers that in fact Raymond is alive at home, liberated before the Nazis could kill him. Destiny is stalking Diego as he arrives at La Chapelle metro, and when he takes Claire and Raymond to a nearby restaurant to celebrate they are interrupted first by supercilious Hugo (decorated as a hero of the Resistance but actually a collaborator who was responsible for Raymond's capture), who taunts Raymond, then by Destiny himself, who obliquely reveals the future of the various characters. Diego misses the last metro and stays at Raymond's apartment, sleeping in their son's room. In the early hours of the morning, the child gets up to go to his gang's secret hideout (he needs to feed a brood of kittens they have saved from drowning) and lets Diego accompany him. Later, when Diego is carrying the child back to bed after he has fallen asleep, he walks into Malou, who has just left her husband. She is also Hugo's sister and is returning from her first visit to their father since he split up with his wife and whom she despises for the way he treated her mother. There is an instant recognition between her and Diego: in a single night they fall in an enchantment of love as they dance and wander around the district in the early hours exchanging confidences. But it cannot last. When they overhear an argument between him and his father, Diego recognises Hugo's voice as that of the mean who denounced Raymond to the Nazis. In their confrontation, Hugo produces a gun, which goes off in the ensuring struggle, although without hurting anyone. Diego leaves Hugo to his remorse and takes Malou to a café. Meanwhile, Malou's husband, distraught and drunk, returns. Learning from Hugo that she is with another man, he confronts the couple. When Malou tells him there is no possibility of her returning to him, in a state of panic, he shoots her with Hugo's gun. He helps Diego rush her to hospital, but the surgeons are unable to save her. Meanwhile, Hugo, disgusted with himself, has gone for a long walk along the railway tracks to face his destiny in the form of an oncoming train.

The film is infused by one of Prévert's most affecting poems/songs, 'Les enfants qui s'aiment':

The young lovers kiss standing
In the doorways of the night
And passers-by mark them out
But the young lovers
Are not there for anyone else
It is only their shadow
Which trembles in the night
And rouses the passers-by to fury
Their fury their scorn their laughter their envy
But the young lovers are not there for anyone else
They are far gone into the night
Very much higher than the day
In the dazzling transparency of their first love

This shadowy love – as transient as it is sublime, as ephemeral as it is profound – is shown to be both the redeeming feature of humans and a mark of their incapacity: 'People don't know how to love'. This is the theme tune Prévert was constantly humming. As always in Prévert, love is the one thing that life offers to justify itself, but this love is neither consoling, nor does it offer hope: it is a moment of contestation (inevitably doomed, at least in so far as one wants to prolong it) of inexorable fate. The kiss is for Prévert the supreme point, but love lives and dies in that moment: there is no continuation. People find themselves in love, but they are incapable of loving: this is the tragedy of the world. As Destiny tells the lovers in *Les Portes de la nuit*: 'You've had one really good night. Isn't that enough?'

Even if it offers no hope, love does nevertheless prevail over human destiny through recognition: the lovers have 'met' before, unbeknownst to themselves, on Easter Island, among myriads of names on the ancient stones; they were each compelled to mark their names next to one another's. As in Tay Garnett's *One Way Passage* (1932, discussed in the following chapter), it is confidence in the encounter, the willingness to submit oneself to objective chance, that offers the possibility of finding true love, even if it may be doomed in its immediacy. When Diego tells Destiny that his name is Napoleon, the latter replies, 'Why not? Napoleon was a man like any other. He was born, he lived his life, he died... Everything is related'.

The title of the film is highly significant. It might be thought that it would be more accurate to call it 'les embrasures de la nuit', since the lovers are to be found kissing only in doorways, and these are doors that do not open onto anything. Nothing, that is, except the night. And this is a theme that runs through Prévert's work: that love is linked to the night, giving access to what is hidden by its darkness. Lovers only experience love in the moment but that moment is all moments. In this way, Prévert's vision does not accept the elemental solitude of human existence we have seen in Buñuel's films, although it remains similarly tragic in nature.

In many ways *Les Portes de la nuit* is Prévert's most significant film. At least, more than any other, it sums up the themes of his work. It is also, perhaps, despite appearances, his most optimistic film. The working through of destiny here is not malevolent, but appointed. Even Hugo is allowed his moment of epiphany as he walks towards the dawn into the path of an oncoming train

André Breton (1987) once wrote that 'expression must be reduced to its simplest form, which is love'. Prévert might have taken this injunction as his starting point, especially in terms of his film scripts. It is remarkable how, no matter what the source material he was working with, we see a similar set of characters and concerns in the majority of the films with which Prévert was involved, even those for which he only wrote the dialogue. On the one hand are those who are open to love and on the other those who close themselves off from it, acting in ways to destroy it in others. In between stand those who act as emissaries of destiny or those who resign themselves to the denial of love.

No film maker has given us so many radiant and sublime lovers as Prévert, not even Frank Borzage. Lange and Valentine in *M. Lange*, Jean and Nelly in *Quai des brumes*, François and Françoise in *Le Jour se lève*, André and Catherine in *Remorques*, Anne and Gilles in *Les Visiteurs du soir*, Michèle and Julien in *Lumière d'été*, Malou and Diego in *Les Portes de la nuit*, Georgia and Angelo in *Les Amants de Vérone*, the Shepherdess and the Chimney Sweep in *Le Roi et le oiseau*, and, most memorably, Garance and Baptiste in *Les Enfants du Paradis*. Each one is singular and each one is dazzling.

Although they are the most unforgettable of these lovers, Garance and Baptiste are also the only ones who never really consummate their love, which is only accepted at a distance. Their failure to act on their feelings is not simply a result of Baptiste's shyness. This simply marks the fact that they are divided from one another by their personalities as much as anything. Baptiste is too dedicated to his art as a mime to commit himself fully to another person, while Garance is too much of a free spirit to abandon herself to one man. In this she resembles the other characters Arletty played in *Le Jour se lève* and *Les Visiteurs du soir*, both of whom are too worldly-wise to wish to transform the world: they are content to accept it as it is and accommodate themselves to it. Like Clara, in the former film, and Dominique in the latter, she is rather an emissary, one who facilitates other people's self-realisation without sharing it. Both Garance and Clara bind themselves to men they do not respect, while Dominique has actually sold her soul to the Devil.

A free woman, Garance would prefer to leave herself open to chance rather than surrender to love. Throughout the film, her love for Baptiste is secondary to her acceptance of her role as being all things to all men, while resolutely belonging to herself. For Frédérik, the Comte de Montray and Lacenaire, she is part of their imaginary world. They realise themselves through her, each in his own way, and the same thing is true, to a lesser extent, of Baptiste. But with each it is part of a performance: their world, after all, is a theatrical one, in which they are constantly playing different roles and are of uncertain identity in themselves.

Garance comes to these men as something of a succubus, of the sort the surrealists had celebrated, who appears to men not so much here to drain them of their energy as to facilitate it. The count tells her: 'You are much too beautiful for anyone really to love you. Beauty is an exception, an insult to an ugly world. Men rarely love beauty, they buy it in order no longer to hear it spoken about, to efface it and forget it ...' The reproach Catherine makes to André in *Remorques*, 'when you want to be sincere, you cannot; you speak obliquely without wanting to, in order to conceal everything', is not one that any of the characters Arletty plays would utter, because they accept people as they are even if, by her presence, she may transform them. Ultimately, then, Baptiste and Garance are incapable of loving one another since both of them are too immersed in their own destinies to reach out to the other. Uniquely among the films Prévert wrote, in *Les Enfants du Paradis* love is never realised, even in the moment; it is glimpsed but not really recognised. At the end, when they do spend the night together, they are too overcome with remorse and regret to love one another as their passion demands. Love makes as devastating an impact here as it does in *L'Âge d'or*, perhaps more so. None of the characters are untouched by it; none of them realise their love.

Les Enfants du Paradis in many ways stands out from the other films Prévert wrote by the extent to which most of the characters are consigned to their own solitude. Their relationships are sustained by respect rather than solidarity, something emphasised by the famous last scene in which Baptiste pursues the illusion of love that Garance represents. In Prévert's original script, this is even more strongly pronounced by the fact that Baptiste, taunted by Jéricho, kills the old clothes man in a furious rage that is redolent of Lange's killing of Batala and Jean's of Valentin. Carné dispensed with this scene, even though it reflects what in fact happened to the historical Debourou, who was acquitted of manslaughter for the incident. In many ways, even if *Les Enfants du Paradis* otherwise may appear to be Prévert's most optimistic film, it might be seen as one of his most pessimistic, since here the characters stay distant from one another and love remains an illusion.

For Prévert, love is the characteristic of those who do not calculate, who are not afraid to surrender themselves to passion. Opposed to the lovers are those who, by their calculation and need for control, do not simply deny love; they also act to destroy it in those who do love. Batala in *Monsieur Lange*, Zabel in *Quai des brumes*, Valentin in *Le Jour se lève*, the Devil in *Les Visiteurs du soir*, Jéricho in *Les Enfants du Paradis*, Hugo in *Les Portes de la nuit*, for instance, are all of a type: their nastiness is unmotivated, having become part of their very natures due to the fact that they have placed worldly values above eternal ones. But each of them pays the price; even the Devil is forced to give way in the face of love.

All of these people are characterised by their manipulative natures, and what they manipulate most is language, treating it as a mere object of their wills. As a poet, Prévert is aware of the power of words both to inspire and to seduce, and his ire is especially directed against those who treat words as things that can be used to manipulate and deceive others. Prévert's own use of language reflects the fact that, as for surrealists in general, language is something to be treated with respect: one does not make demands of it, but caresses it in order to encourage it willingly to divulge its secrets. 'Words make love' in Prévert's dialogues as they do in his poems.

Prévert's characters can be reduced to three or four different types but that does not mean they lack complexity. Each of them is memorable in his or her own way, but Prévert was less interested in the characters as such than in the relation that exists between them. Their simplicity of characterisation is thus deceptive.

Prévert's vision may initially appear to be somewhat Manichean. Yet if in his world evil exists, it is as an active force that is enabled by the denial of the foundations of human solidarity; it is not an absolute characteristic of certain beings. As they act, his 'evil' characters are emissaries of a destiny that is made inevitable by the fact that they have abandoned human feelings to place their faith in material reality. In so doing, they inevitably bring disaster on themselves as well as on those around them. Prévert's world is a strangely ambivalent one in which a glance or a moment's touch offers the possibility of profound transformation that is often prevented by the workings of a destiny they are powerless to act against, since human beings are trapped within a world that is foreign to them. The sense of conflict in Prévert's world is not really between good and evil but between recognition and non-recognition.

For, if love is glimpsed rather than fully realised, it is a glimpse that is dazzling. Founded in a recognition that openness to encounter makes possible, it represents the Sunday of Life, of which Hegel spoke: the sudden realisation that solitude can be overcome in this moment that contains within it the promise of all moments. The tragedy of existence remains: we live in anguish, overpowered by the fate that has carried us here. In Prévert's world the forces of life are too powerful to be harnessed even by love. Or one might put this the other way around: love is too strong to allow itself to be reduced to life, and its appearance tends therefore to invoke death. Human agency may be illusory, but by surrendering ourselves to destiny, we open up the possibility of a glimpse of that supreme point where oppositions, the opposition between life and death among them, are revealed as not being in contradiction to one another. Prévert had a faith in people's sense of solidarity against the organisation of society. His sensibility was that of an anarchist for whom it is the system of society and not an inherent characteristic of human beings that makes for injustice. Kyrou expressed this well: 'Prévert's world is founded in marvellous encounters, unobtrusive looks which overturn the face of the world, liberating rage, avenging humour, cries of defiance, finding love, love without restriction, in the streets, in parks, greenhouses and hovels' (1967: 87).

The commercial failure of *Les Portes de la nuit* did not, contrary to what is often said, directly cause the break-up of the partnership between Prévert and Carné. They worked together on what should have been Carné's next release, *La*

Fleur de l'âge, which had to be abandoned half-way through when the producers withdrew their financial backing, although it was reputedly shaping to be one of their finest films. It was during Carné's next film, *La Marie du port*, from which Prévert withdrew in the middle of filming, refusing to allow his name to appear on the credits, that their partnership came to an end.[3]

Prévert continued to write for films after the ending of his partnership with Carné broke up, and his later work included an adaptation of Victor Hugo's *Notre Dame de Paris* for Jean Delannoy (1956) and the wonderful *Les Amants de Vérone* for André Cayatte (1949). In many ways, though, Prévert's vision may be most fully realised in his final film, which is one of the great classics of animation. *Le Roi et l'oiseau* (1980) made in collaboration with animator Paul Grimault, and not released until three years after Prévert's death. The film had a long genesis, having been conceived in 1945 when Prévert and Grimault worked on a short film which was never completed based on Hans Anderson's story 'The Shepherdess and the Chimney Sweep'. Although released in 1952 as *La Bergère et le Ramoneur*, having been edited against the wishes of both Prévert and Grimault, it was disowned by them. In the 1960s Grimault bought the rights to the film footage and worked with Prévert on a more ambitious project which would incorporate the material into a new feature-length film.

The film is set in the land of Takicardia, ruled by a tyrannical Ubuesque king whom no one dares to challenge. But he earns the eternal enmity of a bird whose companion he kills when out hunting. The king dreams of a beautiful Shepherdess whose portrait adorns his private chamber. But she loves a chimney sweep depicted in another painting. One night the characters in the chamber come to life and the shepherdess and the chimney sweep flee, escaping through the chimney after the sweep throws a tomato at the king's portrait, temporarily blinding him. The king's portrait usurps the king's authority and orders the couple's arrest, but they are able to defy him with the help of the bird.

A brilliantly animated film which has been enormously influential on Japanese anime, especially on the work of Hayao Miyazaki, whose own sensibility appears to have much in common with Prévert's, *Le Roi et le oiseau*, within its fairy tale context, is perhaps the purest realisation of Prévert's worldview. Here expression is reduced to its purest form as true love finally does triumph over tyranny.

Prévert is the poet of the end of the world. But this end is the promise of a new world. In the films he wrote, fate may appear malevolent but it is, more often, facilitatory, allowing a glimpse of a desired life that may be out of reach in more than a momentary way but still gives texture to this life. Fate is conjured up to be negated in the moment. In this respect it plays a similar role here as in the films of Fritz Lang, one of the directors most admired by the surrealists, for the way in which we are given a sense that each moment is both perilous and fragile. Far from regretting the fact, however, we should recognise how this apprehension imbues the moment with a preciousness it would otherwise lack.

CHAPTER 4

Surrealism and Hollywood

The conjunction between Hollywood and surrealism has always seemed anomalous, if not contradictory. Even if, in its heyday, Hollywood was called the 'dream factory', the dreams it manufactured – or at least the ones invoked in this designation – were overwhelmingly ones upon which the surrealists were more likely to choke than be nourished. Applying Taylorist and Fordist production principles to the creative process, Hollywood sought to regulate dreams in ways that annulled any surrealist attitudes of spontaneity and moral rigour, and the list of directors who have been tethered, if not destroyed, by the Hollywood system is a long one. Nevertheless, the Hollywood system still left a place for the imagination. Its producers may have been concerned to control the product they supplied, but they also wanted the best directors, who were usually recalcitrant about incorporation into a production line. The position that cinema held in the social life of the first half of the twentieth century also meant that, simply though its diffusion, it would affect and be affected by the social unconscious and would consequently, if involuntarily, function as a vehicle for the sort of modern mythology the surrealists were intent upon exploring. Equally the vastness of the Hollywood studio system meant that it was unable to control every aspect of the production line, and the very way of life in Hollywood encouraged mavericks and non-conformists. Chance also had its say, intervening in often unexpected ways to disrupt the rationality of the system. At this human level, Adorno was undoubtedly wrong to see Hollywood as a devouring machine (although this doesn't mean he was wrong about its ultimately demoralising impact on the human spirit). Its dreams were in any event not always a sham, as the surrealists recognised. Indeed, the very constraints of Hollywood in its golden age may have aided the process of recalcitrance we argued for in chapter 1 as being an ingredient of popular culture in the early part of the twentieth century.

Surrealism's fascination with Hollywood has been explored before (notably by Kyrou, 1967, 1985; Matthews, 1979; Hammond, 2000) and involves many factors. In the first edition of his book, Paul Hammond argued that 'a mainstream Hollywood film could be surrealist in two ways: accidentally or ethically'. This is something of an over-simplification, as Hammond (1978a) recognised (in revising his text for subsequent editions, he offers a much more nuanced account), but is a useful starting point. It is certainly remarkable how many films made in Hollywood conjoined with surrealism in their thematic concerns or ethical standpoint.

It was genre films that offered the greatest possibilities for surrealist recognition: comedy, musicals, horror films, gangster films and film noir, animated cartoons. In different ways, all of these genres provided fertile territory for dislodging our faith in a realist apprehension of the solidity of reality. Comedy above all was a special domain, at least the burlesque form of comedy that dominated in Hollywood from the twenties until the Second World War. This interest certainly conforms to Hammond's designation: what the surrealists perceived in classic Hollywood comedy was its *moral* value, which can be characterised by the subtitle of one of the two books Petr Král (1984a) devoted to the subject: it was 'Custard Pie Morality'.

The surrealists adored Charlie Chaplin long before it became fashionable to do so, but their special affection was for Buster Keaton, Harry Langdon (Král regarded *Long Pants* as the only film that bears comparison with *L'Âge d'or*), Fatty Arbuckle, Lupino Lane, Harold Lloyd, Larry Semon, the Marx Brothers and W. C. Fields. What united all of these comedians was their taste for anarchy and insubordination, and it was this as much as their humour that attracted the surrealists. Robert Benayoun perhaps sums up the appeal of all of these comedians to the surrealists in discussing W. C. Fields:

> His method was very simple: nothing less that the breaking of *every* rule. He didn't spare one. Logic was his first victim: he twisted its neck good and proper, predicting in many ways the three-dimensional puns of *Hellzapoppin*. All the taboos of the 'American way of life' met the same fate; competitive sport, and its grotesque appurtenances, provided him with themes for his most celebrated sketches. The aseptic cult of the Child-as-God ('I like them fried') inspired his most ferocious struggle with the most horrible little man in the world ('A lad called LeRoy; he maintains he's a baby'), whom he martyrs with impunity in film after film. Another, almost masochistic, cult of the Woman-as-jewel, sanctified by American law, permits him more than one murder. He ridiculed the American idea of success, based on honesty and patience, of which he was the double negative, its politics ('I only vote *against* people'), decency and its puritanical representatives (he created the oath 'Godfrey Daniels' to more than replace the 'God damn' excised by the Hays Office), and last but not least religion ... (1951: 40–1).

Along with a taste for insubordination, classic comedy cut the ground from under our feet. The rational and conventional world was there to be devastated, as Groucho Marx put it, according with a surrealist viewpoint:

> We hold the theory that we shouldn't be repressed. When we see a pompous fellow in a high silk hat swelled up with his own importance and sniffing and sneering at folks as they pass, we do exactly what the rest of the world would like to do. We heave a ripe tomato at the hat. If we suppressed that desire, we would not be normal (Quoted in Eyles, 1992: 9).

The horror film, too, opens up the wounds of society, forcing it to face realities it would prefer to ignore. Freud's famous text 'The Uncanny' offers a psychoanalytical approach to the attraction of horror that chimes with surrealism, but the surrealists didn't need Freud to recognise the way the horror film enables hidden desires and repressed thoughts to emerge into the light of day, having very early recognised the way the gothic novel reflected the forces of social dissolution that underlay the French Revolution. Horror stories take us to the extreme of the problem of our mortality, confronting us with death and dissolution, and often uncovering the more persistent fears and desires that lie buried within our unconscious. Pierre Mabille defines this attraction for the surrealists:

> Fear of death, you give life its value. Fear of the future, you make the moment precious, you give meaning to health, to riches. Fear, you allow us to marvel at the fragile smile appearing on a woman's face, you evoke the intense feelings that come over us when we meet another being who, in the next instant, will be swallowed up into the night... Constant presence of the night, filled with night-black mares, without which there would be no light. Intoxicating dialectic of being and nonbeing which reopens the entire question, which creates anxiety, without which life would cost nothing. Source of all our mind's pleasures. The indissoluble union of fear and hope sadistically makes us think that, perhaps, tomorrow the sun will no longer rise, the equilibrium of the seasons will be destroyed once and for all, the fragile comfort of hard-working societies will be ruined, that nothing will remain of the ordinary circumstances of humanity.
>
> It is necessary to have spent a certain amount of time within the tempest, surrounded by mountains seething in the rains, to have been taken up like a helpless plaything into the frenzied dance of the elements. It is necessary to have known, at night, that gradual cold carried by a horizontal wind when the earth seems frozen for eternity, when life is crystallised, dead... Disturbing limits beyond which life is compromised, you are surely the frontiers and the sources of the marvellous (1998: 89–90).

In film, the great period of the Hollywood horror film was from 1932 to 1935: the stories of Frankenstein, Dracula, King Kong, were enacted as cinematic myths during this era, converging with surrealism in the way they invite us to spend time 'within the tempest'. Films made at this time, such as *White Zombie, The Mummy, The Most Dangerous Game* (all 1932), *King Kong* (1933), *The Black Cat* (1934) and *The Bride of Frankenstein* (1935), in particular, all have an air of strangeness that goes far beyond a simple depiction of fear to reveal some of the more uneasy facets of existence.

In many ways, however, the most remarkable configuration of Hollywood film and surrealism is to be found the treatment of love, in a whole series of films made from the twenties until the fifties. A belief in the transformative power of love has been one of the constants of surrealist endeavour. 'If you like LOVE, you will love SURREALISM' was a motto on one of the earliest surrealist visiting cards, and it was love that was regarded as the marker of that central point of surrealist concern, the determination of the point at which apparent contradictions are resolved.

Taking a cue from the poet Rimbaud, who called for love to be 're-invented', the surrealists sought an extravagant, overwhelming kind of love. It was not something comforting, but represented a rending, a moment of rupture when the identity of the individual self is brought into doubt through an encounter with an other who holds a possibility of effecting its transformation. This love is violent and transgressive for, according to the Mexican poet Octavio Paz,

> it is a choice ... perhaps a free choosing of our destiny, a sudden discovery of the most secret and fateful part of our being. But the choosing of love is impossible in our society. To realise itself, love must violate the laws of the world. It is scandalous and disorderly, a transgression committed by two stars that break out of their predestined orbits and rush together in the midst of space ... Whenever it succeeds in realising itself, it breaks up a marriage and transforms it into what society does not want it to be: a revelation of two solitary beings who create their own world, a world that rejects society's lies, abolishes time and work, and declares itself to be self-sufficient (1961: 198).

Rejecting ideologies of libertinism and free love, the surrealists celebrated the encounter of the unique couple as establishing a desired place of lucidity where it is possible to perceive the point at which the solidity of the world disperses as we become aware of our destiny. By linking the human couple with universal flow, surrealism sees love as the point that links creation and destruction, and life and death, so that existence assumes an*other* meaning. It is an irruption of the eternal into everyday life, assuming the form of an ineluctable necessity, a consecration of destiny that marks a point at which freedom and necessity become one, representing the 'delirium of absolute presence', of which Breton spoke in *Mad Love* (1987: 76).

It is curious to note how, in some of the films made in Hollywood during the thirties and forties, this surrealist understanding of love was given a tangible expression. Breton himself referred to Peter Ibbetson (Henry Hathaway, 1935) as a 'triumph of surrealist thought', considering it on a par with *L'Âge d'or*. An exaggeration, perhaps, as the film contains elements of Christian overlay that are absent from the oneiric novel by George du Maurier from which it is drawn, but *Peter Ibbetson* is just one of many films of the time that have this quality. Paul Hammond (1978a) has brought attention to the way in which the spiritual transcendence of some Hollywood love films may seem to undermine their surrealist content. In so far as the endings of *Peter Ibbetson* or *You Only Live Once* (Fritz Lang, 1937) are concerned, it is difficult to deny that they have a correspondence with the sense of spiritual transcendence recounted by Christian mystics. Yet speaking of You Only Live Once, Ado Kyrou rejects any transcendent interpretation as he writes: 'false words from those who are in the pay of the assassins of love must be rejected with contempt; lovers must do *everything* to live freely, here, on this earth, do everything to know freedom and love, be it only for a single moment' (1967: 426). This materialist article of faith is not borne out by the film, and Kyrou's determination to reject any transcendence in these films in general is hardly convincing. It even seems to go against surrealism, since the supreme point of surrealist endeavour, of which this 'single moment' is an intimation, is precisely not 'here, on this earth', but beyond the dimensions of time and space which form 'this world'. In this respect, there may be a point of intersection with Christian mysticism, except that in mysticism, the transcendent link is one-way: the subject perceives him- or herself united with the godhead. In these films, in contrast, it is through the couple's experience of one another that they are transformed and made aware of another dimension of reality than that which they are habitually used to. In most of these films, though (in *Portrait of Jenny* [William Dieterle, 1948], *Berkeley Square* [Frank Lloyd, 1933], *One Way Passage* [Tay Garnett, 1932], for instance), the recognition of the existence of different realities has little that is Christian about it and seems closer to a pagan acceptance of the way reality is layered through the perception we have of it. In any event, the surrealist appeal of these films lies in the fact that they always take the side of the lovers against social realities and so represent a triumph of the pleasure principle.

In many ways the most remarkable of this series of films is Tay Garnett's *One Way Passage*. In this film, two people meet by chance in Hong Kong. They break the stems of their glasses and join them together as a gesture of togetherness (a gesture that becomes ritualised through the film). They do not expect to see each other again, but later find themselves together aboard a liner bound for San Francisco. Neither of them is aware that the other is doomed: he is a convicted murderer being returned to the States to be executed; she is terminally ill. They spend an idyllic time together, parting at the end of the voyage with a promise to meet again in Aguascalientes on New Year's Eve, both knowing they will be unable to keep the appointment. The film ends in a bar in Aguascalientes at New Year when the barman is amazed to see two glasses spontaneously break and join together their stems.

The faith this film places in love conjoins it with surrealism in a defiant refusal of the given. Time and space are confounded and love makes its home precisely outside of their confines. Normal understandings of time and space are revealed to be equally mistaken in *Berkeley Square*, in which the lovers have to cross the ages to meet, he having been born more than a century after her death. Time also crumples away in *Portrait of Jenny* and *Pandora and the Flying Dutchmen* (Albert Lewin, 1951), while in *Peter Ibbetson*, prison bars, a broken back and the process of ageing are powerless to prevent Peter and Mary from loving each other every night in an enchanted domain. Similarly, in *Seventh Heaven* (1927) Chico and Diane meet each other every day at eleven o'clock despite being separated by hundreds of miles and a world war. In *Seventh Heaven,* too, Diane and Chico are re-united after he has been blinded in the war. Diane sentimentally says she will be his eyes but he, tearing off his bandages, tells her that now he is with her again it is obvious that he will be able to see again. The impossible is the rule because in love everything is possible.

The director of *Seventh Heaven*, Frank Borzage, was one of the two great poets of love in Hollywood's golden age, along with Josef von Sternberg. In their films, the sensibility they revealed is almost at one with surrealism, even if Borzage textures his exploration of love through a redemptive, if idiosyncratic, Christianity. Of his films, *Seventh Heaven* is one of the greatest of all stories of love, but *Street Angel* (1928), *Lucky Star* (1929), *A Farewell to Arms* (1932), *Moonrise* (1948), without mentioning many others, are not far behind (sadly *The River* [1928], perhaps his finest film, has been lost and is only viewable in an incomplete form). Borzage was brought up as a Catholic, but if he remained a Christian, it was of an expansive type, incorporating Mormon beliefs as well as Gnostic ideas, which he probably assimilated as a Freemason. At any rate, an amalgam of beliefs gave rise in his films to a vision of an emancipatory love that converges almost seamlessly with surrealist ideas.

Josef von Sternberg is mainly known for his partnership with Marlene Dietrich and the seven films he made with her are among the greatest cinematic explorations of love, as much for the extraordinary dynamic between the director and his star as for the stories themselves, which are nevertheless magnificent. Sternberg's films provide a fascinating contrast with Borzage's. Where Borzage placed all of his faith in love, Sternberg was a master of ambivalence. In Borzage love is simple: a pure recognition of destiny; in Sternberg it is infinitely complex: to be realised it must pass through a labyrinth of deceptions and disappointments. Love is not something the characters in Sternberg's films in general welcome; sometimes it represents a kind of tidal wave they desperately fight to hold back. In *Morocco*, (1930) when the Dietrich character is asked if she is in love, replies, 'I hope not!' If it exists, it is momentarily: 'I kissed you because I loved you, for a moment', she says in *The Devil is a Woman* (1935). Reciprocal love is never recognised (there is no thunderbolt, 'love at first sight'), but only emerges into the light after a struggle when the lovers have broken down all of their barriers and can finally see each other nakedly. In this struggle they risk destroying one another and at times destruction will win out over love (*The Scarlet Empress, The Shanghai Gesture, The Saga of Anatahan*). Existing in treacherous waters, as elusive as the meaning of a glance, love in Sternberg's films is actively present in the world, activated by desire but also masked by it. One of the most unashamedly carnal of directors, Sternberg never regards the woman as a redemptive figure. In the justly famous ending of *Dishonoured* (1931), Dietrich, who has earlier declared that death is 'just another adventure', makes herself up while awaiting the firing squad. Not an image of vanity, might we infer that she is *preparing to meet her lover*? A greater affirmation that life is not always in opposition to death it would be hard to find, and this shows the extent to which Sternberg's worldview was in harmony with surrealism.

The third director we might consider whose consistently presented worldview approximated to that of surrealism was Tod Browning. Unlike the other two directors, however, love is not a theme of Browning's work; in fact it rarely makes an appearance except in scabrous form. The first great director of horror films, animator of the earliest Hollywood *Dracula* (1930), with Bela Lugosi, his career was closely tied in with that of one of the greatest of screen actors, Lon Chaney. Today Browning is known principally for *Dracula*, which is not one of his best pictures, and for one of the cinema's most notorious films, *Freaks* (1932). Like Borzage, however, he was one of the great professionals of early cinema, producing a string of fascinating and popular films until the controversy over *Freaks* made him partially *persona non grata*. Browning's theme was the irruption of otherness into the realm of normality. In Browning's world the appearance of the world is constantly disrupted in a way that is tinged with black humour. *The Unholy Three* (1925), for instance, is about a gang, consisting of Echo, a ventriloquist who masquerades as a kindly old lady, Hercules, the circus strong man, and Tweedledee, a dwarf, who commit ingenious crimes. Their usual tactic is for the old lady to visit a house with her 'baby' in tow to case the place. On one occasion, the police visit their lair, and they are almost undone as Tweedledee, still dressed as a baby, is sitting smoking a cigar! In *The Devil Doll* (1936), a criminal who has escaped from Devil's Island transforms himself into similarly kind old lady to make beautiful miniature dolls with the purpose of dealing death and destruction on corrupt bankers who ruined him, while in *The Blackbird* (1926) a gangster assumes the identity of a kind crippled missionary. It is in the motif of revenge that Browning's affinity with surrealism is most apparent. His films offer a counterpoint to the explosion of revolt we see in some of the burlesque comedy films, except that what is dealt with through humour in the films of the Marx Brothers or W. C. Fields is here dealt with through violence. In *West of Zanzibar* (1928), as in *The Devil Doll* and *Freaks*, revenge is taken in a way that is as dizzying as it is justified. It is in *The Unknown* (1927) that rage at the world takes on its most astounding form when Alonzo, an apparently armless knife-thrower, spikes the contraption that controls the circus act of his rival in love so that he will be torn apart by two galloping horses. Alonzo was not in fact armless, at least not at the beginning of the film. He was pretending to be in order to escape the police. When he finds that Nanon, the woman he loves (played by Joan Crawford), cannot stand the fact that men have arms, he really has his arms amputated, only to discover that in the meantime she has fallen in love with the circus strong man.

For sheer perverseness, Browning's films have never been equalled, but it is a perverseness that is strangely intoxicating. He is the only film maker who has ever come close to giving form to the sort of glacial cruelty which Lautréamont's Maldoror specialises in. Or at least the only other example that immediately comes to mind is Georges Franju's *Les Yeux sans visage* (1959), but what Franju realised in one film is characteristic of Browning's work as a whole.

We can certainly not say that the world of these three directors is purely 'surrealist', but then nor can we really say that about Buñuel's or Švankmajer's films, since surrealism is not about agreement as to common principles, but about exploring the phenomenal world from a certain perspective. What is remarkable is the degree to which their sensibility converges with or crosses over that of surrealism. In the case of Sternberg, he was almost certainly aware of surrealism and probably integrated his understanding of it into his films. This is, however, irrelevant to the surrealist interest of his films, and may even have worked against it, since he probably understood surrealism as an aesthetic movement. Borzage and Browning, on the other hand, were almost certainly untouched by any direct knowledge of surrealism, yet their respective (if very different) sensibilities were in tune with it to such an extent as to suggest either the existence of some synchronicity of affect that allowed ideas to permeate the sensibilities of people far apart from one another, or that social conditions at the time were such that similar ideas assumed different forms in different places. To some extent, both suggestions have some truth in them. We also, however, have to consider the way in which the production processes of early cinema were responsive to a certain instinctive 'surrealism'.

Before we return to consider this further, however, if we have sketched out the various ways in which classic Hollywood might meet surrealism on the moral plane, what about the idea of finding in films evidence of an 'involuntary' surrealism?

The revelation of finding an 'involuntary' surrealism within certain films is more problematic, involving the disruption of the narrative flow by elements that open up the film to a meaning other than the intended one. In other words, chance intervenes to unsettle the manifest intent and so expose the film to a fresh perspective. This may occur within the structure of the film due to the fact that the different elements of the film are imperfectly meshed together, leaving the film's meaning equivocal or inconclusive. Such an openness of structure leaves the audience free to insert its own meanings into the gaps in the film's narrative. By exploiting such ambivalence, the surrealists were able to imbue certain films with qualities the makers may not have intended to be there. The most complex attempt by the surrealists to do this was not made in respect of a case of involuntary surrealism, however, but in relation to a film they admired: Sternberg's *The Shanghai Gesture* (1941).

This was an attempted 'irrational enlargement' of the film, whereby the surrealists explored their reactions to it in an oblique way, by responding to a set of arbitrarily chosen questions (see Hammond, 2000: 121–30 for full details of the experiment). Some of the questions take the film into another dimension, extending it beyond any rational causality, such as 'at what moment should a snow fall take place?' Others induce the viewer to see what is invisible in it, for instance: When is a river seen in the film? Others are deceptively obvious: 'in what location outside of the action does the film take place?' The answers are no less arbitrary than the questions and do little to tell us about the film itself. What they do, however, is to engage the imaginative process, by feeding reverie and disrupting an obvious audience identification. To ask such an obvious question as 'where the film is located' sets in play questions about our relation to representation, because if the film is 'set' in Shanghai, its actions actually happened in a studio in Los Angeles. It is difficult to imagine that anyone seeing the film, however, experiences it as something that happened in either place: it transports us into a realm that is neither of the city called Shanghai nor of a Hollywood studio (although it contains both). The surrealists' replies to this question are as oblique as one might expect given the determinedly tangential nature of the enquiry, but the indeterminacy of the responses is not entirely explained by this. The 'Shanghai' represented in the film is not a real place but a locus of projected desire. In this sense there is an implicit logic to their responses: they are not as arbitrary as they initially appear but extend possibilities the film contains for amplification. Indeed, to perceive this 'Shanghai' gambling den as existing 'beneath the Sphinx', as Bernard Roger responded (in Hammond, 2000), has a poetic truth which hints at an underlying mythological structure latently contained within the film.

With *The Shanghai Gesture*, the surrealists' 'irrational enlargement' was of a film already largely in harmony with a surrealist perspective. In the Romanian Surrealist Group's exposition of *Malombra* (see Hammond, 2000: 117-20), a rather banal Italian film was transformed by the viewers through the contagion of their desiring lens. In many other surrealist analyses peppered through Kyrou's and Hammond's books, films similarly take on lives detached from the intention of the film maker. That this was possible was due in part to the way that the very rigidity of the Hollywood production line encouraged desertion. An example we might take here is *East of Borneo* (George Melford, 1931), a standard studio melodrama of no more and no less interest than any other, no doubt. It was this film that provided the raw material which Joseph Cornell transformed into his collage film *Rose Hobart*, a founding film of the American avant garde, which saw it as a rejection of Hollywood production methods (although Cornell himself almost certainly considered it to be a homage to its star). If we actually watch *East of Borneo*, however, we will find a very strange film, with a strangeness that is quite independent of, and is not exhausted by, Cornell's transformation of it. It concerns an American couple trapped in a jungle empire of a Sadian maharaja who believes he is descended from the volcano that overlooks his domain and who takes his pleasure feeding prisoners to the crocodiles. Lauded by the avant garde for taking a trashy Hollywood film and turning it into 'art', Cornell's film in these terms fails: it is surely just as 'trashy' as the original and cannot be seen as an artist's triumph over the vulgarity of Hollywood. The surrealist value of

Rose Hobart is elsewhere: it enlarges the original without annulling it, giving us another way of looking at it. As such it represents a similar sort of investigation to that of the surrealist work on *The Shanghai Gesture* and *Malombra*. We see here one of the profound differences between an avant garde and a surrealist attitude.

Is it accurate, however, to speak of films such as *East of Borneo* as revealing an 'involuntary surrealism'? This suggests a certain spirit of appropriation: it gives legitimation to these films because the surrealists saw something in them that others didn't. What we ought perhaps to speak of is an 'involuntary poetry', which, available to all, nevertheless has a particular interest to surrealism because its procedures of automatism suggested just such a possibility. Ado Kyrou, we will recall, urged us to learn to see the worst films because they are 'sometimes sublime' (1985: 276). The surrealists did not extol bad films as such: the worst films Kyrou invoked were rare exceptions. It is significant that he saw this as a learning process, however: one needed to learn to recognise the way such films could become sublime.

There are also films of particular interest from a surrealist perspective even though this is in the sense neither that they share a surrealist morality, nor that they generate a form of 'involuntary poetry'. Two good examples are Charles Laughton's *The Night of the Hunter* (1955) and Alfred Hitchcock's *Vertigo* (1957).

The Night of the Hunter is a film often considered in relation to surrealism, and J. H. Matthews dedicates a chapter to a discussion of it, in which he argues for the surrealist provenance of the film even while accepting that 'There can be no question of supposing [Laughton] embraced Surrealist ideas' (1979: 150). Although it is difficult to disagree with anything Matthews says, his account nevertheless reads like special pleading in the way in which he tries to subsume the film to a surrealist worldview. While it is easy to see the appeal this film has for surrealists (the dream imagery, the story development and especially the dialectical interplay of black and white, the theme of the accursed wanderer, the treatment of childhood and the relations between the human, animal and material worlds), it is nonetheless undeniable that its overall dynamic emerges from a sensibility largely detached from a surrealist point of view. Its dialectic, drawn not from surrealism but from Brechtian alienation techniques, shades too easily into Manichean, if not Christian, dualism, and its sense of moral panic in the face of the forces of disorder (also informed by the English puritanism of its director) suggests anything but a surrealist perspective. *The Night of the Hunter* is one of cinema's great films, and the thematic it explores is indisputably of interest to surrealism (and the surrealists were in fact among the first to recognise its greatness, when it was largely dismissed on its initial release), but the moral positioning of the film is difficult to reconcile from a surrealist point of view (see Hammond, 1979b, for an extended review of it).

Laughton's Protestant puritanism was also shared by Alfred Hitchcock. If we can see in Hitchcock's films elements that chime with surrealism (especially his black sense of humour and atmosphere of terrorised perturbation), in other respects, his moral sensibility, like that of Laughton, seems irreconcilable with it (his collaboration with Dalí in *Spellbound* [1945] is of no significance in considering any affinity he may have had with surrealism). Furthermore, the extent of Hitchcock's control of his films, the fact that he manipulated audience reaction to an extent that one would have expected to preclude any possibility of chance to intrude, would seem to make him a quintessentially non-surrealist director. Nevertheless, in many of his films a certain 'surrealist' element intrudes, especially in 'dark' films like *The Trouble with Harry* (1955) or *North by Northwest* (1959). When we come to *Vertigo* (1958), we encounter a film that might be seen as simultaneously a surrealist film and an anti-surrealist film depending upon how it is viewed.

In this film, the themes of memory and transformation, an obsession with death, dreams and the shifting status of reality are undoubtedly of central interest to surrealism; in fact its dream logic is so impeccable that one might say that the film only makes sense in surrealist terms. At the same time, like his other films, *Vertigo* is so calculated that one has an uncomfortable sense that Hitchcock is interested not so much in exploring the complexities of reality through the above themes as in using it to play games with the possibilities of film to effect and manipulate audience reaction. As he does so, however, the film becomes over-determined in a way that allows chance, thrown out, one might say, through the door of Hitchcock's calculation, to re-enter via the window. There is thus, as there is with *The Night of the Hunter*, a sense of ambivalence that grips the viewer and won't let go.

If in one sense this ambivalence works to make the films of interest to surrealism, it also works against it. It could be said that the effect is the opposite to what we saw with *Les Enfants du Paradis*. In that film, surrealism imperceptibly permeates the film through the contribution of Prévert, while in both *The Night of the Hunter* and *Vertigo*, surrealism enters the films if they are seen under a certain perspective: one might say, if the viewers will it. But the aspects of the films that interested the surrealists can just as easily be ignored. In the fact that both Laughton and Hitchcock were well-informed directors, responsive to intellectual trends coming from Europe, one should not be surprised that surrealism should be one of the elements that found its way into their films. In this respect the two films differ from those of Hollywood's golden age and presage the way in which surrealism will later become part of the methodological apparatus of contemporary Hollywood cinema.

Equally as remarkable as the convergence of surrealist themes in early Hollywood cinema is the fact that such themes had largely vanished from it by the late fifties. It is, for instance, difficult to think of a single significant Hollywood film since *Vertigo* that even touches upon love in a way that corresponds to a surrealist perspective. The burlesque tradition in comedy continued now and again in the films of Jerry Lewis and the early Woody Allen but has appeared only sporadically since, and most comedy films in Hollywood these days are not of a sort to appeal to a surrealist sense of humour. The horror film continues to chill the spine from time to time, but these tend to be purely visceral thrills, lacking in mythological depth, if one excepts George Romero's early films. Not since Tobe Hooper's original *Texas Chain Saw Massacre* (1974) can we say there has been a horror film that really goes beyond superficial chills, even if Wes Craven and John Carpenter sometimes try. The musical as a genre has vanished, while the animated cartoon was largely abandoned to television and continued in the cinema only in the form of prestige productions.

In the surrealist response to Hollywood, genre films were of particular significance because they could elude production codes that dominated the mainstream, but paradoxically it was the demise of the studio production line that put an end to the possibilities of the sort of cinema that would cast up these rich poetic possibilities in a whole range of different films. With the changes in Hollywood production that gradually took effect from the fifties onwards, the involuntary or intuitive affinities with surrealism we can perceive in so many films of the classic age largely vanish, or perhaps assume a different form. With the demise of the B movie, genre films were integrated into the mainstream, something which, along with a greater awareness of inter-textual elements in films among critics and increasingly among film makers as well, has combined to make the involuntary generation of poetry unlikely if not impossible.

Furthermore, surrealism has entered the public domain. This means that today any director can make use of what are considered to be 'surrealist' effects as part of his or her narrative armoury; many films today can be seen as 'surrealist' not, as Kyrou saw it, through the experience of cinema but because they contain elements derived from surrealism that have consciously been crafted into the film.

This is complicated by the fact that surrealism is almost alone among modern movements in painting in not rejecting figurative imagery, its visual veneer gives it a stylistic appeal to film makers that no other movement, not even expressionism, can approach. Such stylistic flourishes do not necessarily reveal anything surrealist in the work of those using them: more often, in fact, it is a sign a paucity of imagination rather than a comment on the paucity of reality in modern life. The common currency surrealism has become makes the evaluation of the surrealist experience of film even more difficult than it was in the past. Surrealism has become an amorphous 'thing' that may, often for no clear reason, be attributed by critics to certain films or directors as suits the analysis they wish to follow.

The name of David Lynch seems to come up frequently in this connection. Personally I have always found the films of this director tedious (his early shorts and *Eraserhead* [1976] offered some promise, and *Blue Velvet* [1986] contained some genuine moments of *frisson*, but the latter film already seemed overblown and to partake of the puritanism it depicts without challenging it). Admittedly, Lynch's films are visually striking and contain resonant images (for instance the splendid encounter between the film maker and his sinister producers in *Mulholland Drive* [2002]) but in a purely episodic way: similar revelatory moments could be found in the work of any number of film makers.

It is apparent that Lynch has learned a lot from viewings of *Un Chien andalou* and surrealist paintings, which have provided him with his essential building blocks, based upon the use of bizarre juxtapositions and details. But this is not evidence of a surrealist sensibility at work; in many ways it is the reverse. The hallmark of surrealist work – the will to change life and transform the world – seems absent (and Lynch's pronouncements on surrealism make it clear he has little real understanding of it). What I find especially lacking is the limpidity I encounter in surrealist work, the sense not simply of looking into the world created, but also of the world of the film, as Breton once said of painting, *looking out* and making a direct communication with the viewer (this is one of the meanings of the surrealist understanding that 'poetry must be made by all'). If anything, Lynch seems closer in spirit to a Cocteau, playing mind games with the viewer. These games may be enjoyable if one enters into the spirit of them, but they are essentially mystificatory rather than revelatory. Lynch's films appear to be made for 'initiates', for those who accept the film makers' points of reference, as well as appealing to a lingering moral puritanism, a puritanism of transgression. They may evoke surrealism in their visual texture, but they do so only to assimilate it to a set of empty signifiers. They represent acceptable shock and reveal a self-consciousness of motive that serves as cover for a lack of motivation in the content of the film.

Of course this may be a blind spot on my part. Lynch's films may have qualities I have been unable to detect in them and it may be legitimate to relate them to surrealism if this could help to illuminate either one or the other. I have, however, never come across anyone who makes a convincing case for such a conjunction: most critics relate Lynch to surrealism purely on the basis of identifying a 'surrealist' visual style in his work, which is fundamentally to misunderstand the nature of surrealism. One could certainly name several dozen Hollywood film makers of the past fifty years in whom we could detect stronger affinities with surrealism: Robert Altman or John Huston (particular favourites of Robert Benayoun), Orson Welles or Robert Aldrich, Francis Coppola or Terrence Malick, Blake Edwards or Terry Gilliam, Sam Peckinpah or Stanley Kubrick, John Boorman or Michael Mann... Would it, however, illuminate our understanding either of surrealism or of the work of these directors to trace out these affinities?

One Hollywood director who does have genuine links with surrealism is Paul Verhoeven. As a young man in the sixties, he was a member of the Dutch Surrealist Group. This is not something he brings attention to, whether because he has ceased to be interested in surrealism, or because, as a genuine surrealist, he doesn't wish to make cultural capital from it. Yet there remain in Verhoeven's work clear traces of a surrealist attitude, even if these are mingled with a deep cynicism (born doubtless of the environment of Hollywood, as well as the considerable difficulties he had making films in his homeland) both gives his films a particular edge while leaving the spectator dissatisfied with an apparent lack of sincerity; at times this cynicism also seem forced, suggesting that it may be a strategy to establish his credentials.

There is nevertheless an undoubted surrealist anger in Verhoeven, even a surrealist rage, but unfortunately it more often seems directed against the film he is making (or more especially the processes of its making) than being used creatively by the director. Verhoeven is impatient with the limitations imposed on him by the commercial process of making films and tries to circumvent them. In the process his films lose much of the charge they might have had through being poorly motivated and written. One has the impression that Verhoeven is so intent upon subverting, or a least introducing content that undermines the limitations imposed upon him, that he loses a sense of the film itself: its content is often a sacrificial victim to the rage he feels. He seems to be saying to himself not 'how can I make the most effective film possible within the limits placed on me?' but 'how can I prevent the film from saying what those bastards want me to get it to say?' One has the feeling he has convinced himself about Adorno's direst warnings about the impact of the Culture Industry, and yet still thinks there is a way to circumvent its conclusive nature.

This prevents Verhoeven from making the most of his material. *Total Recall* (1990) had great possibilities for exploring the complexities of identity and the mutability of time and space, and yet doesn't contain anything like the same charge with which Ridley Scott, a far more compliant – and not at all surrealist – director, managed to imbue *Bladerunner* (1982). Of his other Hollywood films, both *Robocop* (1988) and *Starship Troopers* (1998) in different ways offer sometimes coruscating insights into the incipient fascism that now seems to be engulfing the United States, but in the end don't fully convince. *Basic Instinct* (1992), his most celebrated, or most controversial, American film is a tour de force of suppressed revolt, but it too is frustratingly unrealised in its possibilities. The premise that the Devil in modern society (in the form of Catherine Tremell) would be interested in bodies, not souls, is an intriguing one offering all sorts of opportunities for a surrealist exploration, most of which are not taken up. Catherine Tremell may be the Devil, but there is nothing about her – other than her superhuman knowledge – that sets her apart from mere humans. In so far as she has a motivation, it seems to be simply a very human search to maximise carnal gratification – albeit taken to an extreme – and there is a lack of match between her and her victims that prevents us from regarding her as more than a malicious person. Admittedly a vulgar script that seems to be striving for sensation at the expense of resolving the fascinating intimations its initial premise established made it difficult to realise the possibilities of the idea. Nevertheless, one can imagine the film Buñuel might have made with this material, and to raise this as a possibility is not to draw an invidious comparison between the two directors, but to bring attention to the fact that Buñuel's anger had a calmness about it. He accepted that the world

– and the world of the movies especially – is corrupt, and set about exposing that corruptness when he had the opportunity. Verhoeven recognises the corruption of the world in much the same way as Buñuel, but directs his rage impotently against it, at the expense of manifest content of his work. Verhoeven is often criticised for his ambivalence. From a surrealist perspective, he is probably not ambivalent enough.

It is today still possible to make films that converge with surrealism without the film maker knowing it, but the frame of reference has changed both because the nature of the film industry has changed and because today no one can make films in ignorance of surrealism. It has permeated the social consciousness to such an extent that even the most ignorant of film makers has some idea (most probably a distorted idea, but still an idea) of what surrealism is. This creates a mental barrier that prevents unconscious elements that disrupt the conscious surface from surging forth and entering the film making process. One can say therefore that there are only two types of films: those that use their knowledge of surrealism as part of their own vision, and those that consciously ignore, or reject entirely, a surrealist way of thinking. This does not, however, entirely change the situation. If David Lynch uses the images of surrealism as part of his filmic armoury, the 'surrealism' in the films of other directors like Jim Jarmusch or Tim Burton probably emerges despite any conscious knowledge they may or may not have of surrealism. It emerges rather because they each have a sensibility that merges imperceptibly with a surrealist attitude and is probably contained in elements that they would not consciously associate with their knowledge of surrealism. In the opening of *Mars Attacks!* (1997), for instance, Burton shows us a herd of stampeding cows on fire. There is no explanation for this scene and one imagines that Burton was here striving for a 'surreal' effect to establish the strangeness of the idea of a Martian invasion. It is a shock effect whose intention is not surrealist, since it is too consciously thought out. The scene itself becomes surrealist, however, when seen in the overall context of the film itself and the fact that Burton's sensibility integrates such a shock image into the structure of the film: it ceases to be an arbitrary striving for effect, but rather serves the disorienting impact of the film as a whole. Tim Burton is in fact one of the Hollywood directors in whom one can see a close relation to a surrealist perspective, especially in his love for popular culture in its subversive aspects, his exploration of otherness and sympathy for outsiders and in his sometimes acerbic commentary on American values, seen most particularly in *Edward Scissorhands* (1991) and *Mars Attacks!*

The contemporary American director, however, who seems to have maintained a consistency of viewpoint throughout his work that has most links in with surrealism (although there is no reason to believe that he is especially influenced by it) is Jim Jarmusch. *Dead Man* (1995), *Ghost Dog* (1999) and *Down By Law* (1986), in particular, give evidence of an unstated and no doubt unconscious kinship with surrealism in their attention to the transience of life, the otherness of encounter and the difficulties of communication. But Jarmusch has uniquely refused the inducements of Hollywood and remained outside the system.

If we are right in asserting that the innovations that Griffith introduced were ultimately responsible for diverting the cinema from being a medium for popular culture into one which divided its productions into commercial merchandise, on the one hand, and 'minority' art-house 'foreign' product, on the other hand, the fascination of Hollywood cinema from a surrealist point of view came from the extent to which its films continued to resist this separation, which has now become inclusive. Today, however, the cracks in the productive process that were discernible in earlier eras have been papered over and Hollywood no longer has any special provenance as a medium for the expression of popular culture from a surrealist perspective. Rarely, if ever, does an involuntary poetry surge up to take us by surprise as it once did in films of the classic era. Its films interest or do not interest on an individual basis but collectively do not create any sense of a modern mythology as they did in the first half of the twentieth century.

CHAPTER 5

Surrealism and the Documentary

Very little has been written about the surrealists' engagement with documentary other than in the context of Buñuel's *Las Hurdes, Terre sans pain* (1932). Yet it was quite an important aspect of surrealist film activity and surrealism was a significant influence in the development of the documentary genre. Key figures in documentary film, such as Henri Storck and Luc de Heusch in Belgium and Jean Painlevé, Jean Rouch and Jean Vigo in France, were close to surrealism, while Humphrey Jennings in Britain was a central figure in the British documentary movement. Jacques Brunius also made a number of documentaries, many for the BBC, although most of them seem to have vanished from view. Surrealism was also in many ways a decisive, if not determining, influence on the powerful documentaries of Chris Marker, Alain Resnais and Georges Franju, while the recent American documentarist Les Blank is close to the Surrealist Group in Chicago.[1]

It may at first seem incongruous to put 'surrealism' and 'documentary' together, in so far as surrealism is generally seen as being 'anti-realist', whereas documentary tends to be linked fundamentally with realism. Furthermore, the commonly drawn distinction between the cinema traditions deriving respectively from Lumière and Méliès, which we questioned in chapter 1, has often been seen in terms of a distinction between a 'documentary' and a 'fiction' tradition. Yet there was always a certain 'documentary' element to surrealism in all of its aspects, and this has taken a form which has found a natural, if sometimes uneasy, position within traditions of documentary film. In this respect, as elsewhere, when considering surrealism, we have to question whether making a distinction between the approaches of Lumière and Méliès has any meaning.

In a sense one could even say that surrealism began as a kind of 'documentary' movement. The 'Bureau of Surrealist Research' was founded precisely to document the unexpected aspects of contemporary life. Early surrealist texts such as Aragon's *Paris Peasant* or Breton's *Nadja* are 'documents' of encounter. As a journal, *La Révolution surréaliste* has a strong documentary sense, and of course the journal around which Georges Bataille gathered Breton's discontents during 1929 and 1930 was actually called *Documents*. Against this backdrop, it should not surprise us that surrealism has made a contribution to documentary film.

Indeed, Pierre Prévert's first film, *Souvenirs de Paris ou Paris-Express* (1928), was a documentary (made at the time when the 'documentary', as we now know it, was only just starting to take shape), and the influence of surrealism can easily be seen in some of the other early documentaries, such as Joris Ivens's *Rain* (1929) or Henri Storck's *Histoire du soldat inconnu* (1932). A surrealist element is retained in some of Ivens's later works, especially in the marvellous *La Seine a rencontré Paris*, made with Jacques Prévert in 1957, which deserves a place alongside surrealist explorations of personal geography such as the books of Aragon and Breton mentioned above. Whether Ivens had any real sympathy with surrealist ideas may be open to question since he absorbed influences like a sponge and his work no doubt owes more to realist traditions than to surrealism (at least there is little evidence that he doubted the essentially realist nature of the world). He nevertheless had a poetic sensibility that was in tune with surrealism, which is especially revealed in those films where he is concerned with evoking the relationship between nature and humanity, as in his very last film, *A Story of the Wind* (1988). *La Seine a rencontré Paris* could also be compared with *Aubervilliers*, also scripted by Prévert and directed in 1945 by Eli Lotar, the photographer of Buñuel's *Las Hurdes*, from which it is in turn descended. Both films are lyrical, but where *La Seine a rencontré Paris* is elegiac, *Aubervilliers* is coruscating, finding misery almost as great as that in Las Hurdes in a post-war district of Paris.

Ivens's early collaborator, Storck, however, was always close to the Belgian Surrealist Group and wrote many unrealised and unrealisable scenarios that stand with those written by Soupault, Artaud, Fondane, Desnos and many others as examples of an 'out of reach' surrealist filmography (see Storck, 1981). Although, like those of Ivens, many of his documentaries were made within the confines of a realist tradition, this never satisfied Storck and his work cannot be fully appreciated without taking the backdrop of surrealism into account. Some of his films, like *Misère au Borinage* (1933, made with Ivens) or *Easter Island* (1935), have a force and a ferocity that brings them close to the work of Buñuel. No matter that these films do not challenge the ideology of realism or play upon the problematic between reality and representation in the manner of films whose surrealist provenance may be more obvious, such as Jean Vigo's *À propos de Nice* (1929) or Buñuel *Las Hurdes*, Storck's best films are certainly surrealist in their moral coherence and disposition.

VIGO, BUÑUEL, STORCK

Along with Pierre Prévert's first film, it is Jean Vigo's *À propos de Nice* (1930) that is the starting point for a consideration of the surrealist uses of the documentary mode. Where the Préverts' film is evocative, Vigo's is barbed, offering a portrait of a society in process of disintegration. The Côte d'Azur becomes under Vigo's scrutiny a distillation of capitalist decadence, something Vigo himself stressed in his address on the occasion of the film's opening. Not that there is anything didactic about the film; its 'message' is built up cumulatively through its images, which seem to follow an implacable logic.

Under Vigo's gaze, the resort of Nice assumes a personality of its own as it wakes in the morning and unfolds through the day before expiring at night. It is a passage that seems to presage the coming 'night' that will extinguish the bourgeois order upon which the leisure industry of Nice was founded. Vigo builds upon the surrealist idea of a document, contrasting, on the one hand, the idle lives of the rich in their casinos or promenading on the beach, and on the other hand, the life of toil of the workers who make this life of indolence possible. Excluded from and even invisible to the lives of the wealthy which they serve, the latter are like displaced beings in a world of excess. Imposing nothing, Vigo allows the life of the city to reveal itself. Photographed by Dziga Vertov's brother, Boris Kaufman, *A Propos de Nice* is simultaneously the application of Kino-Eye techniques and their negation: Vertov, one might say, cut with the razor of Buñuel.

Vigo was enormously impressed with *Un Chien andalou*, and this shows in the way he juxtaposes images of the bourgeoisie at play with ones showing the work it takes to make such indulgence possible. This allows the film to reveal without didacticism the extent to which wealth depends upon an exclusion of those who are the real creators of it.

Central to the film is the carnival, assuming a Janus face as a festival of the rich that simultaneously affords the poor with an opportunity to mock their exploiters. The maintenance of social differences is shown to lead to dissolution, and a sense that capitalism is so decadent that no reform can ever alleviate its inequalities. Vigo described the intention behind the film to put on trial a whole way of life. By revealing a decadent society so given over to indolence it had lost its reason to live, he was encouraging the viewer to empathise with a revolutionary solution. In this, he was remarkably successful. Seen today the film is not simply a 'documentary' but has become a social document that reveals the inevitability of a class conflict so entrenched in the thirties that it could end only in violence, even if the conflict that actually took place was not the revolution Vigo expected but a world war that would destroy social certainties and force capitalism to re-model itself on a social democratic model. In the present era when the capitalist system has turned its back on social democracy and re-established new forms of social exclusiveness and exclusion, Vigo's film has lost none of its force.

No one in the history of cinema has embodied revolt as naturally as Vigo, and his approach and vision converge almost totally with surrealism. Even though he was never directly connected with the surrealists, *À propos de Nice* stands with Buñuel's *Las Hurdes* and Storck's *Easter Island* as one of the great unveiling films of the thirties, cruelly pulling back the curtain to reveal the grubbiness within which the stage is set.

If Vigo confronted capitalism in its lair, Buñuel in *Las Hurdes* went to its fringes to observe a marginal people excluded even more completely than the proletariat of Nice. Buñuel's third film, it portrays a 'land without bread' existing in central Spain, only a short journey from Salamanca. This 'filmed essay in human geography', as Buñuel called it, was based on an ethnographic account of the region by Maurice Legendre, a French sociologist, published in 1927. Drawing extensively upon Legendre's work, supplemented by his own experience (and through his collaboration with Pierre Unik, who wrote the commentary, and Eli Lotar, his photographer), Buñuel presented a region that had been left behind by history, marked by a poverty that was intolerable even when judged against the standards of Spain at the time.

Despite this, it is clear that the film is far from a straightforward record of an abandoned people. In fact, it represents a striking challenge to a central tenet of realist documentary tradition, that it should show what is 'really there'. Instead it forces viewers to question what they are seeing. The anthropological gaze is especially brought into question: Buñuel refuses to respect the dignity of his subjects, but insists on subjecting them to a merciless interrogation that implicates the viewer. Vivian Sobchack expresses this well:

If the Hurdanos are monstrous to the narrator and the narrator monstrous to us, then we are most likely monstrous to someone or something else - to history, perhaps. If we are not monstrous objects but human subjects, then so are the narrator and the Hurdanos. There are no villains or heroes to Buñuel - only those who unquestioningly accept the vision of their culture or time, and those who try to see clearly through it even in the knowledge they are doomed to failure (1998: 73).

This is thus a film about seeing as much as anything else. It asks us whether we can believe the evidence of our own eyes, especially in film, where we are caught watching others through the eyes of someone else. Buñuel makes us uncomfortable by the dislocation he establishes between what we are shown and what we are told about what we see. Jeffrey Ruoff sees the film as a knowing subversion of the conventional travelogue: *Las Hurdes, Land without Bread* in its very title evokes, in a negative sense, travelogues that take titles such as *Czechoslovakia: Land of Beauty and Change*. As Ruoff notes, Buñuel had been invited to accompany the Dakar–Djibouti expedition, a major anthropological mission across Africa, as its official film maker. He refused, and in his autobiography he expresses some distaste for such travel: 'I don't have the slightest curiosity about places where I've never been and never will go' (Buñuel, 1982: 167). There is indeed a sense which Ruoff perceives, in which *Las Hurdes* - whether consciously or not - is a critique of the very possibility of ethnographic representation. Ruoff is not the first critic to note the stylistic similarity between Buñuel's film and the early work of Robert Flaherty. Although Buñuel had some admiration for Flaherty's early films, *Las Hurdes* feels like a parody, almost a reversal, of them. Where Flaherty goes to distant places to find human dignity in the 'primitive' fight against nature, Buñuel finds degradation and an inability to cope with the ravages of nature in the heart of a supposedly modern and civilised society; where Flaherty strives for a realism of effect that may ('regrettably', because of the limitations of the film process) require some deviation from actuality, Buñuel invests the scenes he films with realism only in order to make us question the reality of what we are seeing. Everything in Flaherty appears in order, even in the extreme conditions of the Arctic; everything in Buñuel appears out of kilter, even the film making itself. Where Flaherty strives to make the viewer empathise with the subjects of the film, Buñuel distances his viewers, making them uncomfortable and refusing to allow easy identification. The monstrousness that Sobchack speaks of in the film may be another respect in which we may see it as being directed against Flaherty's romantic vision, but it is also a cry of pain against the fact of existence. Marked by the angel of death, Buñuel's film charts another aspect of the disintegration of modern society and its failure to address the contradictions which its emergence has put in place. It is not the least of Buñuel's achievement that he has provided us with a serious document of a people lost in time which implicates the whole of society in the critique it is making, while mocking the very process of representation by which he is addressing the audience. If the film is a social document highlighting *in extremis* the problems the fledgeling Republic of 1932 faced, it thus goes far beyond this specific context to implicate all of us in the process by which misery is created concomitant upon the creation elsewhere of wealth. In this respect, it has something in common with Kiarostami's recent *ABC Africa* (2001), a film which – albeit using completely different strategies – presents Western attempts to address development in Africa as a foolish, not to say arrogant, groping in the dark.

Anthropologist Nicholas Thomas nevertheless finds Buñuel's approach offensive. He sees the film quite differently to Sobchack (and most other critics). Judging it in terms of its ethnographic content, which seems to be the only thing he sees in it, he regards it as 'distinctly colonialist in its reduction of a hinterland people to the status of freakshow exhibits for the Parisian avant garde' (Thomas, 1994: 26).

Many of the criticisms Thomas levels at it are familiar ones which anthropologists routinely cast at films depicting the lives of 'other societies' in ways that do not conform to their rather obscurely formed ideal of what the role of film in anthropology should be. But if Thomas raises some legitimate issues in this respect, one has to question the basis of his approach. Besides anything else, he uses precisely the same strategies in his critique that he accuses Buñuel of using towards the people in the film – he ignores anything positive about it, has a scornful and condescending tone that ignores the context and makes no attempt to engage with what the film is actually saying, frequently misquoting and misrepresenting it. He uses James Clifford's dubious and contentious notion of 'ethnographic surrealism' as an authority in order to set surrealism up as a straw man to be knocked down. He shows complete ignorance of the social and political context of Spain in 1932, bizarrely comparing the film to colonialist missionary films as though they belonged to the same discourse. Most of all, he entirely misses Buñuel's irony and political intent.

Nothing in Thomas's article indicates that he did any research into the situation of the film's making or the political context in which it was set, or that he has compared the details recounted in the film with Legendre's ethnographic account of the region. Ruoff, also an anthropologist, without referring to Thomas, has expressed amazement that 'virtually no Buñuel scholar has since bothered to read Legendre's work' (1998: 47). Ruoff in fact sees *Las Hurdes*, in contrast to Thomas, as a kind of model for what an anthropological film should be and recounts that in great part it accurately reflects the findings of Legendre's ethnography. To assert with Thomas that the film was made 'for the Parisian avant garde' also shows woeful ignorance about the nature of French society in the thirties. No doubt Buñuel had many different audiences in mind when making the film, but there is no question that he would have expected it to be diffused through communist and trade union channels in Spain and France to a largely working-class audience. In fact the film was banned in Spain and not shown in France until 1938.

Despite its dubious assertions and poor scholarship, Thomas's analysis does alert us to the difficulty of representation in general, more specifically of the morality of any form of ethnographic or documentary film making. Do these difficulties, however, become more acute, as Thomas implies, in a surrealist approach to documentation? If from a humanist or realist perspective Buñuel may be criticised for ignoring the humanity of his subjects, and emphasising the negative aspects of their lives, is not such distortion inherent in the process of representation itself, and is it any more acceptable to emphasise the positive aspects of their lives? It might be said that to judge any film by the objectivity of its portrayal is reductive and imposes false criteria of judgement; a film, rather, has to be judged in terms of intent and realisation, in which the context of its making becomes the central consideration. Judgement of the objectivity of portrayal leads us into debates surrounding the 'pornography' of looking, which Buñuel's films as a whole confront. Any documentary film making has an impact on the people filmed in ways that are often unpredictable. There is, however, no reason to believe that Buñuel was in any way more culpable than others who have been held to task for the effect their representations on their subjects (for instance Margaret Mead in the film *Anthropology on Trial* [1981] or Robert Flaherty in *Man Of Aran: How The Myth Was Made* [George Stoney, 1978]). Buñuel was similarly placed on trial in *Buñuel's Prisoners* (Ramon Gieling, 2000), in which the film maker went to the Hurdanos region to investigate people's reactions to the film more than seventy years after the event. Most of the local people had a very hostile relation with it, objecting to the way they thought it represented them, although in fact most had not actually seen the film itself. Gieling took a copy to show in some of the villages and the film ends when the screening begins. Bizarrely, we are not shown anyone's reactions *after* having seen the film, making for a curiously unbalanced view.[2] No one, of course, likes being presented in a negative light but, if it is anthropologically legitimate only to present the positive aspects of the lives of a film's subjects, was it equally illegitimate of Vigo to show the ugliness of the bourgeoisie in *À propos de Nice*? As Octavio Paz wrote, speaking of *Los Olvidados*, another of Buñuel's films, 'reality is *unbearable*; and that is why, because he cannot bear it, man kills and dies, loves and creates' (1986: 154). And here we touch upon another of the profound aspects of the surrealist critique of realism: its refusal to accept the idea that reality is endurable and should be accepted on such terms. It is this that establishes the film's surrealist intentions, and if *Las Hurdes* was Buñuel's only documentary, it cannot be separated from the rest of his films, many of which take the form of 'documents' of certain situations.

Henri Storck's *Easter Island* may be said to stand with *À propos de Nice* and *Las Hurdes* to form a kind of 'surrealist trilogy' of social conditions in the thirties. In the film, made in 1935 as part of an ethnographic expedition to the South Seas, Storck, like Buñuel, turns expectations on their head. If the film is a celebration of the magnificent statues that adorn this isolated land, it turns the idea of cultural heritage against colonialists who were at the time the masters of the island. The scenes of poverty it shows are as rending as those in *Las Hurdes*, and made more poignant by the knowledge of the magnificence of the cultural tradition from which the islanders are descended. Storck's film was made with the co-operation of the anthropologist Alfred Métraux (himself linked with the surrealists) and may be seen as a visual accompaniment of Métraux's ethnography of Easter Island. Like Buñuel's film, however, *Easter Island* also goes against the grain of ethnographic representation in its biting commentary on social conditions in the island which both reveals its line of descent from Storck's social cinema, and marks it as a document in the surrealist sense. It is doubtless the film in which Storck's double interest in surrealism and in the social documentary are brought together most effectively. Where Vigo exposed the hollowness of bourgeois leisure time and Buñuel the conditions of those left behind by the progress of modern society, Storck lays bare the mechanisms of colonialism in a place that had a special significance for surrealism. The three films together have a running time of less than ninety minutes, but the punch they pack is colossal.

JEAN PAINLEVÉ

Another important documentarist to emerge from within the surrealist milieu at this time was Jean Painlevé, who, unlikely as it might seem, was a natural history film maker. Painlevé made around 200 short films, which he usually financed himself, and of which most are about underwater creatures (sea-horses, shrimps, sea urchins, crabs, octopi, etc.).[3]

Painlevé explained his intention as being to bring into question a human-centred way of relating to the natural world: 'How many legends to destroy!

Everything is subject to the most absurd anthropomorphism, completely made for humans and in the image of humanity, explaining it only in relation to humanity, otherwise "it's a waste of time"' (in Bellows et al., 2000: 136).

Painlevé's aim in presenting nature was a long way from an educational one. In fact, his childhood seems to have been marked by intense hatred for school, a hatred he retained throughout his life: he was to refuse an award offered to him by his former school with the comment that 'My aim is to use my modest means to contribute to the complete abolition of secondary education, which has always profoundly disgusted me. Having never frequented my fellow pupils when I was at school, I've no desire to do so now' (in Bellows et al., 2000: 136).

Painlevé had first studied medicine, but rejected it for what he regarded as its cruel treatment of patients and turned to biology. At the Sorbonne, he became friends with the surrealist photographer Jacques-André Boiffard and with Pierre Prévert. He also established a friendship with Ivan Goll, who was pursuing his own short-lived variant of surrealism in opposition to Breton's group. Painlevé published a 'Neo-Zoological Drama' in the first and only issue of Goll's review *Surréalisme*, which appeared in October 1924. Despite the fact that Goll's publication did not continue, Painlevé never participated directly in surrealism, having a personal dislike for André Breton, but he was nevertheless deeply imbued with a surrealist spirit, which is revealed by the above two quotations, as well as by the evidence of his films.

Painlevé intended his films to be taken seriously as scientific documentaries (their principal audience was generally a scientific one, although they were often also aimed at a wider public) and they are as meticulously accurate as those of David Attenborough. At the same time, he was a serious film maker, concerned not simply to describe the natural world, but to confront the process by which film represents it.

The miracle of Painlevé's films is that they retain a sense of wonder at the natural world while engaging with it scientifically. This wonderment is very different from that of a natural history film maker like David Attenborough, whose enthusiasm is contained within a sense of detachment that anthropomorphises the animal kingdom while enclosing it as something separate from the human realm. Serious scientist though he was, Painlevé refused such scientific detachment, recognising as a film maker that it played a deceptive role and served to elide the relationship between the scientist, the subject of study and the audience. For Painlevé easy identification between viewer and subject was a snare. He presented the creatures of the natural world as being out of reach to human interpretation just as they are illuminating about human behaviour.

This creates a kind of anthropomorphism *à rebours*. In a way similar to Buñuel's use of insects, under Painlevé's gaze sea creatures reflect and illuminate human depravity without participating in it. In this there are clear links with Roger Caillois's work in the thirties on the behaviour of insects and the way they provide us with a measure of life that is psychologically revelatory of human actions, and yet doesn't quite fit with those. This is revealed most forcibly in *The Vampire* (1939-45), made during the war when Painlevé was active in the anti-fascist struggle and on the Nazi wanted list, and in which the activities of the vampire bat are used as a biological archetype for an understanding of the motivations of fascism.

Painlevé knew Buñuel and was close friends with Vigo. In his films he incorporated what he had learned from these two film makers to create films in which the relation to the world is questioned rather than accepted for what it is. Painlevé did not reject explanation, but he refused to accept its finality. His quest had certain resemblance to that of Charles Fort: he wished to reveal the gaps in our knowledge, and that these were gaps we should never be able to able to overcome because they were integral to our relationship with the world. To believe that we are able to explain the world is nothing but a sign of human arrogance. It is not enough simply to understand the behaviour of other creatures; we need also need to understand the process by which we are doing the understanding. Painlevé's work may be seen as an attack on theories of evolution, which it undermines not by disputing their truth, but by showing how they are too simplistically constructed, especially to the extent that they reveal the human creature as the summit of creation, the focal point both of evolution and of the method by which it is investigated. In Painlevé's films, anthropomorphism is turned against itself. He shares with other film makers linked to surrealism a fascination with the relationship between humanity and the world, and to this extent his films are fundamentally about communication, seeking to chart aspects of its topography.

The world presented is one of disjunction, a disjunction not inherent to this world, but emerging as a result of humanity's will to grasp life as a continuum. In 1931, Painlevé set out his distrust of the way we seek to domesticate the unknown by means of knowledge, which we use 'to predict, from a safe distance, phenomena in a variety of fields and to produce more numerous and more fruitful hypotheses that we hope will finally explain Nature once and for all... But compared to Nature, Man's imagination provokes weak revelations' (in Bellows et al., 2000: 119). This doubt about the human capacity to master the world is a characteristic of surrealism that Painlevé shares. He also recognises the way in which film, in its documentary capacity, does not serve as a transparent medium by which reality may be held in suspension as an object of study, as positivism would like, but as often as not serves as an opaque screen that masks as much of reality as it reveals. This is emphasised by accompanying music that may appear incongruous but functions as an organic complement (which may still be discordant) to the images, acting, like Buñuel's use of music, as an 'irrational enlargement' of what is visually represented. What is celebrated in most of Painlevé's films is the pure energy which constitutes the dance of life and alone offers the means to understand the continuities existing between different species in life's plan. In this one might see Painlevé's work as representing a fourth aspect, placing the natural world in evidence in a way that parallels the way the human world is treated in the films of Vigo, Buñuel and Storck.

HUMPHREY JENNINGS

On the face of it Humphrey Jennings was a more engaged surrealist than any of the film makers we have so far considered, even Buñuel. At least, he was an active member of the English Surrealist Group and one of the organisers of the 1936 International Surrealist exhibition in London. However, his films raise some questions since they seem to pull in different directions and at times even seem to be working against a surrealist perspective.

The contradictions in Jennings's work arise from three principal factors. The first was that he had to function within the context of a British documentary movement established on positivist lines by John Grierson, and expected to have an educational, not to say didactic, purpose. The second was that most of his films were made during the war as contributions to the British war effort, something in itself in conflict with fundamental surrealist principles. The third, and perhaps most significant, was that his sentimental attachment to an English romantic tradition of identification with the land at times sits uneasily with his surrealism.

Joining the GPO Film Unit in 1934 at the same time as Alberto Cavalcanti (who also had a distant relation with the French surrealists), Jennings nevertheless brought to his films a poetic sensibility that was in tune with surrealism. His first significant film, *Spare Time* (1939), is probably his most interesting from a surrealist point of view, in so far as it explores the marvellous aspects of everyday life in filmic terms in a way that allowed him to play with sound and image.

Jennings's subsequent films are no less rich, but were marked by the shadow of war and the fact that most were made as part of the war effort. If Jennings was able to present us a unique portrait of Britain at war, from a surrealist perspective, these films are tarnished by the fact that they were propaganda films designed principally to maintain the public spirit. As such they promote or reinforce a sense of British identity that is fundamentally at odds with surrealist internationalism, even if Jennings always sought to situate his films in universal terms and tried to make it clear that Germany was not the 'enemy' in the war.

It would probably be more true to say that Jennings used surrealism as an element in the way he made films rather than that his films contribute to surrealism. His films were too marked by the war. Had he begun making films earlier or later (that is, after the war), he might have made a significant contribution to surrealist cinema. As it is, he gave us a handful of great films in which surrealism is not a negligible factor, but it is only a factor. The contingencies of the time meant that these films ultimately were working in a way that was often alien to surrealism.

CHRIS MARKER, ALAIN RESNAIS, GEORGES FRANJU, JEAN ROUCH

If the documentary movement in which Jennings worked was largely indifferent if not hostile to surrealist ideas, forcing him to work against its grain, in France the documentary tradition was profoundly marked by surrealism, which even might be said to have become its dominant influence during the early fifties. Michel Zimbacca came to surrealism in the forties as a film maker and made several documentary shorts on anthropological themes in collaboration with Jean-Louis Bédouin and Benjamin Péret. The two most well-known are *L'invention du monde* and *Quetzalcoatl, le serpent emplumé*, both made in 1952 and based on Péret's researches into American myth. Zimbacca did not make any further films and his work has fallen into undeserved obscurity, but in their attitude towards non-Western cultures they undoubtedly had an influence on the young documentarists emerging in France in the fifties, such as Alain Resnais, Chris Marker, Georges Franju and Jacques Baratier, all of whom, although they did not directly participate in surrealism, were deeply imbued with its spirit, and of whom it might be said that their documentaries in general are surrealist in all but name.

This is especially apparent in the film made by Resnais and Marker together, *Les Statues meurent aussi* (1951), which bears comparison with Storck's *Easter Island* as an assault on colonialism, and the film seems to be directly inspired by the uncompromising anti-colonial attitude of the surrealists. This film outraged the French government, which banned it for forty years. The narrative technique in Resnais's other documentaries, such as *Nuit et brouillard* (1955), his devastating exploration of the Nazi concentration camps, or *Le Chant de Styrène* (1958), clearly owes much to Buñuel and Vigo, while the approach to the material, especially the way in which text and image are used, is evidence of Resnais's avowed accord with surrealism. *Les Statues meurent aussi* and *Nuit et brouillard* are complementary films: both are about destruction and death; if the latter is about the death of people, the former is about the no less rending death of culture.

Les Statues meurent aussi raises key questions about colonialism, the nature of art and its place within the framework of society. By placing African statues in Western museums, Marker and Resnais's film argues that a form of cultural genocide is being enacted which transforms living cultural forms into dead objects of contemplation. *Les Statues meurent aussi* takes further the implied critique made by Storck in *Easter Island*. Where in that film, the statues of the island stand as mute witnesses to a barbarism committed against the descendants of those who made them, in the film by Marker and Resnais, the objects themselves are taken away from their place of origin and laid to rest in the museums of the conquerors and, their power dissipated, made into items to be contemplation.

Les Statues meurent aussi is a film about the power of the gaze and a commentary on the effect of museums on the perception of art. This could be the story of any art, but in the context of the film, it invokes a specific relation to African art and its appropriation as part of colonial subjugation. It reveals how African statues function in their own societies in ways that are incommensurable with Western understandings of art, and thus to place them in museums is paradoxically to destroy their power while giving them another life, one that serves the story of colonialism. In the process, they die as such, being torn from their ritual context and use-value, while being reborn as props serving a Western order of art. Museums act to suspend art in a timeless zone that renders moribund the stories they told in their original contexts. Marker and Resnais's film provides one of the most poignant verifications of Walter Benjamin's comment that 'there is no document of civilization that is not at the same time a document of barbarism' (1970: 256).

Resnais ceased making documentaries after he made his first feature, *Hiroshima Mon Amour* (1959). Marker, on the other hand, has remained principally a documentary film maker. Too eclectic in his interests and tastes to be considered entirely within a surrealist purview, his best work still seems imbued with its spirit, and his recent *Remembrance of Things to Come* (2002), about surrealist photographer Denise Bellon, gives a testimony of the extent to which his own trajectory has been tied in with surrealism. In many of his films, and especially his masterpiece, *Sans Soleil* (1984), his concerns with memory, representation of otherness and not least the legendary aura in which he enfolds his own life show a clear link with a surrealist perspective.

This is perhaps even more explicit in the case of the documentaries of Georges Franju, three of whose films in particular, *Le Sang des bêtes* (1949), written by Painlevé, about the Paris slaughterhouses at La Villette, *En Passant par la Lorraine* (1950), about a steel mill, and *Hôtel des Invalides* (1951), about the Paris museum for war veterans, are fine examples of the surrealist idea of a 'document' that powerfully places in evidence out-of-place elements of modern society. *Le Sang des bêtes* in particular is as rending as Vigo's and Buñuel's films as Franju forces us to confront questions of the pain of existence, our sense of mortality and the complex relationship we have with animals. The surrealists expected a lot from Franju, but he largely disappointed them when he turned to making feature films, most of which are frustratingly insubstantial (the exception being his eerily oneiric *Les Yeux sans visages* [1959]).

The extent to which the films of Jean Rouch can be considered under a surrealist rubric is also problematic. Although he was never a member of the Surrealist Group, Rouch maintained his links with surrealism more explicitly than Resnais, Marker or Franju. Rouch also has a claim to be the most significant ethnographic film maker yet to emerge, and his films of ethnographic documentation, such as his series on the *Sigui* (1966–81), providing moving testimony of a vast Dogon ritual, are of undoubted surrealist interest purely due to the fact that Rouch brings a surrealist eye to bear on the ethnographic details he observes. The surrealist provenance of his work as a whole is more difficult to determine, especially of his films from the early sixties, when he became linked with the *nouvelle vague* and founded a *cinéma vérité* style derived from Vertov, something that made Kyrou decidedly uneasy: 'neither cinema nor truth can be found in that muddy pond' (1985: 43). Although this notion in Rouch's hands was more complex than Kyrou thought – Rouch was not entertaining a naïve realism, but questioning the nature of filmic realism – it is not easy to see how it could be compatible with a surrealist perspective.

One of Rouch's films, however, certainly stands alongside the other films we have considered as contributing to a specifically surrealist application of documentary. This is his most controversial film, *Les Maîtres fous* (1955), and the controversy it generated has to be seen to be at the heart of the problematic of his later work.

Set in the Gold Coast (now Ghana) under British colonial rule, *Les Maîtres fous* documents a possession ritual carried out by group of Songhay and Zerma people, recent immigrants from the then French colonies that now comprise the countries of Niger, Mali and Burkina Faso. The Hauka cult depicted in the film was not part of traditional Songhay ritual, but emerged in Niger in the twenties, almost certainly as a collective psychological response to the trauma of colonialism. At least, this is the impression given by Rouch's film, in which colonial administrators are added to the pantheon of traditional spirits.

Les Maîtres fous is a vivid and visceral film that disturbs the senses. In it the participants go into trances and become possessed. They assume personalities other than their own, becoming, for instance, Commandant Mugu, the wicked major, or Gomno, the governor-general. In such spirit form, they break religious taboos, eating forbidden food and transgressing normal behaviour as well as assuming super-human qualities which enable them to put their hands into fire or boiling water without being burned. In such a guise, too, they are able to insult or parody their masters, the 'mad masters' of the title. At the end of the film, Rouch shows the participants back at work in Accra, apparently content, or at least normal, members of the community. Rouch's commentary asserts that the performance of the ritual was a form of a therapy enabling them to deal with their difficult situation in everyday life, living in a city alien to them and under colonial rule.

Les Maîtres fous was made at the request of the participants in the ritual themselves and appears to have satisfied them. It offended most everyone else directly concerned with it – the British and French governments, anthropologists and black intellectuals – having been controversial ever since its first screening at the Musée de l'Homme in 1955, when Marcel Griaule, Rouch's mentor, urged him to destroy the film. The film was banned in Britain and its colonies and has been shown with circumspection elsewhere. The objections to it took different forms for different groups. For the British government it was an insult to colonial administrators and, by extension, to Britain as a whole and the authority of the Queen. It was also condemned for its violence and for the cruelty to animals it depicted. Anthropologists were uneasy at the film's representation of the native culture in its concentration on a supposedly 'barbaric' ritual, something that was equally disturbing to black intellectuals, especially at a time when they were seeking independence and trying to show that they were as 'civilised' as Europeans.

For surrealists, of course, none of such objections pertained; in fact the only surrealist criticism of the film would doubtless be of the way in which Rouch explains the ritual as being a healthy psychological outlet to enable the participants to come to terms with in their everyday struggles in colonial society. The value of the film rather was the way it placed in evidence the function of transgressive ritual as being at once a communal celebration and a revolt against colonial authority. At the same time, the film raises similar questions about the nature of ethnographic representation to those we have already considered in relation to Buñuel's *Las Hurdes*. Paul Stoller asserts that Rouch '*documents* the existence of the incredible, the unthinkable' (1992: 160), which may be true for some. The surrealist provenance of his films, however, inheres in the extent to which he also brings into question this sense of the incredible or unthinkable.

In most of his subsequent films, however, Rouch retreated to safer ground. Although he refused to renounce *Les Maîtres fous* and continued to defend it vigorously, one feels that he did lose confidence in the power of filmic representation. Instead of using film to place social relations in evidence, he became obsessed with exploring the relation between fiction and truth and the problems of representation, especially when it was a matter of non-Western cultures being represented by a European. The controversy generated by *Les Maîtres fous* seemed to hang over his subsequent films like a sword of Damocles, making him over-cautious and careful not to offend sensibilities. Becoming obsessed with allowing his subjects to participate in the film making in order to establish a form of 'shared anthropology', he ceased to place his material in evidence through film, but made the film itself an event. Whatever their other qualities, films like *Moi, un noir* (1958), *La pyramide humaine* (1959) or *Chronique d'une été* (1960), are ultimately neither revelatory nor challenging and one feels that Rouch's obsession with the difficulties of representation prevented him from really penetrating African cultures, leaving him content to explore his own obsessions through Africa. At least, one might say that after the furore over *Les Maîtres fous* Rouch appeared becalmed in his subsequent films. In this we might compare him to Jennings. Both film makers, although for very different reasons, were forced to work within frameworks that did not allow the full exploration of their surrealist sensibilities.

If we can generalise about surrealist documentary practice, we might say that it assumes a pure form founded in the way the early surrealists used evidence. When it comes to film, this involves taking film literally as a 'document' divested or any pedagogic, didactic or informational role. Such a document serves rather to place in evidence a relation between the film maker and the world, asking questions about the material it presents. Documentation is a not insignificant aspect of surrealist endeavour (see Walker, 2002, for a cogent exploration of the surrealists' use of documentation in still photography) and in many ways the documentary may even offer the most natural means for the exploration of surrealist themes in film. It tends to be characterised by a focus on evidence as such, used not, as with most documentaries, to prove or illustrate a point, but to stand for itself. Evidence is generally presented to the viewer in the films discussed in ways that have something in common with the presentation of evidence in a law court, except that neither a prosecution nor defence case is made and the audience, although in some ways placed in the position of both judge and jury, are not asked to bring a verdict of guilty or innocent, but to recognise themselves in the indictment. Its aim is to expose the very foundations of our certainty of the possibility of either guilt or innocence at the same time that it disturbs our belief in the solidity and tangibility of the 'real' world.

CHAPTER 6

Nelly Kaplan and Sexual Revenge

As the only female film maker linked with surrealism, Nelly Kaplan's work raises the complex and controversial topic of the surrealist relation to women. Although she denies any feminist agenda and, like most of the women associated with surrealism, is suspicious of feminism as an ideology, insisting that her work exists beyond gender, Kaplan's work has been taken up by feminist film critics and her films help to elucidate the theme of sexual relations in the context of surrealism. If it cannot be denied that issues of sexual politics are present in her work, it would be a serious error to reduce it to this.[1] Kaplan addresses us in a tone of intimacy. She is concerned not to convince us, but to take us into her confidence. She demands accomplices rather than viewers, and it is in terms of a sense of complicity that her link with surrealism has to be understood: she is surrealist above all in the faith she places in revolt as a moral principle, pure revolt that has its own justification irrespective of the conditions that have given rise to it or the consequences it may have.

Born in Buenos Aires in 1936 into a family of Russian/Jewish extraction, Nelly Kaplan ran away from home when she was 17, buying a one-way ticket to France. She has never looked back: since then she has lived continuously in France. Her passion as a child was the cinema, mainly Hollywood films, since Europe was mostly cut off due to the war. In Paris, she represented the Argentine Cinémathèque at an International Congress and made contacts in the film industry by doing menial jobs.

In 1953, she met Abel Gance, and became his assistant, working on his last four films: *La Tour de Nesle* (1955), the elaborate three-screen *Magirama* (1955–61), *Austerlitz* (1960) and *Cyrano et d'Artagnon* (1964). She has made two films about Gance, *Abel Gance, hier et demain* (1962) and *Abel Gance et son Napoléon* (1983). In addition, she has published three books: *Le Manifeste d'un Art Nouveau* (1959, about the making of *Magirama*), *Le Sunlight d'Austerlitz* (1961) and *Abel Gance's Napoléon* (1994), about her mentor's films. Her involvement with Gance would seem to be in conflict with her interest in surrealism, since Gance was among those directors the surrealists had never liked. Buñuel, in fact, burned his bridges with the avant garde by refusing to work as Gance's assistant in 1928, and it is curious that Kaplan would, by a strange coincidence, a quarter of a century later, take up the role Buñuel refused. Gance's position in cinema had, however, radically changed in the meantime: in 1928, he was perhaps the leading director in France, but by the fifties he had become a marginal figure whose projects fitted with neither the mainstream, nor the agendas of the emergent younger generation. Kyrou specifies what the surrealists objected to: 'Gance remained ... an explorer, but his researches always remained technical and, what is worse, they were placed in the service of subjects as questionable as *Napoleon* or *Le Maître des Forges*' (1985: 30). For Kaplan, however, this did not represent a conflict of interest, and for her Gance was an inspiration.

If her decade as Gance's assistant was to lay the foundation for her career as a film maker, it was under the sign of surrealism that she sought her intellectual weapons. In fact, she tends to wears her surrealism on her sleeve like a medal of honour, even whilst maintaining a certain distance from it: there are constant references to surrealist myths and ideas throughout her work and her heroines are generally marked by their surrealist tastes. As with so many of the people we have looked at, too, collaboration was an essential aspect of her work, and a mention should be made of her close partnerships with Claude Makovski and Jean Chapot, the latter association ending only with the death of Chapot in 1997. Both men had some involvement in the making of her films, as she has in the films they directed themselves.

Kaplan made her first film in 1961, *Gustave Moreau*. The crystalline quality of Moreau's work greatly attracted her (she illustrated one of her first collections of stories *La Géometrie dans les spasms* with Moreau's lithographs and his images appear later in her feature films). Her film, shot at the Gustave Moreau Museum in Paris (which itself has the quality of a privileged place), perfectly captures the luxurious and clairvoyant atmosphere of this painter's work. In fact she often met Breton at the Moreau Museum, which was very near Breton's home and was a place in which he related that 'beauty and love were first revealed to me' (1965: 363). In Moreau's paintings the terror of women's presence is given a powerful form, and Kaplan sees in his images 'for the woman – equality'. With a commentary alternating between a female and a male voice (spoken by Breton himself), she beautifully captures the divided personality that created these images of splendour and torment.

This film was followed by a further six short films about artists: *Rodolphe Bresdin* (1962); *À la source, la femme aimée* (1964); *Dessins et merveilles* (1965); *La Nouvelle Orangerie* (1966); *Les Années 25* (1966); and finally a fifty-two minute film about Picasso, *Le Regard Picasso* (1969). *À la source, la femme aimée*, about André Masson's lithographs, was initially banned for obscenity and was only much later shown in its complete form. More than straightforward commentaries, these films have their own force and deserve a place alongside the films of Henri Storck as some of the finest explorations of the work of particular painters committed to film. They have been unjustly neglected.

Kaplan made her first feature film in 1969. According to her, the original idea for *La Fiancée du pirate* came from her collaborator Claude Makovski, but its theme – woman as witch and as eternal avenger – is one that was close to Kaplan's heart and seems derived from one of her best stories, 'Prenez garde à la panthère', in which a woman whose mother was wrongly burned as a witch is in consequence turned into a panther during the day, while at night she resumes her feminine, human, form to seduce men.[2] The memory of the witchcraft burnings is a theme that runs through all of Kaplan's work, giving a stimulus for the avenging role that many of her women characters assume.

La Fiancée du pirate is a Cinderella story which concerns Marie, a nomad who lives in the small village of Tellier with her mother but without money or papers. They live in a miserable cabin and Marie becomes the village drudge, exploited by everyone, especially by Irène, her 'landlady'. When her mother is killed by a hit-and-run driver, she inherits the shack. No one wants to bury her mother but she uses her 'inheritance' to hold a wake – she buys wine, food and cigarettes and makes herself up using the juice of berries and the charcoal of burned matches, to the approval of her pet goat. She invites the villagers, who soon get very drunk, but organises them sufficiently for them to bury her mother. The priest arrives, concerned that it is not a proper Christian burial, but he is ignored. Realising that she has a great power to attract men, Marie refuses to work any more for Iréne. The men talk about how Marie has put a spell on them and one of the wives tells them she has seduced her husband. The villagers chase her to her hut; she bolts the door against them and they take out their fury by shooting her goat. She becomes the village whore and, as she is much in demand, keeps upping her price, spending the money on consumer goods for which she has no use, using them as decorations. Systematically seducing all the men in the village, she prepares her revenge. Finally she burns down her cabin and dutifully sets off for the village church, where mass is being celebrated. She puts a tape recorder on an inaccessible shelf high in the tower and leaves it to play the in-criminating conversations she had had with the men who have visited her. The enraged villagers race to Marie's cabin and destroy all of her remaining material goods (which she has formed into a kind of surrealist tomb that functions as her mother's tomb), but Marie is elsewhere: walking down the road without a care in the world.

Picasso said of *La Fiancée*, 'this is insolence raised to a fine art', a comment which succinctly expresses the film's impact. As in all of Kaplan's work, there is at play a will of vengeance against everything that is sordid in life which is force-fully articulated through the playing of Marie, who, Kaplan makes clear, is herself an embodiment of the sort of convulsive beauty that Breton called for.

The insular village world which *La Fiancée* calls up recalls the atmosphere evoked by Huysmans in *En Rade*, a novel which constituted part of the surrealists' armoury as they sought to construct a modern mythology. Marie is a foreign element which cannot be incorporated into the closed, inwardly directed society in which she lives. As such, she is the perpetual outsider who is both part of the society and excluded from it. By confronting this role and refusing its iniquity, she becomes the catalyst which explodes the social order from within. This social order is thereby shown in its inflexibility to function in a way to suffocate the life of the whole community. Its rejection of Marie is simply one symptom of a sick order of things, which has its effect on the other characters in the story, all of whom are circumscribed by their petty jealousies, small-mindedness and self-hatred and so prevented from realising themselves.

Marie, living outside of society and pure in her wildness, is an uncorrupted symbol of the life-force that, once unleashed, cannot be contained by the inflexible norms under which the society is held together. Associated with the Devil in his incarnation as a nature god through the goat she keeps as her pet, Marie is in a contact with nature in a way that is as natural as it is unconscious, and it is when the villagers kill her pet goat that she makes her vow of vengeance and becomes transformed. In this sense her link with the world of witchcraft is an elemental one: her 'otherness' is not simply to be seen in terms of her outsider status, but also, and perhaps more crucially, because her sensibility is not of the modern world. It belongs to a medieval sensibility which scorns worldly endeavour and especially the capitalist spirit of accumulation and parsimony. Her 'sacrilege' is less in her rejection of the church and its teachings as in her contempt for money and personal possessions. She fleeces the village through her sexuality, only to squander what she amasses on fripperies. Kaplan shares the lascivious humour of the surrealist painter Clovis Trouille, whose scandalous representations of Christian iconography are not so much blasphemous as disdainful. Like Trouille, Kaplan mocks Christianity as a marker of the authority that facilitates and upholds the mean spirit of the village.

La Fiancée du pirate was a stunning debut film. Kaplan's second feature, *Papa, les petits bateaux* (1971), was less successful. The story concerns rich, spoiled Venus de Palma (known as Cookie by her friends), who, after escaping from prison (she has been arrested for undressing while being driven around the Champs d'Elysées, and her father has asked for her to be locked up to teach her a lesson), is kidnapped by a gang of small-time bandits who expect this to be their big job which will make them all rich. But things don't go as planned. From the start, when they have difficulty opening the chloroform bottle, they are a group who hardly inspire confidence. Marc (the gang leader with pretensions of grandeur), his girlfriend, Marylene (a phony clairvoyant), Luc (a dandy who thinks he is Casanova) and Hippolyte (alias Polite, alias Popol, alias Popeye, whom Cookie calls Podane) are all lumpenproletariats out of their depth, and it soon becomes apparent that they will be no match for Cookie: when they finally get her to their hideout, they find that she is not the frightened victim they had expected, but a forceful woman more accustomed to giving than taking orders. When Papa de Palma refuses to pay the ransom money, they are unable to decide what to do. Cookie is able to play them off against one another. Two of them are killed, and two more ruthless gangsters, Jeannot the Corsican and Mateo Falcon, appear on the scene demanding a cut. Since Palma is continuing to refuse to pay the ransom, Cookie starts to take charge, telling them only she can persuade her father to pay, but if she helps them, she wants a share of the ransom. While Marc and Jeannot go to collect the payment, Cookie turns Marylene and Mateo against one another, leaving both of them dead. Jeannot is killed in an argument after he and Marc return with the money, and Cookie turns the gun on Marc, inflicting on him the humiliations she had suffered at his hands. In their struggle, he is accidentally killed. Cookie buries the money and blows up the house. Concocting a story to satisfy the police, she returns home, wondering whether she should now 'kidnap daddy'.

A sort of reverse *No Orchids for Miss Blandish* in which it is Miss Blandish who ends up with all the orchids (it may in fact owe a debt to *On est toujours trop bon avec les femmes*, Raymond Queneau's spoof of Hadley Chase's novel), *Papa, les petits bateaux* unfortunately doesn't entirely work. The idea for the film, a homage to Tex Avery and Max Fleischer, is much more original than that which founded the later Jim Carrey homage to Avery, *The Mask*, but its realisation doesn't allow it to take full advantage of this originality. It seems to be an over-determined project, in which the concept overwhelms the spontaneity of the film making. It also seems to be pulled in different directions, unable to decide whether it is principally a comedy or a thriller. In the event it is neither one thing nor the other: not wacky enough to succeed as a comedy; too self-parodying to be taken seriously. Kaplan said she wanted to 'create a perverse Betty Boop' (though perhaps a female Screwball Squirrel might have been more appropriate), but Cookie is not sufficiently sympathetic as a character for this to work. A spoiled rich kid, she displays little real intelligence, but has a remarkable facility to manipulate situations for her own benefit. Her 'revenge', unlike Marie's, is empty, and the film fails to follow up occasional suggestions that it is the gang, not Cookie, who are the exploited. Despite Marc's protestations of criminal descent (his grandfather died on the guillotine, he proudly tells Cookie), they are just small-time crooks, losers. At one point, Marc tells Cookie that if Palma pays the ransom, then he will still be rich, but they will no longer be poor, but the film ignores the implication of this statement. Instead it prefers to concentrate on Cookie's outwitting of her kidnappers. Yet she seems an empty, superficial character, one who is embedded in the system of exploitation against which her kidnap might be seen as the real act of revolt. The more positive characteristics of the bandits are suggested but then rather passed over. Marc seems to be aware of Rimbaud and Marylene has some magical qualities (admittedly very minor ones, but ones which the 'Popeye' scene implies are not entirely false). What sticks in the mind is Marc's resigned phrase: 'Sun, rain, all thieves, all mad', a recognition that as criminals they are but amateurs compared with Papa de Palma and his daughter. Indeed, we learn that there was from the start a complicity between father and daughter. Aware of the possibility of a kidnap, they had agreed that a ransom would be paid only if Cookie used a password to indicate she felt in real danger. At the end of the film, Cookie does not walk away from exploitation as

Marie does at the end of *La Fiancée*. With her money safely stashed away, she is now considering whether she should kidnap her father. Despite some tantalising possibilities, by apparently unreservedly approving Cookie's actions, *Papa, les petits bateaux* ultimately sanctions bourgeois criminality and amorality rather than revolts against it.

The heroine of Kaplan's next film, *Néa*, is also a spoiled rich kid, but a much more endearing one than Cookie. The only one of her projects to be an adaptation of a book rather than an original story, *Néa* (1976) is supposedly based upon a novel by Emmanuelle Arsan of *Emmanuelle* fame. Made soon after the success of Just Jaeklin's version of the original *Emmanuelle* novel, but before the series became a franchise, *Néa* is a pure surrealist love story whose real inspiration appears to have been Michelet's history of woman as witch, *La Sorcière*, which we see the heroine reading at several points in the film. Kaplan recounts that when she spoke to Emmanuelle Arsan about adapting the book, the latter gave her a free hand other than insisting that two aspects be retained: the age of the heroine and the 'extraordinary mechanism of her revenge'. In the event, these are about the only two things the film does retain from the novel, and what probably interested Kaplan was nothing more than these details, and perhaps an epigraph from Cyrano de Bergerac, used by Arsan as a chapter heading and which might stand as a thematic metaphor for Kaplan's work as a whole: 'this land is so luminous it resembles snowflakes on fire'.

Michelet wrote: 'Nature has made her sorceress. It is the genius appropriate to Woman and her temperament. She was born Enchantress. By a regular return of exaltation, she is Sibyl. By love, she is Magician. By her delicacy, her (often temperamental and beneficent) malice she is Sorceress, and casts the, at least hidden, spell that eludes the curse' (1966: 2).

Néa is prefaced with a quotation from Fourier that became something of a surrealist watchword: 'attractions are proportionate to destinies'. The film concerns 16-year-old Sibylle, the wilful daughter of a rich industrialist. She lives on the margin of different worlds: on the threshold between childhood and adulthood, she is also caught between the business world of her family and her rich erotic imagination. She has, separate from the family house, her own grotto, to which she allows access to no one other than her cat, Cumes. Cumes, in fact, is a key character in the film, playing a similar role as the goat in *La Fiancée* as an intermediary between the human and natural worlds, but also acting as an initiating character for Sibylle (the very endearing creature who plays the role was a stray which Kaplan found during shooting). One day she is caught stealing erotic books from publisher/bookseller Axel Thorpe. Provoked by her insolence and her claim that she can 'write far better than any of these people', he releases her without going to the police. They meet later at her sister's birthday party and at the height of a thunder storm Axel wants to know when she will write the book she promised. Next day they agree a contract which requires her anonymity since she is still a minor. At first her writing goes well, but she soon encounters writers' block due to her lack of personal experience (she is still a virgin). She asks Axel to initiate her. At first he refuses, but then agrees to this 'new clause in the contract'. Now initiated, Sibylle completes the novel at one sitting and delivers the completed manuscript to the still sleeping Axel. The book, *Néa, un grand roman érotique*, becomes a *cause célèbre* and Axel insists that, in order to protect her anonymity, they must not meet again 'until the snow melts from the Saint Ravine chapel'. He then haughtily refuses to see her, other than to give her the money the book has earned, and even implies on TV that he has written the book himself. In frustration, she burns down the chapel, and goes to see Axel, only to find him making love with her sister. Sibylle plans her revenge, a superbly realised fake rape. Axel becomes a fugitive but, when he returns for counter-vengeance against Sibylle, they come to accept their mutual love and leave together in the early morning mist, crossing Lac Léman in Sibylle's boat *Le Pirate*.

Néa is a return to the themes of *La Fiancée du pirate*, although Sibylle is not an exploited outsider but an assertive, fully paid-up member of the bourgeoisie. From the beginning she has a self-confidence that shades into arrogance even if it does not hide a certain inner insecurity (it is one of the strengths of the film that this delicacy of feeling comes through without needing to be stressed). She does not have to face any of the abuse heaped upon Marie. Nevertheless, she shares with her a singularity of revolt by which she attains a victory over the surrounding society and enables others (her mother, Axel) to realise their own potential. *Néa* is thus very much an affirmation of surrealist values at a time when they were decidedly unfashionable. There is a certain irony in the fact that she did this through the medium of Emmanuelle Arsan's novel, which extolled the then fashionable morality of pleasure without responsibility. At one point, Sibylle accuses Axel of being afraid of mutual commitment: 'the absolute exists', she insists. Axel's refusal to accept the commitment she demands, his rejection of the absolute, arises not from a desire for independence but, as Sibylle tells him, from fear, the fear of confronting his need for another person, and his failure to accept the consequences of free choice (it is significant that Sibylle's sister is promiscuous and far more 'liberated' than Sibylle herself). Kaplan's film articulates in a powerful way the fearful attraction of sexuality in its multiple configurations. The heavily stressed Dracula/Bluebeard persona of Axel is indicative of both his emotional coldness and his fear of Sibylle's purity of feeling.

In the beautiful scene when Sibylle first crosses Lac Léman in her small boat, overwhelmed by darkness, to pass through underground passages into Axel's threatening house, which has all the ambiance of Dracula's castle, to find Axel making love, which Sibylle wondrously and voyeuristically watches in an apparent enchantment, before returning across the lake in the night's serenity, the effect is that of a powerful metaphor of the essentially forbidden quality of the sexual act, in which Sibylle's transgressive and secret journey is an active, if unknown, participant. The sense of transgression, here and elsewhere, is one of the strong features of the film. It is especially given its most powerful representation in the fake rape scene, carried off with such panache by Sibylle that we hardly have any sympathy for Axel, even though he has actually, in conventional terms, 'done nothing wrong' (i.e. he has not raped her). We are nevertheless convinced that he has hurt her as badly as she claims by his betrayal and that her revenge is a just retribution.

Nevertheless, despite its fascinations, *Néa* lacks the force of *La Fiancée du pirate*. Partly this is because Kaplan, as ever treating her audience as accomplices, asserts more than she shows about the characters. It is as though she expects us to take her view of the characters on trust, without providing sufficient evidence to satisfy us that this is how things really are. This is especially so in that Sibylle's revolt is not shown to have anything causative behind it. Unlike Marie, she is not an outsider, and we might wonder whether she is simply going through a rebellious phase of adolescence before being re-integrated into her high bourgeois family. In this respect, we may question the portrayal of the father and the sister, who are asserted as negative characters even though nothing the sister does justifies such an assertion, while we might sympathise with a father at his wits' end in trying to control a wilful teenager and deal with a situation in which his wife spurns him. Similarly the *amour fou* between Sibylle and Axel is not altogether convincing and doesn't always communicate what one feels Kaplan was trying to express. Axel's persona as a sophisticated man of the world who is intellectually responsive but emotionally dead is perhaps too well conveyed, especially through Sami Frey's performance, for it to be convincing that it would be eroded by such a supercilious teenager as Sibylle. Although Kaplan insists, as a good surrealist, that there are no messages in her films, one does get the feeling at times that she uses her characters to convey a meaning she imbues them with rather than allowing them to take full shape as characters in their own right.

In order to appreciate Kaplan's work fully, her films cannot be treated in isolation from her writings, because she is a significant writer and her fictional texts are integrally related to the films. In fact, one of her published books is also one of her 'films'. This hybrid text is *Le collier de Ptyx*, a 'ciné-roman' published in 1971. It is not clear why this was not made into a film, whether it was not possible to find the finance for it, or whether it was intended simply to be part of the library of imaginary films the surrealists were fond of writing. However, since the published text is a completed screenplay with camera directions included, this seems unlikely.

The heroine is a more fully realised version of Sibylle, who becomes embroiled in a splendid plot involving nefarious Latin American dictators and a range of characters as colourful as those in her novel *Mémoires d'une liseuse de draps* (1974), which is her major literary work.

Kaplan published several stories in small volumes during the sixties before gathering them together in *Le Réservoir des sens*, first published in 1966 and re-issued in 1988 and again in 1995, each time with additional material. The original publication appeared under the pseudonym of Belen, or perhaps it would be more accurate to describe this character as an assumed persona, in which the elements of her personal mythology – a world or sorcery and transformation – is established. Belen, whose name, according to André Pieyre de Mandiarges, 'may be solar, but the flag she bears is black', is far more than a pseudonym, but takes on Kaplan's own identity as an *other* aspect of herself. In fact it is Belen (rather than Kaplan) who appears in the role of Nostradama in Kaplan's later film *Charles et Lucie* (1979).

Mémoires d'une liseuse de draps is presented as Belen's autobiography. Born of a sailor (a kind of fantastic pirate) and an unknown mother, Belen spends an idyllic childhood as a daughter of the sea aboard her father's ship, *The Sperma*. Although she is doted upon by the loving crew, her only childhood friend is a lion named Griffy. When she is 8, she receives her name, conferred on her in the course of a lubricious ritual making her aware of her sexuality. Reaching the Galapagos Islands, they come across a massacre carried out by agents of the sinister CIA (Company of American Indies) in order to destroy the revolutionary community established there by Jaguar Bronstein and devoted to erotic and political freedom. Kidnapped by the reactionaries, Belen's execution is ordered by the CIA's evil head, José Acero Stalin, but *The Sperma* is following behind and her friends are able to rescue her. Belen participates in the revolutionary movement which succeeds in Angola, after which, reaching Amsterdam when she is 16, it is time for her initiation as a woman. She decides that her father should be the man to take her virginity. The ritual is performed in a strange apartment in Amsterdam, but as they are returning to their ship, they are apprehended by Acero's men. Belen is captured and her father killed, while *The Sperma* is set on fire. The other crew members lie low, but Griffy is captured and sent to an animal sanctuary. Escaping to the China Seas after seducing the millionaire Van Ryn Susy, who is in Acero's pay, Belen finds refuge in a pleasure district in Shanghai, where she becomes aware of her strange gift: the ability to read the future in the deposits men leave on the bedclothes. Her fame spreads and she becomes fabulously rich. Learning that Griffy is held prisoner in Persia, she goes to try to rescue him. Persia at this time is under the control of the Great Matriarchy, whose representatives are sympathetic but unable to help as Griffy is being held by a group of religious fanatics, who intend to sacrifice him. Belen, therefore, must rescue the lion on her own, in which task she succeeds. Momentarily united with Griffy (woman and lion couple in their excitement at being together again) and the other members of the crew, she discovers that José Acero is in Buenos Aires; she travels there, in the guise of the adventuress Léonie d'Ashby (the heroine of *Le Collier de Ptyx*), and lures him into a seductive trap in order to kill him. Her mission accomplished, she retires to an island in the Sargasso Sea, where she writes the stories contained in *Le Réservoir des sens*.

Like *Néa*, *Mémoires* takes as its epigraph Fourier's proposition that 'attractions are proportionate to destinies'. The novel encapsulates the themes that run through all of Kaplan's substantial oeuvre of writing and film making: commitment to freedom in which it is freedom of the senses as much as political freedom that is at stake; it is the freedom of revolt, the freedom not to succumb to anything that is sordid in life. But this freedom is as far as could be from the freedom supposedly defended by our political masters in today's world. It is a freedom that bears the black flag and it is essentially the freedom to *feel*. It is also a powerful celebration of the eventual. *Voyeur* and *voyeuse*, Kaplan is equally committed to the pleasures of sight as an opening up of the potentialities of existence. 'Eroticists of the world unite', she once proclaimed. 'You have only your chains to lose and a whole wide sensual world to gain' (1964). Freedom is thus never given; it demands a process of purification, through a cleansing or a catharsis.

Kaplan's 1979 film *Charles et Lucie* was unusual – a love story of people of 'a certain age'. Charles and Lucie are a middle-aged couple living in difficult circumstances. She is the concierge of an apartment block; he is unemployed, making a little money by selling trinkets at the local flea market. Then one day their world is turned upside-down when a lawyer visits them and tells them they have inherited a villa in the south of France. They sell their possessions in order to pay the death duties and buy a car. When they reach the Côte d'Azur, however, they discover that they are victims of a hoax: the villa does not exist and the car they were sold had been stolen. They therefore find themselves on the run from the police. Their misfortunes multiply until they are reduced to total destitution when a gang of hooligans steal their clothes. Left literally with nothing but themselves, sleeping naked in a field, Charles is woken when a snake dislodges an apple from the tree above them. Stealing the clothes of a scarecrow, they remake their lives from scratch. Having re-discovered their love for one another through their travails, their desperation also leads them to discover their talent as entertainers, when, about to be thrown out of a café because they are unable to pay for their meal, they recount their adventures with a vivacity that could only come from experience and enchants the other diners. At the same moment, the police arrive, not to arrest them as they expect, but to identify the people who swindled them. It appears that what the crooks were after was a portrait of Lucie's great aunt, which, unknown to them, was painted by Van Gogh! Benefiting from a windfall after all, they nevertheless return to the road as modern troubadours, reciting the tales of their misfortunes to enthralled audiences around the land.

Charles et Lucie is audacious – and perhaps unique – in positing *amour fou* among a couple of fifty-somethings The satire here is gentle, perhaps too gentle. What happens to Charles and Lucie is outrageous but not atypical of the sorts of things that are happening every day to people at the lower end of society. It is only the cumulative nature of their misfortunes that marks them as being remarkable. One might therefore expect the film to be more angry, and it would perhaps have gained in comic force if it had been. At no point in the film do Charles or Lucie lose their sang-froid; even when Lucie is pushed close to suicide, it is out of a sense of despair at their predicament rather than at the injustice of what has happened to them.

Where *Papa, les petits bateaux* drew upon slapstick comedy, here the model is the screwball comedy of the thirties, with which it shares not only the humour but also the problematic social relations, which it resolves in a similar sort of way. Charles and Lucie triumph over adversity, transforming their lives in the process, but the social conditions which gave rise to their problems in the first place are left untouched. *Charles et Lucie* is thus a film of great charm but one that is somewhat lacking in depth.

Kaplan's most recent film, *Plaisir d'amour* (1991), is a subversion of the Don Juan legend. Replete with mythological references, it also offers a discreet – if unconscious – homage to one of the surrealists' favourite films, *The Most Dangerous Game*, made by Irving Pichel and Ernest Schoedsack in 1932. In that film, a famous big game hunter, Rainsford, is returning after a productive trip to Africa. The ship on which he is travelling sinks and he is the only survivor, washing up on an island in which he encounters Count Zaroff, a mad nobleman who has grown tired of hunting animals and stalks human beings instead. Rainsford's assumptions of the inherent superiority of humans over animals are thus brought into question. In *Plaisir d'amour*, the hero's prey is women rather than wild animals, but he, like Rainsford, finds his values being turned upside-down when he finds himself the hunted rather than the hunter. Guillaume de Burlador, the 'last descendant of Don Juan', having grown tired of chasing after women, is on the point of suicide (the film opens with an eerie scene in which he drives to 'the cauldron of Hell', the edge of a volcano where he screams out his complaints against the world). But he doesn't cast himself into the inferno. Finding an invitation to become the tutor to a young girl on an isolated Caribbean island, part of the possessions of someone who had earlier come to the spot to kill himself, he decides to go in the place of the dead man. He is welcomed there by three women, Clo, Do and Jo, the mother, grandmother and sister of the young girl. Despite their isolation on the island, the three women are fully 'in the world': Do is a scientist who is friends with Einstein; Clo is a mechanical genius; while Jo is a writer and storyteller. His 'pupil', however, remains elusive, and these three furies play with Guillaume like cats with a mouse as they each allow him to seduce them in turn while tantalising him with the expectation of the young girl's arrival. Flo, the pupil becomes his obscure object of desire, as 'real' or as 'illusory' to him as Conchita in Buñuel's *Obscure Object*.

The film is set in the thirties on the estate of 'The Savage Orchids' on Anatha, a imaginary island straight out of the paintings of Henri Rousseau. That Guillaume is entering an upturned world we know from the beginning, when he encounters the gardener of the estate, Rafaël, creating a strange object (which bears some relation to the tomb Marie made from consumer objects in *La Fiancée*), while standing on his head in the pose of the tarot figure of the Hanged Man, who signifies, of course, division and separation: an end of one path and the beginning of another. There is little indication, however, that Willy (as the women call him) is ready for such a transformation. In fact, quite the contrary, he brings to the island all his old obsessions and phobias and is unable to adapt in any way to the potential his new environment offers him. At the end of the film, he flees the island, apparently having been driven insane.

The idea that fate is 'spun', as widespread ancient myths assert, has some significance in a surrealist context. That existence is not simply arbitrary but responds to some hidden and inaccessible order is central to surrealist ideas and founds the notion of objective chance. In Greek myth, three goddesses took turns in presiding over a person's fate. They were Clotho, who selects the threads of a person's life and spins its strands together; Lachesis, who, as the drawer of lots, measures the threads and acts as the guardian of the life force; and Atropos, who cuts the threads that bind a person to life. Representing, like the heroines of Kaplan's film, the three ages of woman (youth, maturity and old age), they are also linked to the moon in its three phases, waxing, full and waning, as they are born of the union of the sun and the waves. The fates are among the oldest deities: in Greek mythology they pre-date the gods themselves and preside not only over the destinies of humans but over those of the gods as well. Eternal, but ever-changing, they represent metamorphosis in its active form in a way that reminds us that freedom does not comes from without (as, for instance in Sartre's existentialist notion of becoming) but is established in relation to destiny. Another trio of women in Greek myth who may have visually inspired the film through a painting by Gustave Moreau are the three Furies. In *Orestes and the Erinyes* the Furies appear to have been conjured up by Orestes himself, emerging from a lantern and hovering above him. In Kaplan's film, the three women seem to combine elements both of the Fates and the Furies, since they spin Willy's fate while also effecting a female revenge on him.

Here Fourier's 'attractions are proportionate to destinies' joins with the Hegelian/Marxist demand for a freedom that lies in recognition of its unity with necessity. Indeed, the way in which Marx saw freedom as emerging through recognition of necessity may be regarded as coterminous with the surrealist supreme point. *Plaisir d'amour* shows that in terms of gender relations, Kaplan follows a line of surrealist interest in the transposability of men and women, represented by Marcel Duchamp's assumption of the character of Rrose Sélavy or Claude Cahun's and Pierre Molinier's transformations of identity taking them beyond gender to a realm of indifferentiation in which it is possible to be male and female at the same time.

'Who will deliver us from men and women', a phrase in one of Kaplan's stories, is a constant refrain within her work, and the tests Willy is given on the estate in *Plaisir d'amour* are tests of his transformability: is he able to imagine beyond his male destiny? The estate of the 'Savage Orchids' is precisely a domain that has been given over to indifferentiation. In this sense, the women are not precisely women and the men (other than Willy) not precisely men. In fact, just as the three fates are not really three but one, we might see Rafaël not as a separate character, but as another emanation of the destiny to which Willy has been submitted. The Hanged Man of the tarot stands at a point of transition between realms. He is both identity and its negation. The encounter with the Hanged Man is precisely an encounter with fate, which offers the possibility of a renewal based upon confrontation of one's own shadow. But such a confrontation is too much for Willy: he reverses the Hanged Man, tries to put him the 'right way up'. In so doing he fails to recognise the transformed realm of which he is now part and remains confined to his male identity, which causes him to become his own victim as he confuses reality and fiction. His deception is complete when he 'sees' Flo and chases her into her bedroom to find only a mannequin dressed in her clothes. This presages his departure from the enchanted domain: his 'fate' is to be returned to the realm of sexual appearances in which identity is fixed.

Kaplan follows in a surrealist line that is profoundly out of sync with proponents of identity politics who seek new forms by which to change oppressive gender relations. It is important to understand the focus of the surrealist demand for *transformation*, which relies not upon a rational calculation of possibilities, but upon a plunge into the unknown. The sense of revenge running through Kaplan's work, although it is generally effected by women on men, is not principally retribution for male oppression of women. In so far as men have oppressed women, this has been part of a more generalised oppression of the possibilities of existence against which Kaplan's work is constant protest.

Plaisir d'amour is Kaplan's most complex and, despite its deceptively light-hearted tone, her darkest and most troubling film. It is a film in which she seems to come closest to Buñuel: the themes particularly bring to mind not only *That Obscure Object of Desire*, but also *El*, in which a man's self-centred obsessions draw him into insanity (it is not without significance that both *El* and *Plaisir d'amour* have roots in Spanish drama of the Golden Age, in which the consequences of rigid adherence to social conventions was a perennial theme). It was, however, not very commercially successful and does not appear to have gained any English language distribution (although its initial idea – of a weary Don Juan on the verge of suicide – was lifted for a subsequent Hollywood film, *Don Juan de Marco*, starring Marlon Brando and Johnny Depp) and she has not succeeded in gaining finance for any further films.

Nevertheless, Kaplan has been far from inactive since 1991. Although no further film projects have come to fruition, she has a wealth of ideas which she still hopes will reach the screen. She has published a novel, *Aux Orchidées sauvages* (1998), based upon *Plaisir d'amour*, and an updated version of *Mémoires d'une liseuse de draps* published under its original title of *Un Manteau de fou rire* (1998) as well as a new work, *Ils furent une étrange comète* (2002). A further novel, *Cuisses de grenouille,* appeared in 2005, which continues her explorations into sensual emancipation under the sign of Eros and Thanatos. She is currently trying to raise funds to make a new film based upon this story.

Kaplan's world is resolutely her own and she has stubbornly resisted pressure to modify it despite the vagaries of a French film industry largely hostile both to the tradition of quality cinema to which, through her apprenticeship with Gance, she belongs, and to the tradition of ideas devolving from surrealism in which her intellectual formation was immersed. Her concern to work with popular genres rather than fall in with accepted standards of art cinema has also contributed to her marginal status with film critics. Unfortunately it has not at the same time enabled her to make genuine contact with the popular audience she would like (another sign of the grip maintained by the dichotomy between the entertainment industry and art cinema). She has also had to deal with the marginality that arises from being a woman in a male-dominated film industry. Like the characters in her work, she has prevailed as an outsider in a hostile world.

Kaplan's surrealism is founded in a sense of complicity that begins in personal encounter but extends through elective affinity to those who participate in her world. Although never a member of the Surrealist Group, surrealism is integral to her work and in a sense she creates her own imaginary surrealist group with whom, like the crew of *The Sperma* in her novel *Un Manteau de fou rire Mémoires d'une liseuse de draps*, she embarks on a sensual adventure founded in revolt and passion.

CHAPTER 7

Walerian Borowczyk and the Touch of Desire

There has never been a Polish Surrealist Group, but surrealism has been a strong undercurrent in Polish cinema, especially among those directors who emerged during the fifties. It has a noticeable influence, in different ways, in the films of Andreij Wadja, Wojciech Has and Roman Polanski, each of whom has expressed his debt to it. The Polish director whose sensibility is closest to surrealism, however, is undoubtedly Walerian Borowczyk, who has also maintained direct contact with surrealist ideas through his friendships with surrealist writers, notably Robert Benayoun and André Pieyre de Mandiargues, several of whose stories Borowczyk has used as the starting point for his films.

Borowczyk is an important film maker who has fallen into obscurity, his reputation damaged by the pornographic films he made at the end of the seventies. Nevertheless, his early films undoubtedly represent high points of surrealist film making. Borowczyk was one of several film makers who were asked to discuss surrealism in 1965 by the journal *Études Cinématographiques*. His response was one of the least guarded and most uncompromising in terms of a commitment to a surrealist will of transformation: 'Surrealism has prescribed absolute non-conformism, in life and in poetry, which also means in the cinema. I'm in favour of it' (see 'Surréalisme et Cinéma', 1965: 155).

Borowczyk has made most of his films outside Poland, having lived in France since 1958. He has had a strange career. In the sixties he established his reputation as one of the great animators, making a series of inventive and starting films. In 1967, he made his first live action film, and for the next decade concentrated on a series of beautiful and complex films on surrealist themes. From the mid-seventies, his films increasingly came to be dominated by eroticism, notably his outrageous *The Beast* (1975). After that, however, he seemed to lose his way, and his next few films are generally dismissed as no more than high-class pornography. These later films are certainly uneven, and represent a disappointment after the brilliance of his early work. Almost all of them, however, contain interesting elements and do not deserve the obscurity into which they have fallen.

The films Borowczyk made from 1957 to 1976 remain audacious and stunningly complex, and are marked by their visual and tactile qualities. His long involvement with animation made him particularly attentive to subtle detail and the visually resonant image. No other film maker comes close to approaching his eye for the materiality of objects, which almost become characters in their own right (it has been said that he directs his actors as though they were inanimate objects and his inanimate objects as though they were living beings). This is not done in an arbitrary fashion, however: the material world in his films complements the world of living humans, to the extent that one may be said to be the emanation of the other. Borowczyk's world seems to be close to the ideas of Schelling, the romantic philosopher of nature, in the way he sees the material and living worlds as being qualitatively indistinct, distinguishable only by their different arrangement of atoms. This foundation opens up access to another sense of reality. In Borowczyk's films time seems to be functioning under different rules, or is rather subject to a different perception to that under which we habitually perceive it. Borowczyk does not show us the temporal world of everyday, ephemeral experience, but one with the gravity of stone: rather than being active participants in a perishable human setting, the characters seem to be alien beings in a world defined by the immobility and impassivity of objects. It is thus a universe which humans do not control, and it offers a surrealist challenge to Enlightenment conceptions of the mastery of nature. Like the world represented in a Magritte painting, too, the familiar assumes a disturbing tinge. The way in which Borowczyk uses light is unique as well, accentuating the fact that the world is also a sensuous one in which the repression of desires inevitably leads to explosions of cruelty and vindictiveness that no one can control and ultimately destroys the very order it is meant to protect.

In all of his films, Borowczyk creates a world that is simultaneously apart from this one but inseparable from it. Everything within the film is important, and no element is more significant than any other. People, animals, objects, scenery, are all participants in a psychic drama in which neither animate nor inanimate is privileged. For Borowczyk as for Jan Švankmajer (although his sensibility is more tragic and less cruel than Švankmajer's), the world is a dynamic whole, but human action is an intrusive element which impinges on the world's unity. Human beings are out of kilter with the rest of existence by virtue of the very fact that they consider themselves to be above it. This leads to their exclusion from the harmony of nature, but it is an exclusion they have brought upon themselves by trying to rationalise what cannot be rationalised. In this, too, Borowczyk's world is close to that of Švankmajer, except that, as we shall see, for Švankmajer the inanimate world assumes a much more active role: it is not simply alien to humans, but almost seems to have declared war on them, to the extent that inanimate things come to life almost, it seems, in order to commit mischief. In contrast, in Borowczyk's work, it is the very impassivity of the natural world that presents the threat to the human world, the fact that it resolutely *refuses* to come to life.

Borowczyk was born in Kwilcz, Poland, in 1923. An accomplished artist as well as a film maker, he was trained first in drawing and lithography at the Warsaw Academy of Arts. He had also been involved with film making since 1946, and made his first serious film, *Glowa*, in 1953. It was when he began working with Jan Lenica in 1957, however, that he really came to notice, most especially for *Dom* (1958).[1] He also collaborated with Chris Marker on *Les Astronauts* after emigrating to France in 1959.

During the sixties Borowczyk made an amazing number of short films, many of them of extraordinary power. Not all of them were animated. Like Švankmajer, again, he occasionally combined live action with animation and some of these films, like *Rosalie* (1966) and *Gavotte* (1969), were entirely live action. Borowczyk's animation is extremely complex. He uses a range of different elements: drawings, photographs, animated figures, inanimate objects, picture postcards, are combined to create a kind of animated photomontage, or even a film that is itself an object. This is especially seen in *Renaissance* (1963), in which we already see the extent of his tragic vision, in which all things are overwhelmed by entropy. Beginning with an empty screen, an explosion gives access to a room that seems to have suffered from the effects of fire, or perhaps it is merely the effect of age on an old photograph, a memory of a lost past. From a pile of rubbish, different elements take shape: a stuffed owl, a trumpet, a picture, a table, books, the penal code, a prayer book. The trumpet celebrates and other objects form, notably an alarm clock, which becomes attached to a hand grenade which eventually explodes and returns everything to rubble.

Described thus, the film may seem overly schematic; in fact it is anything but. Working as a compelling depiction of the emergence of order from disorder and the inevitability of its collapse, it reflects Borowczyk's worldview, in which the instability of things and the fundamental *perversity* of the human will to impose order on nature combine to create tragedies that cannot be contained.

In *Jeu des anges* (1964), Borowczyk used his own watercolours to evoke, in oblique way, the experience of living under occupation. Where *Renaissance* portrayed in a general way the collapse of order, *Jeux des anges* doubtless recalls Borowczyk's memories of the Nazi occupation and the collapse of civil society it involved. Borowczyk's pictures thematically recall Fautrier's hostages series and this comparison is by no means excessive: in *Jeu des anges* the resonance of the images is no less powerful in the way it forces us to confront the reality of persecutions that reached their culmination – if not their end – in the Nazi concentration camps.

Equally impressive is *Rosalie* (1966), in which a young servant woman in nineteenth-century France, played by Borowczyk's wife Ligia Branice, recounts in detail the death of her new-born twins, the result of having been raped by a soldier. As she tells her story, however, the evidence points us to another, unstated but perhaps even more tragic, story. It is precisely in Borowczyk's use of understatement, his ability to suggest multiple layers to what at first appear simple stories, that the power of many of these films lies.

In 1967, Borowczyk made his first feature, a remarkable animated film, *Le Théâtre de M. et Mme Kabal*, an extension of one of his shorts, about the adventures of a grotesque couple seemingly inspired by Alfred Jarry's Ma and Pa Ubu, although they are more endearing than Jarry's monstrous pair. When a director has made his name through a long apprenticeship with shorts, it is not easy to adapt to the demands of feature films. Nevertheless, despite occasional longuers, *Mr and Mrs Kabal* maintains its length with great facility. Moreoever, with his first live action film, *Goto, Île d'amour* (1968), Borowczyk showed that he had made the transition almost seamlessly.

In both of his first two live action features, *Goto* and *Blanche* (1971), we are presented with isolated, inwardly directed societies that are unable to contain the human passions within them. As a consequence, they are in constant danger of imploding. In *Goto*, we have a society that may superficially bring to mind North Korea. It is an island that became cut off from the rest of the world following a disaster (an earthquake, it appears) that occurred in 1887. Since then it has been ruled by a series of governors called Goto. As we learn from a school lesson at the beginning of the film, the governors are three aspects of a single image, which the teacher illustrates by means of a trick portrait. Is this some sort of comment on the Christian trinity, or a manifestation of the divine right of kings, or is something more subtle intended? It could be a commentary on the way that reality changes depending on the angle from which it is viewed, or an illustration of the philosophical point made by Parmenides that change is merely a matter of appearance and in reality nothing changes. In this world marked by inertia, reflected by the fact that the clocks don't work, one feels that any action, any sign of passion, might immediately bring down the social order.

The story concerns Gonzo, a thief subjected to trial (or, rather, sentence, since he has already been found guilty) by combat: he must fight another criminal for the right to live. Defeating his opponent, who is consequently condemned to death, Gonzo is appointed as assistant to Gozo's father in law, Gomor, and is responsible for looking after the dogs, getting rid of flies, and cleaning the shoes of the governor and his wife, Glossia. Meanwhile, Glossia is having an affair with her riding instructor, Gono. Together, they intend to escape from the island in a rowing boat, but when Goto takes Glossia down to the sea, he destroys the boat. Meanwhile, Gonzo is using his position to insinuate himself into the ruling order. First he murders his master Gomor and then reveals to Gozo Glossia's affair with Gono. Mortified, Goto allows Gonzo to kill him. Gonzo covers his traces and it is first thought that Goto has committed suicide, but then Gonzo frames Gomor as the murderer. When he is executed, Glossia escapes from Gonzo and throws herself from the top of the building. Gonzo carries the apparently lifeless body to the bed, but in the final scene, we see that Glossia is still breathing and in the final image she cautiously opens her eyes …

In the society depicted in *Goto* the themes Borowczyk had developed in his animated films come to life in a startling way. We are reminded that all film is a form of animation in so far as it depicts life through the use of dead matter by means of light, celluloid and machinery. The mechanical way in which film is made – and this is something that is constant in Borowczyk's work – seems complicitous with the immobile world in which the characters act, so underlining the feeling one has that the human characters are enclosed by the world. There is no escape: in many ways this could be the message that runs through all of his films. And there is no escape because everyone is subject to the same regime. No one – be he a king or a dictator with absolute power – eludes the inexorable pressure of the material world.

In *Goto*, there is little distinction in terms of gratification between the lives of the inhabitants, who toil daily in the quarries and enjoy the pleasure of the brothels which the state provides for them, and the aristocrats, whose lives of leisure are equally empty. The immobility and passivity of things is almost contagious, and even the love-making of Glossia and Gono is strangely subdued. The most powerful image in the film is perhaps Glossia's tearful face when the king destroys the boat she was expecting to convey her to a new world. His motivation for this wanton act is unclear. There is no suggestion that he has any suspicion of his wife at this stage. It is almost as if he must destroy anything that suggests any possibility of existence outside of that of the island.

A deeply repressed and authoritarian world though it is, the society of *Goto* seems to be more in thrall to the environment than to human tyranny. The governor in fact seems to be quite an amiable soul, distanced from the population and despotic, but taking no pleasure in cruelty and considerate and affectionate towards his wife. The tale brings to mind Kafka's *In the Penal Colony*, in which justice is dispensed in an arbitrary way and cruelty is inscribed into the social structure rather than being the result of human malevolence. The moral, however, seems to be the opposite of Kafka's, since in Borowczyk's film, it is the introduction of jealousy and spite through the agency of Gonzo that destroys this world. This makes for a profoundly disturbing film.

The unsettling mood of *Goto* is even more pronounced in *Blanche*, Borowczyk's next project, and his most exquisite and dazzlingly constructed film. Set almost entirely within the walls of a castle in thirteenth-century France, *Blanche* has its genesis in *Gavotte*, Borowczyk's 1967 short in which a gavotte by Rameau provides harpsichord background against which a pair of dwarfs are observed sitting on a wooden chest. They are restless, apparently awaiting the occurrence of some event, which is never revealed. Finally, it seems that one of them strangles the other and stuffs him in the chest. We are never sure that this is what actually happens, however. In a similarly ambivalent way to *Rosalie*, Borowczyk inscribes doubt into the very evidence he places before us, forcing us to confront the uncertainties of what our senses perceive. In *Blanche* this sense of doubt is amplified to the extent that it permeates the whole film.

The film begins with a stunning credits sequence. There can be few films that have set up the themes to be explored during the course of the film with such dazzling brevity. Blanche (Ligia Branice once more) is being made ready for a reception with the king, who will arrive later in the day at a medieval castle presided over by an ageing (not to say decrepit) lord (played by the great actor Michel Simon in one of his last performances), to whom we learn Blanche is married. As she emerges naked from her bath, in scenes intercut with shots of the castle, of musicians practising, and of a caged dove, Blanche is dried and dressed by her attendants in a way that suggests nothing so much as that she is being prepared as a sacrificial victim, which, we will learn, is hardly different from the truth.

The arrival of the king sets in motion a train of events which, through a series of avoidable misunderstandings, lead to an ultimate tragedy that is as inevitable as it is senseless. The catalyst is provided by Blanche herself, as 'innocent' as she is beautiful, who becomes the object of desire first of the king's mischievous page, Bartholomé, and then of the king himself. The machinations of the two men as they each unsuccessfully strive to seduce her cause Blanche herself to recognise, and reveal, her love for the baron's son, Nicolas.

As in *Goto*, suppressed tensions are unleashed that tear apart an apparently stable world. The old baron becomes an increasingly ridiculous figure as he strives to maintain his authority as lord of the castle and the husband of Blanche. This is not so much because he desires a young woman as his wife, as because of his lack of awareness of the effect his actions have as the events unfold around him. So determined is he to protect his honour that it does not even occur to him to ascertain the truth of what has happened; instead he blindly persists in acting on what appearances suggest might have occurred. In this he reveals his total obliviousness to the fact that his marriage to Blanche is a sham; he desires her only as a kind of trophy and subjects her to an emotional confinement that is symptomatic of how he controls his domain in general. This is immediately apparent to the king on his arrival in the castle. His first words to Blanche are: 'You must feel like a caged bird in this castle.' Like Goto, the baron has unknowingly erected an apparatus of repression that suffocates the whole community. This creates the sense of tension that can be contained while the authority of the baron remains supreme, but when the king appears with an entourage over which the baron has no control, the pressure becomes too great to be confined.

Blanche becomes the catalyst for the release of these tensions by her very presence, rather than by her actions. She stands as a constant provocation to which the men in the story are doomed to succumb in different ways. The king sees her as another conquest, for his page she is a way of asserting his virility, and the son of the baron is in love with her. For the old baron she may be merely a trophy, but it is a trophy he will jealously guard and not relinquish under any circumstance. Blanche herself, however, is an emblem of freedom. As such she reveals the lack of freedom of the world in which she moves. Blanche's purity is, in true surrealist fashion, dangerous if not subversive. Subversive, in the sense that it reveals the shams and hypocrisies of the surrounding society at the same time as it provides a point of entry that enables love to be recognised. In a sense she is less a character than a cipher. Indeed we never really learn anything about her:

so enclosed is she within herself that her desires cannot be read. Not, that is, until circumstances force her to reveal her love for Nicolas. When they become aware of the fact of this love, the page and the king both relinquish their lecherous designs on Blanche. She thus brings out the best and the worst in people. In the end, only the Baron, enclosed in his pride and stubbornly clinging to the appearance of things, is unable to recognise things as they are. In this respect, the film is a contribution to the age-old theme of the infirm sovereign unable to renew his kingdom by giving way to a successor.

The film is charged with a unique atmosphere. Few films have so successfully conjured up a medieval world in a way that so reveals its alienness to modern sensibilities and yet is so recognisable in the passions and longings it depicts. We are constantly made aware of what distances us from this world, which disconcerts as much by its familiarity as by its alien quality. By reducing the depth of focus and flattening perspective, Borowczyk's conjures up images that call to mind medieval painting. Yet at the same time we are given a sense that this world exists not in the European past, but in a parallel universe that is both of and not of the modern world. It lies, in fact, *elsewhere*.

Of course, the atmosphere is resolutely 'gothic', not in the sense in which the word tends to be used today to describe any impression of menace, but in the claustrophobic mood in which we feel that so much is repressed that anything might happen at any moment. The castle, with its winding stone staircases, gloomy corridors and rooms full of caskets and objects, is a major character in the film, giving us the disconcerting – if not paradoxical – sense, as so often with Borowczyk, that, in its very indifference to human activity, the inorganic world is somehow complicit with (if not the initiator of) the passions which inexorably lead the action to tragedy. In this, as in all of Borowczyk's films, the situating of the audience as voyeur is interesting. We are placed in a position in which we observe the drama in a way that draws us in so that we too become complicit with the fact that within the film everyone appears to be watching everyone else. The only exception to this being the baron, whose complete blindness to everything that is going on around him is therefore set further in relief.

A mention should also be made of another important element we will find in many Borowczyk films: the role of animals. Intermediaries between the world of matter and the world of the spirit, animals often appear to be more intelligent than the humans. Here we have not only the caged dove which acts as a counterpoint to Blanche's own confinement, but also the mischievous monkey, a veritable Harpo Marx of disruption, which often seems to be mocking the actions of the human characters as it interrupts the framework of the usual.

The film is so rich, and constructed with such attention to detail, that we feel every action is redolent with meaning. Yet, at the same time, Borowczyk is enough of a surrealist not to use symbols as simple signifiers. Even as it may seem obvious that the caged dove symbolises Blanche's confinement, there is something which doesn't fit such a neat designation. The bird acts rather as an avatar of difference;

the fact that it lives at the end while most of the human protagonists have died signifies yet again in Borowczyk how the human world in the end is no match for the world of nature.

That Borowczyk should follow up such a delicate and unstated film with *Immoral Tales* in 1974, a film that 'leaves little to the imagination', at least in terms of sexual explicitness, may seem anomalous. Only those who have little imagination in the first place, however, would fail to perceive the continuity in Borowczyk's concerns.

Immoral Tales is a portmanteau film bringing together four (or, more strictly, five) stories of eroticism. In the first, taken from a story by surrealist writer André Pieyre de Mandiargues, a young man initiates his 16-year-old cousin into the nature of sexuality by taking her to the beach and requiring her to perform fellatio on him in tune with the waves of the incoming tide. 'Thérèse Philosophe', the second story, is based on an anonymous sacrilegious eighteenth-century novel about onanistic pleasures through which Thérèse enters into mystical communion with God. The tale neatly encapsulates Mimi Parent's surrealist definition of masturbation: 'the hand in the service of the imagination' (in Anon., 1970). The third story is a re-telling of the historical case of Erzébet Bathory, taken from the study by surrealist poet Valentine Penrose, *The Bloody Countess*, who terrorised her Hungarian province in the seventeenth century in search of blood and eternal youth. The final story is also based on a historical figure, this time the equally infamous Lucrezia Borgia and her exploits at the court of Pope Alexandre VI (especially incest with her father and brother), and is set in the context of the persecution of heresy.

A consciously transgressive film, *Immoral Tales* was directed as much against religious as sexual repression, although a lot of its force in the former respect was lost on an English-language audience, whose religious repressions are not founded in the Catholic ritual so central to French society or more particularly to that of Borowczyk's native Poland. Its first two episodes are probably the best, especially the first, in which Borowczyk effectively manages to illustrate the continuity existing between female sexual awakening and the rise and fall of the tide. Overall, though, the film is a minor work in which Borowczyk's deeper concerns are subsumed by his apparent eagerness to push at the boundaries of what was considered to be at the time acceptable in terms of the representation of sexual activity.

The fifth of the 'immoral tales' was taken out of the finished film to re-worked into a feature film, *The Beast*, that would become Borowczyk's most outrageous work. Before that, however, Borowczyk returned to his native Poland to make *Story of Sin* (1974), a film as scintillating as *Blanche*. Adapted from a novel by Stefan Zeromski published in 1908, Borowczyk's film seems a continuation – or extension – of the themes explored in his short film *Rosalie* which we discussed earlier. *Story of Sin* is a story of *amour fou* that stands alongside *L'Âge d'or* as one of the great explorations of the disruptive impact of love on social relations.

Eva is the pious daughter of a down-at-heel bourgeois family forced by circumstances to rent out rooms in their claustrophobic apartment in order to make ends meet. When Lukasz Niepolomski, a young anthropologist who has come to Warsaw to obtain a divorce, takes up residence in one of the rooms, Eva falls madly in love with him. We are never sure whether this love is reciprocated, whether Niepolomski is taking advantage of her, or whether he is simply unaware of its intensity. Eva's love, however, is unqualified: she will follow him if necessary to the ends of the earth. And in fact it will prove necessary: she is impelled to undertake a journey across Europe that will take her into the depths of the soul, which will involve infanticide, blackmail, murder and prostitution. Defying her haridan mother, she abandons her home and job and offers herself up to the vagaries of fate, in the process experiencing degradation, dishonour, ruin and redemption in pursuit of an impossible amorous sanctification she will not relinquish at any cost.

This melodramatic, and not always coherent, plot is simply the barebones of a subtle and complex tale of human motivation. Like Blanche, Eva is a woman whose purity acts as a magnet, drawing men to her in a way that brings tragedy upon them, as well as upon herself. Unlike Blanche, however, she is not a passive catalyst of the tragedy, but actively participates in it and it is through her own actions that it unfolds. A difference of affect is also apparent. Where Blanche is confined by the rigid protocols of a medieval court, Eva's confinement (which is just as great) is less immediately apparent, since she has a freedom of movement denied to Blanche. Nevertheless, the structures of the surrounding society in nineteenth-century Poland are equally constraining, if anything more so, because they act in a spiritual sense to drain the life out of people, which is one of the reasons this is the 'story of sin'.

Borowczyk denies the Christian notion of sin, while showing the way in which it permeates Western society: sin is not an individual fault but inheres in the structure of society. When we first see Eva she is in a confessional box. The priest admonishes her to avoid sin, whose inner cause is 'imagination and lust' and whose outer cause is 'other men'. The household is dominated by her tyrannical mother and the atmosphere around her is charged with hypocrisy and repression. The house itself is as oppressive as the castle in *Blanche*, and although Eva escapes from its confines, she never divests herself of the order that pervades it since it is the order that dominates the wider society from which there can be no escape, only different degrees of confinement.

It is tempting to see *Story of Sin* in counterpoint to Buñuel's *That Obscure Object of Desire* in so far as Borowczyk was concerned to show the effects of female enslavement to the object of desire as Buñuel was later to deal with male desire. It also bears comparison with the films of Sternberg or Ophuls (especially *Letter from an Unknown Woman* [1948]) in the way in which it treats female desire. Yet Eva is very different from the heroines of either of these directors' films in the destructiveness of her purity. It is by taking an active role in pursuing her object of desire that she ultimately brings down destruction on all of the men (except Niepolomski) who enter her life, not intentionally but through the way in which their own machinations turn against them. Eva acts as a catalyst for the evils men conceive. In contradistinction to Mathieu in Buñuel's film, too, her pursuit of love is less a self-delusion than a release from the codes of the repressive society in which she is condemned to live. That this release leads only to a different form of confinement does not invalidate the initial revolt that gave rise to it: this is a case, as Breton put it, of revolt that 'is its own justification, completely independent of the chance it has to modify the state of affairs that gives rise to it' (1994: 89).

Story of Sin also differs from *Goto* and *Blanche* in being set in a recognisable social milieu of Poland at the end of the nineteenth century. This social context is not a mere pretext for the story, but is subsumed within the general theme: ultimately this is *the* story of sin: Eva, as she tells us in the course of the film, is the first sinner. But in what does her sin consist? Like Viridiana in Buñuel's film, Eva strives to obey church strictures about purity only to be overcome by the pressures that living in the world places upon her. Like Viridiana, too, she does not bring sin into the world; it is the world that brings sin to her. It is her purity, her will to submit herself to the absolute, that subjects her to sin. In a corrupt world, it is purity that contaminates.

After completing *Story of Sin*, Borowczyk returned to France to rework the omitted fifth part of his immoral tales into a full-length feature film. The result was *The Beast* (1975), one of those sexually explicit films from the seventies that, along with Bertolucci's *Last Tango in Paris* (1972), and Oshima's *Ai no corrida* (1977), was instrumental (Pasolini's *Salo,* which one might add to this trio, really functioned in a quite different sphere) in confronting the pusillanimous way in which sex could be represented in the cinema.

Borowczyk seems with *The Beast* to have sought to confront repression head on rather than document its effects. The plot of the film seems to have been loosely derived, like so many erotic vampire movies, from Sheridan Le Fanu's *Carmilla*. It is set on the country estate of the Esperance family, who have arranged to marry their uncouth son Mathurin to English heiress Lucy Broadhurst. When Lucy arrives she becomes fascinated with a story she reads about the ordeal of Romilda D'Esperance, an ancestor of the family, who was raped by a strange beast in the estate woods. That night Lucy has a dream in which she relives Romilda's ordeal, something which has a startling effect upon her own wedding preparations.

The Beast is an ironic, scabrous fairy tale in which Borowczyk's eye for detail and corrosive humour is still fully apparent. The way in which he uses sound – especially music – also shows a continuity with his earlier films. In other respects, though, it is difficult not to see in the project of *Immoral Tales* a fundamental change of direction by which Borowczyk abandoned his charting of inner states to engage with questions of expression. It almost seems that he became a militant for a cinema that would both challenge censorship and awaken the viewers' sensual capacities. Instead of exploring questions of repression and domination, Borowczyk decided to concern himself with liberation. This shift could loosely be seen as a move from a cinema of ideas to a cinema of the senses (or at least a change of emphasis, since all of Borowczyk's films are sensuous films centred in ideas). But if he might be seen as being successful, one has to wonder at its import. Borowczyk's films are never salacious – even *Emmanuelle 5* contains a sly humour – and the eroticism is always contextualised *sensually* in relation to its setting. Nevertheless, the new openness these films helped to bring to the depiction of sexual activity on the screen did not destroy the sense of shame with which sexuality is regarded in modern society, it merely displaced it. Sensuality was 'liberated' only to be reduced to a mechanical function which did nothing to address the repression and sense of shame that underlay it.

In 1975, Borowczyk was at the peak of his powers. He had made three films that deserve to be regarded as classics of the cinema. If *Immoral Tales* and *The Beast* were not in the same class, they were still outrageously provocative films that showed the extent of his authority as a film maker. His almost immediate 'fall from grace' therefore seems incomprehensible.

One might be tempted to believe that Borowczyk became a victim of his own choices, that he had become 'typecast' by producers as the maker of erotica. Borowczyk's 'mistake', perhaps, was that, unlike Oshima or Bertolucci, he did not follow up *The Beast* with serious, largely unerotic material.

This is contradicted, however, by the fact that his next two projects were both based upon interesting source material in which the erotic element did not need to be emphasised. The first, *La Marge* (1976), was an adaptation of an excellent – and eminently cinematic – novel by André Pieyre de Mandiargues. The second, *Behind Convent Walls* (1977), was taken from a story by Stendhal. Perfect material, one would have thought, for Borowczyk's sensibility. Yet these two films seem to have sealed his fate by giving critics the ammunition they needed to dismiss Borowczyk as a simple purveyor of pornography, and it is certainly difficult to understand how he could have made two such ordinary, even vulgar, films from such promising material.

La Marge is especially disappointing. Mandiargues's story is a tale of passion set in Barcelona which is represented as a city under a curse or evil spell cast by Franco's fascism. This suggestive notion seems perfectly attuned to Borowczyk's temperament, and offered the possibility for a transposition of the themes from his earlier films into the modern world. Instead he eschews this whole theme, setting the *La Marge* not in Barcelona at all but in Paris and the film appears to be little more than a vehicle made to cash in on the vogue for classy eroticism made acceptable by the phenomenon of the *Emmanuelle* films (in fact it starred Sylvia Kristel, the heroine of the first *Emmanuelle* film). The film is not so much an adaptation as a betrayal of Pieyre de Mandiargues's novel, something that seems especially incomprehensible given that Borowczyk and Pieyre de Mandiargues were friends. *Behind Convent Walls* is a rather better film than *La Marge*, with some striking sequences and characteristic Borowczyk touches, but is equally much less than one might expect from Borowczyk and did nothing to dispel the feeling that he had become an exploitation director, more concerned with the effect of the eroticism on the audience than with the story's thematic concerns.

It is probably the case that with these two films Borowczyk had created a ghetto for himself, whether consciously or not. Most of his subsequent films appear to have been made primarily for an exclusive video market and have rarely received a theatrical release. Even when they have, they have usually passed unnoticed by critics.

While Borowczyk never recovered the power of his earlier films, many of the later works are far from negligible. He followed up *Behind Convent Walls* with *Les Heroines du mal* (1978), again taken from a story by Mandiargues, and *LuLu* (1980), drawn from Wedekind, both of which have faded into obscurity, but which from all reports are much more interesting than the previous two films. *The Art of Love* (1983) is another tale of sexual initiation, this one based on Ovid's *Ars amors*, a film which perhaps more than the others reveals the bind into which Borowczyk had cast himself as he seems to be seeking, not always successfully, for a balance between titillation and serious content. Here the politics of ancient Rome provide a background for the action and Borowczyk seems to be looking back to *Blanche* as he strives to create a sense of the otherness of a distant age. The Rome we see turns out to be the dream of a young French archaeologist on her way back to Paris after participating in a dig. Unbeknownst to her, while she has been travelling her lover has murdered her professor out of jealousy. Ovid's treatise thus penetrates across time, infecting the present. However, what had been sublime in *Blanche* here seems like indulgence and only occasionally convinces. Although the film does contain some lovely moments and scenes (Claudia bathing with fishes, lovers playing the harp as they play with their bodies are a couple that deserve mention), and is worth seeing for the splendidly insolent cockatoo which plays the same trickster role as the monkey in *Blanche*, overall it lacks coherence.

Borowczyk restored his reputation somewhat with *Dr Jekyll and Miss Osbourne* (1984), a bloody updating of Stevenson's story, but in 1986, his career reached its nadir when he directed *Emmanuelle 5*. The film is not entirely worthless. With some characteristic Borowczyk visual flourishes, it is doubtless the best of the series. Yet despite some unsettling moments, Borowczyk makes little attempt to undermine the ethos of the *Emmanuelle* franchise, and one can only lament the fact that a film maker of Borowczyk's stature should be reduced to producing such lame and vulgar work.

He did, however, make at least one further film that is worth a serious mention. *Love Rites* (1987) is another adaptation of a story by André Pieyre de Mandiargues. It concerns Hugo, an antiques dealer who one day becomes fascinated by a woman he meets in the Paris metro. Her name is Miriam and she tells him about her traumatic childhood and how she has become an actress enacting the role of a prostitute who picks up men on the metro. She takes him to a church where she continues her story, telling of how her brothers had raped her and sold her into prostitution. They go on to a secret boudoir, the home, she tells him, of the mysterious Sara Sand, who allows Miriam to use her apartment when she is away. Their erotic activities begin tenderly, but soon take a violent turn. Miriam assumes a Sphinx-like appearance and attacks Hugo to punish him for his masculine pride. At first Hugo thinks that this is part of the performance, but she disabuses him: 'This is no act. I only told you it was in order to lure you here.' At this point the film becomes genuinely disturbing, evoking a primal world of sexual terror. At the end, Hugo must cleanse himself in the river, where he dies a death that is not a death as it is activated though another strange encounter with a woman.

The title, *Love Rites*, changes the emphasis of the Pieyre de Mandiargues story from which it derives, but otherwise the film shows the extent to which the worlds of Pieyre de Mandiargues and Borowczyk are coterminous, something that makes the wretchedness of *La Marge* all the more incomprehensible. The title of the original story is *Tout disparaître*, which is a more evocative title that gives us clearer hints of what the tale is really about. This might be translated as 'all things pass away', although this only conveys part of the meaning, since it implies a natural process of the world, whereas what 'tout disparaître' suggests is a more active – or accelerated – process in which the mutability of things (more specifically of one's self) is revealed. *Tout doit disparaître* is also the sale sign used by French shops: everything must go; and this sense is also alluded to directly in the dialogue, implying that one should entirely surrender one's own identity in order to become free: one needs to relinquish what binds one to everyday existence.

Miriam has already accomplished this task. She tells Hugo: 'I've wiped the slate of my past clean with acid.' But not quite: the fact that it required acid implies this. For there is one thing from her past she still remembers, which is the occasion when she was raped by her two brothers who abused her and sold her to rich men. 'Life wasn't a stage in those days,' she says. In threatening 'no mercy for men who refuse to surrender their male pride', she is taking her revenge for the humiliations forced on her. But she is more than a succubus who devours men: she is also an initiatrice into another world beyond the ordinary one Hugo inhabits as 'just a simple man'. Miriam is his destiny. She plays with him in a way that recalls the three female fates in Kaplan's *Plaisir d'amour*.

It is difficult to sum up Borowczyk's work. He made some of the most striking, and disturbing, short films ever made and several features whose unique atmosphere ought to mark him as one of the cinema's great directors, even if one considers that his career constitutes an extended and incontrovertible *faux pas* after 1976. None of his films are devoid of interest, and even in the worst of them, he retains an eye and a sensibility, as well as a taste for provocation, that is at one with surrealism, as much as it may at times seem misdirected.

Borowczyk's eroticism is entirely within the surrealist tradition, in which provocation is not divorced from humour or tenderness. Even at its most extreme or
most libidinous, it is underwritten by love, conceived in a resolutely surrealist way.
In their dark humour, their refusal to accept the given, and commitment to the
cause of human freedom, the films of Borowczyk conjoin with surrealism. Like
Kaplan, Borowczyk is among those who embark on the pirate ship displaying the
black flag of surrealist refusal.

CHAPTER 8

Jan Švankmajer and the Life of Objects

Surrealism has been a pervasive presence in Eastern Europe. There have been important surrealist groups in Romania and what was then Yugoslavia, although in neither country does this appear to have had any substantial impact in film. In Poland, as we have seen, surrealism was enormously influential, but there has never been a Polish Surrealist Group. In Czechoslovakia, in contrast, surrealism as an organised movement has been a continual presence since the thirties and has profoundly affected the film culture. It has also produced one of the most original and productive of all surrealist film makers in Jan Švankmajer.

The evolution of film in Czechoslovakia and its relation with surrealism has been well charted by Peter Hames (1995). Švankmajer distances himself from much of the 'surrealising' trends we may discern in Czech cinema: 'I am not interested ... in people who are "influenced by surrealism". For them, Surrealism on the whole signifies aesthetics... Surrealism is everything else - world views, philosophy, ideology, psychology, magic' (in Hames, 1995: 104). We can see the working of this 'influence' most clearly perhaps in Jaromil Jireš's *Valerie and Her Week of Wonders* (1971), drawn from a novel written by Vítězslav Nezval in 1935 when he was an active member of the Surrealist Group. Jireš's film is interesting and is largely 'faithful' to the letter of Nezval's book, but it uses surrealism for purposes that are alien to surrealism itself. Hames explains that the film 'is ultimately (and intentionally) reassuring. Valerie's relations with her father, mother and brother, and with other girls, run the whole gamut of sexual threat and temptation without ever threatening her innocence' (1995: 28). This raises an important point about the distinction between being influenced by surrealism and using it as an element of one's own work. With *Valerie and Her Week of Wonders* Jiriš made a fine film which pays a certain homage to surrealism without partaking of a surrealist attitude (and Jiriš never appears to have had any contact with the Surrealist Group in Prague). The point Hames makes about Valerie's innocence is also an important one that provides us with a point of entry into the world of Jan Švankmajer's films. The relation between childhood and adulthood, the focus of *Valerie and Her Week of Wonders,* is a major theme of Švankmajer's work, but in Švankmajer, as in surrealism generally, 'innocence' does not exist (or if it does, as we have seen in Buñuel and Borowczyk, it not as an inherent quality, but a counterpoint to the corruption of the world). This is, as we shall see, a key theme in Švankmajer's work. Unlike the film by Jireš, in which adolescence is treated as a time of terrors to be overcome as we pass into adulthood, for Švankmajer the terrors are never overcome. It is because they remain with us and affect our adult life that there is an imperative need to return to them in order to evaluate their continuing effects.

Švankmajer is in fact the only major film maker whose work has been sustained by active participation in a Surrealist Group for almost the whole of his career. Born in 1934 in Prague, he learned his trade as a film maker principally as a member of the Magic Lantern Theatre group, which he joined in 1960. Švankmajer has been a member of the Czechoslovak Surrealist Group since 1970, serving on the editorial board of the group's journal *Analogon*, a heightened environment from which his work has emerged intimately. His films are very much a collaborative expression, and his partnership with his wife Eva, as well as his participation in surrealism, is at the heart of his work, something emphasised by František Dryje (in Hames (1995).

Švankmajer therefore represents the exception to the argument made earlier about the impossibility of being a surrealist and a professional film maker. The exception that proves the rule? Perhaps, but the Stalinist system under which Švankmajer established himself was not subject to the monolithic production and distribution practices that control the economics of Western cinema, and thus paradoxically offered a space for an oppositional cinema, although this was only possible because the censors regarded animation as something for children. If he were an aspiring film maker today it is doubtful that it would now be possible for Švankmajer to establish himself as a film maker in the uncompromising way he did in the sixties and seventies.

Švankmajer's career bears an uncanny resemblance to that of Borowczyk, except that Švankmajer has never given in to commercial pressures as Borowczyk did in his later works. Both established themselves first as original animators using the short film as vehicle before turning to feature films. Both distrust simple animation techniques and seek to integrate different elements into the process of animation. They also share an interest in tactility and the life of objects. Their treatment of objects, however, is markedly different. Although both directors see the world as being dynamically active in the way in which the animate and the inanimate respond to one another, Borowczyk always respects the distinction between what is animate and what is inanimate. In Borowczyk we never see objects actually coming to life, as we do in Švankmajer, something that represents a significant difference of sensibility between the two directors. Another major difference is the relation to childhood. Children do not seem to exist in Borowczyk's world. The only child I can recall in any of his films is the baby to whom Eva gives birth in *The Story of Sin*, whom she promptly kills. The world of the child, on the other hand, is central to Švankmajer's thematic explorations.

Although Švankmajer's work has been well appreciated, to the extent that where he has become something of a cult figure, in Britain the critical reception of his work has suffered from a poor understanding of his relationship with surrealism, as well as from some ignorance of Czech social realities. In the latter respect, much of the commentary about him suffers from what might be called a certain 'ethnocentrism', which sees Czech culture not in its own terms but as an adjunct to the West. This leads to a tendency to consider him a dissident of Stalinism. While this is not inaccurate in itself since Švankmajer was opposed to the Stalinist system, to emphasise it severely distorts the significance of his work. Švankmajer, and the Czech surrealists in general, always saw Stalinism as a symptom of a wider sickness of modern society, not as a phenomenon that could be isolated from it. As he put it: 'the ulcer of Stalinism would never have appeared if the whole of civilisation itself had not been diseased' (in Hames, 1995: 118).

In regard to surrealism, while there is acknowledgement of Švankmajer's irrevocable linkage with surrealism, its significance for his work seems often to be poorly understood. Many of his admirers seem to be entranced by the technical brilliance of his films without appreciating their theoretical underpinnings. This has not been helped by the fact that Michael O'Pray, one of the leading commentators on his work and one who otherwise writes with some sensitivity about it, fatally misunderstands surrealism and Švankmajer's relation to it, even as he acknowledges its centrality. O'Pray appears to have been responsible for a depiction of Švankmajer as a 'militant surrealist' (1986: 224), a phrase that has been frequently repeated even though it is a contradiction in terms: surrealism is never 'militant' (I am uncertain whether Švankmajer ever described himself in such a way; if he did it was undoubtedly in a spirit of provocation which O'Pray has misunderstood). O'Pray has an unfortunate tendency to coin internally contradictory descriptive terms. He has described Švankmajer as a 'mannerist surrealist', which makes no sense (although he may be a mannerist *and* a surrealist). He is also responsible for conjuring up a category of film makers, into which he would like to plant Švankmajer, whom he defines as 'alchemists of the surreal'. This phrase is a *non sequitur*. O'Pray justifies this category in these preposterous terms: 'They are alchemists in the sense that they blend disparate materials in the service of fantasy; they endow the real, the very materiality of the world – its objects, surfaces and textures – with an aura of strangeness and the fantastic' (1989: 254). A more complete misunderstanding of both surrealism and alchemy it would be difficult to find since surrealism and alchemy in different ways are both concerned with the investigation of reality and with the transformation of life, not with turning it into some fantasy realm of the 'surreal'. Švankmajer does have an intimate interest in alchemy, but, as we shall see, it has a completely different basis than this.

O'Pray's unfortunate way with words is symptomatic of his lack of under-standing of surrealism. Throughout his writing he seems to find Švankmajer's commitment to it slightly embarrassing, and something that needs to be explained away in a variety of ways. This is necessary, it seems, because O'Pray regards sur-realism as an art movement which had its heyday in the thirties and is no longer relevant. He seems to be among those whom Švankmajer referred to when he noted how surrealism 'is passé for snobs who "move with the times"' (in Hames, 1995: 104). Unable to detach Švankmajer from surrealism, O'Pray tries to twist surrealism into a form that suits his perception of Švankmajer's importance as a film maker. He thus tries to separate Czech surrealism from French surrealism, to subsume it within Czech traditions (hence the 'mannerist surrealist' label) and to extend the definition of surrealism into an amorphous realm where it loses all specificity. In a particularly insidious passage, he even seems to be implicitly accusing Švankmajer of bad faith as he emphatically states that 'the entire Czech New Wave betrays a Surrealist sensibility' against Švankmajer's assertion that it had nothing to do with surrealism. This sort of arrogance is frequently encount-ered among critics who appear somehow to know better what surrealism is than the surrealists themselves do. The centrality of surrealism to Švankmajer's work is apparent and has to be taken as read; it cannot be qualified in this way.

Švankmajer's film career begins in 1964 with *The Last Trick of Mr Schwarzwald and Mr Edgar*, in which his technical brilliance as both film maker and animator are already apparent, as are some of his major themes, even though the film is only eleven minutes long. Here the relationship between the characters is already defined as problematic: the conjurers Mr Schwarzwald and Mr Edgar, as they seek to outdo one another in the audacity of their tricks, pass from respect for each other to deadly combat. Their encounter is marked as one in which the relationship between things is a fundamentally destructive one, and this is something we encounter again and again in Švankmajer's work.

The breakdown of communication is particularly apparent in his first feature, *Alice* (1987), when the white rabbit orders Alice (mistaking her for one 'Mary Ann') to fetch him some new scissors. Protesting that she is not Mary Ann, Alice nevertheless obeys the command and goes to the white rabbit's house, where she finds a drawer full of scissors. Instead of taking a pair back to the white rabbit, however, she inures herself in his bedroom and refuses to let him enter, so that he is forced to lay siege to his own house, eventually having to call upon an army of the dead to assail Alice. When they finally trap her, they force her into a vat of a milky substance that turns her into her own plaster effigy, which enables them to expel her from their world, although it doesn't take her long to find the key that allows her to find her way back into this other world again. It is only when she has done so that the white rabbit is able to find his scissors. Communication takes place, but in a very roundabout way and one that is not at all reassuring.

Švankmajer's films might be said to be 'anti-dialogic', at least to the extent that dialogue is seen to be a matter of direct verbal communication. This is so at both a formal and an informal level. In formal terms, meaning is rarely conveyed by means of dialogue, and many of Švankmajer films are without speech at all, especially the short ones, but even in the features the characters rarely speak *to* one another, more often communicating by means of signs and gestures. In *Alice* hardly anyone ever responds to the little spoken discourse there is, which is nearly always articulated through Alice's mouth. The Mad Hatter's question 'Why is a raven like a writing desk?' is never answered. Equally, all of Alice's entreaties of the white rabbit are either ignored or responded to with violence (on one occasion he even throws the baby he has been tending at her, which then transforms into a pig). Only the caterpillar actually offers any positive help, but even this is only in a reluctant way. The characters in fact never seem to be speaking *to* one another, recognising that talk tends to result in misunderstanding. In *Faust* (1994), too, the characters usually speak past one another, and when speech is used to communicate it is more likely to be used to confuse than to impart useful information. *Conspirators of Pleasure* (1996) dispenses with dialogue altogether. In other films, the images may turn what seems an innocent conversation into something quite sinister, as for instance in *The Garden* (1968), where Josef's words, without apparently saying anything explicitly threatening, cause Frank to agree to give up his freedom and join the living fence surrounding his property. In this film, the confrontation between the two main characters reveals the manipulative way in which we may be induced into acting against out own interests and obey orders that have not even been verbally articulated, but are contained in the very form of the dialogue being used. We see this most clearly in *Dimensions of Dialogue* (1982), where scepticism about the possibility of dialogue is explicitly addressed. In the three sections of this film, dialogue not so much fails as leads either to exhaustion, as in the last dialogue, or to a reduction of diversity to a common reality that reproduces itself according to a uniform pattern, as in the first dialogue. Only in the second of the sections is genuine communication achieved by the couple in their love-making, but this soon degenerates into conflict and destructiveness.

There is thus in Švankmajer a profound distrust of the word, and understanding emerges, when it does, from touch and recognition of what is contained within the power of images. The superiority of images over words for Švankmajer appears to lie in their mutability: it is precisely because images can lie that they can also tell the truth. Of course, this is not immediately apparent: if one takes images at face value, they may be even more deceptive than words. It is necessary to engage with them; to question them and draw out their meaning. In contrast, the word, due to its immutability, is always false because it ties meaning down to one possibility. In terms of what he is attempting to do in his films, therefore, Švankmajer might be putting into effect Adorno's perception that 'art is magic delivered from the lie of being truth' (1974: 222).

Švankmajer has nothing to do with the puritanism that sees images as inherently false; on the contrary, it is only through images that genuine communication can occur. And this is precisely because images – at least if they are used well – impose nothing on the viewer. By the use he makes of framing, colour, shade, context and most especially texture and tactility, Švankmajer draws the viewer into his world without coercion. These images are not necessarily, or principally, visual: they may also take a tactile form; in fact they assume a greater veracity when they are sensually – and not simply visually – present. This is why Alice warns us to 'close your eyes, otherwise you won't see anything'. Unlike a spoken dialogue, which always calls for a response, through his use of images Švankmajer seeks to allow us the luxury of choice: of whether to be seduced or not; of whether to enter or not enter. This attitude, at once profoundly anti-Platonic and anti-Christian, functions at all levels in his work. It allows for a kind of embodied knowledge to emerge, which incorporates visual and tactile modes of knowing into a framework within which the meaning of the work is allowed to communicate in a way that goes beyond a sense of rational understanding.

That Švankmajer is one of the great directors when it comes to invoking touch hardly needs to be said. Along with Borowczyk he is almost alone among modern directors in having the ability to communicate the tactility of things.[1] The facility with which he allows the viewer to experience the physicality of what he represents is probably without parallel in film, certainly since the end of the silent era, a reflection of the fact that his formation, like that of Méliès and other silent film makers, was by means of magic theatre rather than through the learning of film montage, which has been the characteristic foundation of most film makers since the thirties. Touch, of course, is the most elemental of the senses. It is through touch that we begin to communicate with the world, that we recognise even that there is a world out there that is separate from us and with which we need to learn to communicate.

Food and the process of eating are even more important to Švankmajer than they were to Buñuel, but the emphasis is very different. In Švankmajer the communal aspect of eating is absent (in fact his characters generally eat alone). Eating for him is rather a primary communication with the world. Švankmajer is interested in the act of consumption itself as it involves the incorporation of dead matter into the living being. It is thus linked both with the sexual act and with death itself. But the action of eating – and by implication the act of creation itself – is ultimately destructive. This is taken to its logical conclusion in *Little Otik* (2001), this being which through its creation is able only to devour and digest everything and does so without reciprocity.

František Dryje has brought attention to the way in which everything in Švankmajer's films tends to end up being destroyed. Destruction 'breaks into each of Švankmajer's films for no apparent reason, as an act which is – immediately – unmotivated: decay, ruin, the spontaneous disintegration of objects, an ever-present threat' (in Hames, 1995: 127). This might be better expressed in more positive terms by saying that he never allows anything to be preserved, because preservation stifles the life out of things. It is appropriate that when Švankmajer made a film about heritage with *The Ossuary* (1970), it was a heritage devoted to death.

This is not to say that Švankmajer is unaware of or uninterested in tradition. Quite the contrary, it is precisely because of the need to communicate with the past that he is so interested in bringing alive what is on the face of it inanimate. The past is not for Švankmajer an inert recital of ancient events but, like the objects that comprise its evidence, remains a living presence that resounds into the present. The way the past reverberates in his films is as a residue that is contained not so much in the memory of people as in the very texture of the objects and products that have borne witness to a history that is far longer and broader than anything that can be encompassed by human history or memory. Thus the images of *The Ossuary* function to enact the presence of death in life so that the sense of horror which may overcome us at the sight of the thousands of bones situated there is simultaneously a process of remembrance and communication as it links us with the lives of those people whose flesh once animated these unresponsive bones. In Švankmajer's other films, the stuffed animals, dolls, bones, tools, clothes and other detritus of everyday existence are not so much dead as eternally present as witnesses or participants of the events occurring around them, ready to take animate form when necessary. In this respect, his approach in *The Ossuary* very much ties in with what we observed in other surrealist approaches to the use of documentation and the construction of documentary film.

This is also why in Švankmajer's world animate and inanimate are inter-mingled, to such an extent that what is living and what is not living are con-founded. Nothing stands still; it is a world of constant motion in which creation and destruction grow out of one another. Švankmajer is firmly situated within the Czech traditions of puppet theatre, and draws very much on styles of mannerist painting and alchemy. All of these traditions are based in the idea that the world cannot be divided into living and lifeless matter because everything is given its own life form through processes of representation and realisation, or more specifically by means of the construction of a stage upon which the life of objects can be revealed.

As an animator Švankmajer has always been concerned to open up the inner life of objects, both in relation to human activity (as repositories of memory and witnesses of events – as he says, they 'conceal within themselves the events they have witnessed' [*Afterimage*, 1987: 13]) and in terms of their own integrity that is independent of their human 'masters', in which they may be seen to have a life at variance with human objectives. Humans are not the centre of this world: life is fragile and objects are likely to have revenge on whoever abuses them.

The effect is to create a disquieting atmosphere at once threatening and comical, something embodied by Lewis Carroll's idea of the Jabberwock, that creature which mocks our sense of reality, being beyond possibilities of repres-entation and yet at the same time containing so many of our deepest fears that nothing could be more 'real' to us. In bringing the inanimate to life, Švankmajer is engaged on a path that leads in the opposite direction from that which preoccupied Dr Frankenstein. He has no concern to understand the mystery of life, but rather seeks to bring attention to the way in which the animate and inanimate participate together in a primal drama.

Nevertheless, Švankmajer dislikes being regarded as an animator. In a sense he does go against the whole tradition of film animation, and he has little real affinity even with those animators who have most enchanted the surrealists. His approach actually undermines the usual assumptions of animation as he uses it to disturb the relation between the tangible and the intangible worlds, rather than, like most animators, as a medium that enables the free play of the imagination. Max Fleischer's assertion that 'if it exists in reality, it isn't animation' finds little favour with Švankmajer, who rejects the distinction it contains. Even though animation is a domain particularly responsive to a surrealist sensibility as it enables reality to be bought into question, Švankmajer, in his own work, eschews such a possibility, preferring to situate himself in a realm in which reality is not so much brought into question as expanded into a domain that is beyond usual perception. We can perhaps see this if we compare his white rabbit with Tex Avery's Bugs Bunny: where the latter remains fully anthropomorphised, even as Avery confounds such anthropomorphisation by making Bugs *more* than human, the white rabbit in Švankmajer is always *other* than human (or beyond humanity) even as he takes on human characteristics. Where Avery – like virtually all American animators – uses animation to explore ideas, Švankmajer's animation conjures up an *other* life that brings the human domain into question. That said, however, there is certainly more than a little thematic affinity between Avery and Švankmajer: *What's Buzzin' Buzzard?* (1942), to take one example, might almost stand as a dry run for Švankmajer's *Food* (1992). At least it must surely be the only comparable film in the ferocity with which it represents the daily struggle for survival.

Thus, Švankmajer claims that his mode of animation is not about giving life to inanimate things, but rather about coaxing another life out of them, a 'life' that isn't life but which enables them to reveal themselves by means of magic ritual. In an interview with Vratislav Effenberger, Švankmajer expressed this in these terms:

> Objects conceal within themselves the events they have witnessed. That's why I surround myself with them and try to uncover these hidden events and experiences. Sometimes objects speak immediately as one looks at them, or touches them; at other times it takes longer, occasionally years, for them to speak out. People were touching the objects and things in certain situations in life, while experiencing various tensions or moods and they have deposited their own feelings and emotions in them through their touch. The more an object has been touched, the richer its content. I have always tried in my films to 'excavate' this content from objects, to listen to them, and then illustrate their story. In my opinion, this should be the purpose of any animation: to let objects speak for themselves. This creates a meaningful relationship between man and things, founded on a dialogue, not on consumer principles. This way the objects free themselves of their utilitarian function and return to their primaeval, magical meaning. The first things man created were indeed alive and it was possible to converse with them (*Afterimage*, 1987: 33–4).

Thus, Švankmajer is not playing with the possibilities of animation. No matter how complex the technique he uses, it is always subservient to the process of communication through which he imbues his objects with a 'life' that is their own. The animation in Švankmajer's work reflects an animist sensibility in which again he is close to Borowczyk in so far as Borowczyk, too, listens to his objects and seeks to uncover what they have witnessed. Švankmajer, however, expects more of them: he wants them not simply to reveal what they have witnessed, but also to enact it.

In Švankmajer anything may come to life at any moment. What is really disturbing about this process is less the mutability of phenomena, the sense of the closing of the barrier between the material and the living world, than the suspicion that these things choose to come to life in order to play with – and at times abuse – living things. The usual order of the world is thus overturned. Instead of dead matter serving life, it is matter itself that dominates life. Perhaps nothing in Švankmajer's work in this respect is more troubling than the white rabbit in *Alice*. Self-created and supposedly in the employment of the royal court (which is peopled only by cardboard figures which are neither alive nor dead but simply entities that subsist through empty rituals), he is the trickster attired as a mere messenger who in fact controls everything. His self-creation, as he transforms himself from a stuffed creature nailed in a glass box into a living being with a life very much its own, is one of the more unsettling scenes in all cinema.

The white rabbit's role is reprised in a still more complex form in *Faust*, where he appears as Punch, whose direction of the action is not so assured; in fact it constantly threatens to spin out of control as he tries to act as intermediary between the hapless Faust and the forces of light and darkness that surround him.

It is in *The Flat* (1968) perhaps that we see the most severe representation of the malevolence of the material world. In a film that most reveals Švankmajer's debt to Kafka (not least in the direct reference at the end when we learn that the name of the hero is 'Josef K'), the assault is unrelenting. Nothing obeys its ordinary function and the trap into which the protagonist has fallen is definitive: there is no escape from this world of entrapment. It is as though the hero has been condemned as irrevocably as the man sentenced to death by the Inquisition in *The Pit, the Pendulum and Hope* (1983).

In Švankmajer there is something fearful about an encounter, any encounter. This fear is centred in childhood memory and it is one of the reasons why so much of his work is concerned with childhood. In Švankmajer's world, as we have noted, there is no innocence: childhood is not a privileged state. Or at least if it is, it is by reason not of its innocence but through its character of play, although it is a play with little that is reassuring about it, since it is situated in fear and desire. There is no security in a child's world: it is a world that is menaced from outside, through the intervention of adult reality as well as by capture by the inanimate world (the child making less of a distinction between living and non-living matter than an adult is able to do).

Childhood fears are startlingly depicted in *Down to the Cellar* (1982), in which a little girl's descent to collect potatoes from the cellar becomes an initiation into awareness of the dangers of the world. The film vividly illustrates a common enough childhood fear of darkness and the unknown in a way that brings to mind familiar fairy stories like that of Red Riding Hood as well as certain cinematic memories, like the fateful and fearful child's errand to buy groceries that opens Jacques Tourneur's *The Leopard Man* (1943).

Švankmajer's view of childhood is not sentimental. If the world of the child is fearful, it is also marked by cruelty. This is especially revealed in *Jabberwocky* (1971), Švankmajer's major exploration of the child's sensibility. No child actually appears in the film, other than the one who is having his bottom smacked, but the film is a powerful realisation of childhood memory. Perhaps Švankmajer's most brilliantly edited film, it is about the way in which a child creates its world, through a process of experimentation with what surrounds it, in which creation is soon followed by destruction. The child, it seems to suggest, has no sense of creating for permanence but creates precisely in order to destroy; this double process of creation and destruction is its own rationale, and maintaining the stability of the world offers no comfort. This, Švankmajer seems to be implying, is where the child's world most differs from that of the adult. The child is content to be in the world and does not wish to control or dominate it. In *Jabberwocky* the dance of the knife offers a striking example of the inter-relation of life and death, creation and destruction, in the child's universe. It animates itself and playfully whirls on the table, cutting apart the white tablecloth on which it performs before suddenly stopping and falling, at which point, as its switch-blade closes on itself, blood flows from its now inanimate body.

The world of the child may be cruel, but it is a cruelty of a quite different order to that of an adult. One of the major themes of Švankmajer's work is the exposure of the way in which a child's cruelty, rather than being tempered by society, is harnessed into a direction that suits the organisation of society. He strongly disagrees with the attitude society takes towards children, of trying to protect them from the harmful aspects of adult society whilst simultaneously preparing them to become an 'adult'. For him this is profoundly mistaken, if not perverse. Arising from Christian guilt, it takes human evil as a given. As a surrealist, Švankmajer cannot accept that we were born in sin. He does not admit primary guilt. In his world there is neither guilt nor innocence. Evil is a human creation founded in social relations and it can only be addressed by acting on the processes that have caused it to emerge.

The failure to address this problematic has resulted in a human society that is sick, and which reproduces that sickness in its attitude towards children. For Švankmajer, however, it is a sickness that needs to be diagnosed and cured. Instead of trying to prepare children to enter a world that has been made evil, we should be confronting the sickness in its actual manifestations. Just as he rejects original sin, so Švankmajer does not believe we come into the world as a *tabula rasa*. If humans are born cruel there is nothing specifically human about this cruelty: it is the condition of life itself. Nor is this cruelty equatable with evil: it becomes evil only when subjected to the fault-lines within the social process.

Although Švankmajer treats the world of childhood, his vision is never that of a child's: he is always aware of the distance that separates him from childhood, to the extent that we might speak of him as an 'anthropologist' of childhood. At least, he treats childhood as part of the otherness that both surrounds us and is within us: as adults we can only experience it as an alien territory, even though it is a territory we have passed through ourselves in the form of an intimate encounter. In this respect, Švankmajer speaks of his relation with childhood as a form of combat. As he explained in an interview with Petr Král,

> The vision of childhood as a lost paradise is very deformed. There is already nothing very nice about our coming into the world. Equally childhood is filled with prohibitions, injustices and cruelties. Children are moreover propelled to become adults – an error certainly analogous to the idealisation of childhood which comes to us with age. No one knows how to be as cruel as a child…But I do not want, for all that, to disavow my childhood. I want only to retain an 'active' attitude towards it. It may even be that I engage it in a kind of combat (Král, 1985b: 42).

In addressing himself to the world of the child in his work, Švankmajer is thus striving not to capture a childhood experience, but to enter that world in order better to be able to see the world of the adult from outside. He shares the doubt and apprehension the child has for the adult world, but not for the same reasons as the child. Where the child both dreads and looks forward to becoming an adult, Švankmajer has seen the adult from inside and doesn't like it. He therefore strives to return to a perspective by which he is able to place a certain distance between himself and the adult world in order to view this world through the perspective of the untutored eye of the child he once was.

Nevertheless, he does not regard the adult world as one of a corruption from which children need to be protected. Making such a separation is part of the problem: it does not treat children as children but infantilises them. Children are thereby not considered in their own terms but treated as prospective adults, so that childhood becomes merely a stage in a progression that leads into the maturity of adult society. This is a significant part of the sickness of society: in a sense it forecloses childhood, causing adults to regard it as merely a stage through which they have passed and left behind and so they disregard their own childhood wisdom. Švankmajer regards this as a serious error. Rejecting childhood innocence, he sees the child (as did Freud) as having a different (or an *other*) system of wisdom which it is important for us as adults not to lose contact with. If we do so, we treat children purely in adult terms and this reduces the possibilities we have to act on the world in a way that can effect the transformation that surrealism sees as being essential. It is for this reason that he says

I'm not at all sure that any work of art is unsuitable for children. When children are confronted by something they can't understand, [they engage with it] so that it works by analogy, or they simply reject it and carry on as before. Adults have a very distorted idea of a child's world; they are crueller, more animalistic, than we like to admit (*Afterimage,* 1987: 51).

It is therefore necessary to re-visit to terrain of our childhood, and to engage with it is as part of the process of communication we have identified as a major theme of Švankmajer's work. Švankmajer's quest appears to be to try to place himself in a state of grace in relation to childhood. As Vratislav Effenberger perceived, he invokes' natural phantoms which seem to have escaped natural science registration only to be discovered by the imagination of a recalcitrant child not bowed by "adulthood" into humble domesticity and determined to protect poetic freedom' (1994: 17). Effenberger further charted the links in Švankmajer between poetry and childhood vision through humour and play:

The secret of Švankmajer's humour certainly lies in the fact that if lyric pathos and raw reality are set against each other, the rawness and pathos both evaporate and the lyric reality becomes what it is in the eyes of the child or a poet: a game that contains nothing either noble or base. Coarseness stops being coarseness, cynicism ceases to be cynicism, cruelty gains the butterfly wings of the dream and dream fosters the miraculous... (in Dryje, 1998: 12).

This also brings us back to the importance of touch in Švankmajer's work. As the most elemental sense, touch belongs to childhood, and the injunction 'do not touch' is part of the initiation into adulthood. Defying this prohibition, Švankmajer's engagement with the tactile is part of a spirit of demoralisation of the adult world, one which most specifically links his work with alchemy, the tradition of which has remained alive in Prague as nowhere else.

Švankmajer is not, as far as I know, an expert on alchemy (unlike his friend and fellow surrealist Martin Stejskal), but alchemy permeates his work (his home in Prague is actually an old alchemist's house), especially in the way in which the material world is pared down to its essentials. Indeed, the second stage of the alchemical work, the 'melting' or 'coagulating' stage, is referred to as 'child's play', and it is this stage that seems to foreground much of Švankmajer's work. In this stage the alchemical task is to draw out the properties of things. It is concerned with decay, and since Švankmajer thinks the modern world is in a process of irresistible decay, his concern with alchemical processes is linked to his dissatisfaction with contemporary society, seen as part of a civilisation which has lost its way. It was in fact in rejecting alchemy that science set Western society along the wrong path.

The surrealists have always had a fascination with alchemy, in which they saw the germ of a critique of modernity that complemented their interest in the

Freudian unconscious, on the one hand, and the Hegelian dialectical analysis, on the other. The second stage of the alchemical process is doubtless of particular interest because it offers a means to explore what Švankmajer sees as a society in decay and needing renewal, as he explained in discussing his film *Faust*: 'When any civilisation feels its end is growing near, it returns to its beginnings and looks to see whether the myths on which it is founded can be interpreted in new ways, which would give them a new energy and ward off the impending catastrophe'.

Although simply called *Faust* in the English-language version, Švankmajer's film should really be called *The Faust Lesson*, which is the literal translation of the Czech *Lekce Faust*. The film is not so much another version of the Faust legend as, precisely, an exploration of what the legend can reveal to us today. Faust, of course, is associated with Prague and with its alchemical tradition, more precisely with the point at which alchemy starts to go wrong, that is, when it becomes detached from a disinterested quest for knowledge and becomes self-interested.

In fact, in Švankmajer's film Faust appears to enter into the diabolic pact not from any great desire, but out of boredom: he can't be bothered to resist, and barely protests when the Devil doesn't keep his part of the bargain. This is partly a comment on the way in which people came to accept Stalinism. We should, however, always remember that for Švankmajer Stalinism was nothing but a particular emanation of the sickness of modern civilisation: the fact that consumerism has come to replace Stalinism does not reflect any improvement in the structure of society.

It is in the will to modify the environment so that is serves human needs that Švankmajer sees the sickness of modern society as essentially residing. From his earliest films, he has been concerned to question the way we tend to try to reduce the world to our own dimensions. The futility of human endeavour is most expressively set out in *Et Cetera* (1966), in which the actions of humans to rise above their circumstances simply turn on themselves in a form of eternal return. In one episode a man who finds himself unable to enter a house sets about destroying it and then rebuilding it with himself inside it. Now, however, he is unable to leave it. A failure to recognise the distinction between inside and outside, or rather the desire to enclose oneself and expel the outside, re-appears in many films and reflects the way humans arrogantly see themselves as standing above nature. *Et Cetera*, however, is a somewhat crude film, satirising human endeavour without offering any alternative. This is something we find in many of the films that precede Švankmajer's entry into surrealism. What surrealism thus provided him with was a way to 'negate the negation' his early films represented. It is in this respect, too, that Švankmajer's attraction to alchemy takes shape. Like many surrealists, he saw in alchemy a means of regeneration, an intimation that change did not have to be destructive and that there was a way of re-energising the world without placing human needs first. Through both surrealism and alchemy, he saw the possibility of a transmutation which was not imposed from outside but emerged as part of a difficult process of personal transformation in which one questioned one's own relation to the world. Vratislav Effenberger, again, recognised this aspect of Švankmajer's work:

> Even if the change to another civilisation calls for unimaginable sacrifice in proportion to all the threats which derive from formalised technical automatisms, and even if it is drawn out in proportion to the devastation of the human element which is taking place, this human element cannot die without trace. Although the deforming pressures of the end of the cycle will devour most of humanity's energy, they cannot eliminate the anthropological constants such as the dream, eroticism and sexuality, the dialectic of consciousness and unconsciousness and so on (quoted by Dryje, 1998: 11).

It is against the background of this devastation of the human spirit, which Effenberger sees as the condition of the modern age, that we need to see a film like *Conspirators of Pleasure*, in which pleasure assumes a furtive form since each of the characters is fundamentally alienated from the others, although tied together through their unspoken 'conspiracy' (of the existence of which they may even be unaware).

Although not made until 1996, *Conspirators of Pleasure* was conceived in the early seventies and doubtless had its genesis in the major exhibition the surrealists held in Prague in May 1968 devoted to 'The Pleasure Principle'. It may therefore have a certain anachronistic feel to it and may too easily be subsumed to a sixties counter-cultural discourse. This would, however, be to miss the underlying critique the film contains: the conspiracy of pleasure the film invokes contains no liberating potential. Quite the contrary, in fact: it reflects the passivity of the population under a repressive regime, the way people adapt themselves to conditions they have not chosen. Of course, their conspiracy is not without consequences, as the 'innocent' games in which the characters indulge turn out to have a tragic impact on their daily lives. To make the film in 1996, when seeking egotistical pleasure no longer had any social stigma attached to it, reflected the fact that Švankmajer saw little difference in the social conditions pertaining then than in the early seventies.

The films of Švankmajer are one of the major achievements of surrealism, as they are not simply marked by the personal interests of Švankmajer, but also coloured by the collective involvement of the Surrealist Group itself. Among film makers he holds a unique position in that his surrealism can be described without any qualifications.

CHAPTER 9

Panique: A Ceremony Beyond the Absurd

Panique was a configuration of three figures from the fringes of surrealism who came together in the early sixties not, apparently, for any fixed purpose, but simply to share ideas, especially on the transgressive and transformative possibilities they perceived in theatre. Their common inspiration was to be found in the theories of Antonin Artaud and his idea of a Theatre of Cruelty, developed in the thirties and aiming at liberation through cathartic violence.

These three figures were Alejandro Jodorowsky, a mime artist and theatre director, Fernando Arrabal, already a well-established dramatist and novelist, and Roland Topor, a cartoonist and storyteller. They appear to have met one another at a meeting of the Paris Surrealist Group when they decided to work together, feeling that that context of the Surrealist Group was insufficiently dynamic to satisfy what they wanted to achieve. All three of them later had a link with film, the first two as directors, the latter as a writer.

Panique was never a movement, or even really a group. It appears to have been no more than a point of convergence for three disparate personalities to explore ideas they had in common, a 'joke', as both Arrabal and Jodorowsky describe it. It is mainly known for the organisation of theatrical spectacles, later called 'happenings', an early form of performance art, of which their 1964 production 'Sacramental Melodrama' seems to have been a characteristic example.

Despite its lack of any clear programme or objective, the experience of *Panique* seems to have marked its members' subsequent careers, or at least given them a common starting point which they have explored in the multi-media careers and left a mark on their respective film works.

ALEJANDRO JODOROWSKY: DEVIATIONS FROM THE NORM

Of the three, Alejandro Jodorowsky has made the strongest mark on film. Jodorowsky was born in a small seaside town in Chile in 1929, the son of Jewish Russian immigrants. In 1953 he travelled to Paris to study mime with Marcel Marceau. Since then he has lived principally in France, although with long spells in Mexico, where he has made most of his films.

Jodorowsky is a controversial film maker, both for surrealism and for broader film criticism. A sometime cult figure whose reputation has waxed and waned, his films lie within the orbit of surrealism, but constantly threaten to spin out of it. He has an ambiguous relation with surrealism generally, and his comments on it over the years have not always been consistent. It is not clear whether he was ever really a member of the Surrealist Group, although at times he was certainly close to it, especially through his friendship with the surrealist artist Jean Benoît. As Jodorowsky tells it, his first encounter with André Breton was hardly propitious. According to him, upon arrival in Paris, the first thing he did was to telephone Breton at three o'clock in the morning to announce himself. When Breton asked, 'Who is Jodorowsky?' he replied, 'A young man of 24 and I've come to revive surrealism, here I am. I want to see you.'[1] Breton's response was that it was too late and they should meet the next day, which to Jodorowsky signified that Breton was insufficiently surrealist for him and he kept his distance.

How much credence one puts in this seductive story depends most probably on the extent to which one wishes to be seduced by the personal mythology Jodorowsky has constructed around himself. The story as Jodorowsky tells it is unlikely, given that when he arrived in Paris he could, by his own admission, hardly speak a word of French, and Breton, we know, was unable to speak Spanish. That a young man from Chile who, according to other testimony by Jodorowsky, was still unsure of himself would have had the confidence to telephone Breton in the middle of the night, demanding to meet him immediately when they did not even share a common language, is difficult to accept. If it really did happen, the surprising thing about it seems to be Breton's patience. Yet the telling of the story is revealing about Jodorowsky's own personality, in which arrogance and insensitivity go hand in hand with charm and naîvety. Whether such an incident did indeed take place or not (and perhaps it did, although doubtless a few years later than Jodorowsky tells it), the anecdote reveals, in microcosm, what links Jodorowsky to surrealism, and also what distances him from it.

The fact that he would expect Breton to see him immediately in order to 'revive surrealism' indicates a tendency towards hero worship and messianism which we see throughout Jodorowsky's work. He appears to have always been looking for guru figures (and to regard himself as one), and in this way to have regarded Breton as an embodiment of surrealism, something fundamentally opposed to its collective spirit. That Breton should have disappointed such hopes is hardly surprising. In fact, to contact Breton in such a way would, I think, have been regarded as a breach of surrealist etiquette. One generally needed to be introduced into the Surrealist Group through personal contact. To approach Breton (or anyone else) expecting instant access would have represented a misrecognition of the nature of surrealism.[2]

Although Jodorowsky related this incident as what caused him to reject surrealism, on other occasions he has claimed to be a member of the Surrealist Group until *Panique* emerged, when he abandoned it as he saw that as a more dynamic movement. He joined the group, he says, through his friendship with Breton's wife, Eliza, a fellow Chilean exile.

Whatever the case, Jodorowsky's passage through the Parisian Surrealist Group has left little trace (he never published anything in any surrealist journal or signed any of their tracts) and his relation with surrealist ideas is complicated. In some ways one might see him as a comparable figure to Salvador Dalí. Jodorowsky has something of the same dazzling and extravagant qualities the young Dalí brought to surrealism, but this is only a superficial comparison. On closer inspection their personalities could hardly be more different: Dalí's imagination was highly original and focused; Jodorowsky's is derivative and ill-defined. There is also genuine depth to Dalí's best work. Jodorowsky, in contrast, dazzles with his superficiality and his ability to engage in multiple activities in a way that impresses but in the end fails to convince. At the same time, he has an integrity that Dalí lacked. We may look askance at some of his projects, but he has never been guilty of the opportunism that characterised Dalí after he split from surrealism. For all its flaws, his work seems to be deeply felt. The problematic of Jodorowsky's work in relation to surrealism is something that runs through it from the beginning; Dalí, on the other hand, betrayed his early unquestionable surrealist credentials in his later work. Let us, however, look at Jodorowsky's film work to try to elucidate the contribution he has made.

Apparently, Jodorowsky made his first film, *The Severed Head*, in 1955, but no trace of it seems to remain. His next film, *Fando y Lis*, made in Mexico in 1967, was also for a time considered to be lost, but has recently been re-discovered. It cemented Jodorowsky's position as a controversial figure when most of the scandalised audience apparently walked out of its first screening at the 1968 Acapulco Film Festival and Jodorowsky had to make a getaway to escape the angry crowd that had gathered outside the cinema. The film was banned in Mexico and subsequently seems to have received a few screenings in the United States before vanishing from view, re-appearing only in the last few years.

Fando y Lis was adapted, or more accurately remembered (since Jodorowsky ignored the text), from a play by Arrabal which Jodorowsky had produced for the theatre. As the film begins, we see a young woman, Lis, eating roses, while sirens sound. The commentary tells us that a catastrophe has caused all cities to collapse, except one: the fabled city of Tar, where all dreams come true. With her boyfriend Fando, Lis sets out across a devastated terrain to find this legendary place. Unfortunately she is crippled and Fando needs to push her in a cart. They first encounter the ruins of a city where a jazz band continue playing, appreciated by a chic bourgeois audience as oblivious to the collapse of civilisation as the diners in *L'Âge d'or* were to the violent incidents occurring in their midst. The piano burns as the pianist continues playing and Lis is returned to her childhood, when she was raped in a theatre, while Fando is taunted by a group of mostly women in a game of blind man's buff. He is humiliated when he is induced to kiss a man under the impression that it is a woman. They escape from the destroyed city as Lis has a sad premonition of her death when 'no one will remember me'. Fando promises he will visit her grave and they play games in a cemetery before venturing into the desert landscape that will lead them to the land of which they dream: 'If Tar doesn't exist, we can invent it.'

On the way they encounter a motley collection of characters: a crazy old man who dances around a naked pregnant woman, a group of people who wallow in mud, transvestites who perform for them before dressing Fando in drag, an old man who craves blood and takes some from Lis's arm which he drinks like wine. They are a quarrelsome couple, and Fando often abandons Lis only for them to be re-united after he has experienced a trauma usually connected with his parents. First he is tormented by a group of women whose bikini-clad, whip-wielding leader forces him down a hill as the other women bowl bowling balls after him. Finally they throw him into the open grave of his father, who rises from the tomb to meet him and tries to bury Fando in his place. Later he encounters his mother, who force-feeds him eggs, and then he strangles her as he recalls in a dream how she was responsible for the death of his father by firing squad. Lis's childhood rape is also re-enacted, before, following an argument during which she enrages him by breaking his drum, Fando savagely beats her. She dies, killed by Fando; her body is sanctified in a cannibalistic ritual before he buries her as a final vision ends the film in which they encounter one another in a beyond-death state, the city of Tar finally attained, one presumes. The end titles tell us that 'When the reflection faded away in the mirror it gave way to the word "freedom".'

Set up as a fairy tale through its credits sequence, *Fando and Lis* is a some-times powerful, sometimes tiresome, and often incoherent film that enchants as much as it annoys. As a film about loss – the loss of childhood, the loss of civilisation, and finally the loss of life – the film is often affecting but in the end lacks resonance. As with other Jodorowsky films, the images are frequently self-indulgent and the incidents in the story lack motivation. The strange people Fando and Lis encounter on their quest appear to have no other reason for existing than that they are strange. Jodorowsky, one feels, wants to give us images that shock us without thinking through how they contribute to the story he is telling.[3] The trouble with this is that images played for effect soon lose that effectiveness. *Fando and Lis* may have outraged audiences in 1968, but what may then have been shocking today merely seems quaint and indulgent.

Jodorowsky's next film, *El Topo*, was made in 1971, and is the one around which his cult reputation is founded. El Topo (The Mole), played by Jodorowsky himself, is a leather-clad gunslinger who rides through the desert with his naked 7-year-old son (played by Jodorowky's own son Brontis) in tow. His son carries a picture of his mother, which El Topo tells him to bury, since he is now a man. They come to a village where a massacre has taken place. El Topo tracks down the killers and exacts revenge on them, castrating the leader. He is attracted by Mara, one of the village women, and rides off with her, leaving his son alone. The woman tells him he must defeat the four masters of the desert in order to prove himself. He defeats each one in turn, the first by trickery, the second by distraction (the Master is obsessed with his mother and El Topo puts glass under her feet, causing the Master to go to her aid and making himself vulnerable). The third shoots El Topo in the heart, but he has protected himself with a copper ashtray and so recovers to kill the Master. The fourth is the most impressive of all the masters, able to catch bullets in a butterfly net. He defeats El Topo but then kills himself to show how unimportant life it. Mara then apparently kills El Topo and rides off with her lover. Twenty years pass and we discover that El Topo survived and is doing penance in the mountains. He encounters a group of outcasts, whom he promises to lead to the town by building a tunnel. In the town he comes across his abandoned son, who swears to kill him, but agrees to wait until the tunnel is built. When the tunnel is completed, the outcasts go down to the town, where they are massacred. El Topo appears and exacts revenge, killing all the inhabitants.

Looked at today, it is very difficult to see how *El Topo* managed to establish its cult reputation. It has all of the weaknesses of *Fando and Lis* with none of the earlier film's charm. As a film, it is badly constructed and even more poorly motivated than the earlier film. In terms of ideas, it is disorganised, incoherent and unbelievably self-centred. One can only imagine it appealing to New Age fantasists of a particularly masochist bent.

Those who are enthusiasts for the film seem to regard Jodorowsky as some kind of visionary genius, but the striking thing about it is how derivative it is: images and themes taken from Fellini, Kurosawa, Buñuel, Peckinpah, Leone and doubtless a dozen other film makers seem to have been drawn upon with little sense of how they contribute to the story Jodorowsky is telling. *El Topo* most particularly resembles Glauber Rocha's 1968 film *Antonio das Mortes*, of which it seems almost to be a narcissistic re-telling, with all of the guts and content of the original taken out. Rocha's film was also overly eclectic in the elements it cast into its brew, but it did have a firm grounding in Brazilian folk traditions that provided it with a framework which is entirely lacking in *El Topo*.

There is so much in the film, it pulls in so many different directions, that reflecting on what it is trying to say is a tiring task. One is simply left with a series of questions with no answers. Why does El Topo embark upon his quest to kill the masters? Why do the outcasts want to find a way to the town? Why do the townspeople kill them? These are just a few of the more obvious questions the film forces one to ask. Meshing together biblical symbolism with Asian philosophy, one imagines that it is supposed to be a spiritual quest. But if so it is one in which nothing seems to be learned at all. El Topo ends the film as he began it: by massacring people.

For all that, the film was a great success in 1971. Among its admirers was John Lennon, who convinced his manager Allan Klein that he should finance Jodorowsky's next film, *The Holy Mountain*, made in 1973. Like *El Topo*, it is a quest film in which a motley group of characters who either come from or are associated with different planets ascend a mountain in search of enlightenment. They include a chief of police (associated with Neptune), a financial adviser to the President (Uranus), a Warhol-type artist (Jupiter), a weapons manufacturer (Mars) and a particularly sinister character who makes children's toys that will condition them to hate their enemies (Saturn). They will go together to seek the nine immortals who live on the mountain and hold the secret of enlightenment.

Quite why these characters would wish to embark upon such a quest is not, of course, explained. And their quest simply ends with the platitude that they need to seek enlightenment within themselves: the 'secret', such as it is, is that they are in a film! *The Holy Mountain* has a rather better grounding than *El Topo*, based as it (very loosely) is on *Mount Analogue*, an unfinished novel by René Daumal, a surrealist 'dissident' in the thirties, whose knowledge of Oriental philosophy and esoteric traditions went far deeper than Jodorowsky's. It is also a far more original film than its predecessor: if it draws on other films it does so in a less obvious way. And some of the imagery is genuinely disquieting, with a few marvellous set-pieces: the re-enactment of the Conquest of Mexico with toads playing the parts of Conquistadors, for instance, is splendidly realised. In terms of ideas, however, the film is pretty much the same arbitrary meshing together of notions taken from different religious and esoteric traditions.

Jodorowsky's only other significant film is *Santa Sangre* (1989), which is by far his best. A colourful, outrageous story of a serial murderer, it works better because Jodorowsky finally breaks free from the portentous tones of his earlier quests for enlightenment. Admittedly the cod philosophy is still there, but it is held within bounds by the power of the images allied with the fact that it actually tells a story and there is some motivation behind the characters' actions. Based upon an actual case of a serial killer called Gojo Cardinas, whom Jodorowsky happened to meet in a bar in Mexico after he had served his sentence, it works well because it highlights what Jodorowsky is good at. He is adept at capturing the vivacity and excitement of circus life with all of its colour and pageantry, and the intricacies of mime and conjuring tricks are explored with a fine eye.

And while Jodorowsky may be unable to perceive otherness, he does have a marvellous affinity with physical and mental difference. Not since Tod Browning has a director been able to represent abnormality and physical disability in such an uncondescending and unassuming way. The pleasure the Down's syndrome children take in playing their roles in *Santa Sangre* is evident and comparable in this sense with the scene with transvestites in *Fando and Lis*.

We can nevertheless still see a wide gulf between Jodorowsky and a genuinely surrealist perspective. Writing about *Santa Sangre* he said: 'I like to take reality and put it into an imaginary context. But I work with real scenes – where you see the prostitute at the beginning, this is real. But I mix it with the non-real. And when I take reality and put it in my work, it becomes a masterwork' (1990: 120). The way in which he makes a distinction here between 'real' and 'imaginary' is hardly surrealist, since it assumes a separation between the two which surrealism does not recognise. Surrealism does not mix the real and the non-real: it endeavours to find the point at which they are not perceived as being contradictory to one another.

In an excellent documentary devoted to him, *The Jodorowsky Constellation* (director: Louis Mouchet, 1994), Jodorowsky complains about Breton's limited taste: 'he didn't like rock music, he didn't like science fiction, he didn't like pornography...'. Whether this was so or not, Breton's interests and concerns were much broader than Jodorowsky's and were integrated through an overall sense of values: Breton's dislikes came as much from passion as his likes. Jodorowsky, on the other hand, cobbles together whatever serves his purposes without any apparent sense of unifying judgement: pornography or rock music seem to have the same status in his mind as Zen philosophy or alchemical treatises.

There is a void in Jodorowsky's films, an emptiness that emerges from the fact that he is seeking something but seems to have no clear idea of what it might be. It is a quest of 'liberation' but from what and for what? From the self, from society, from his own personal obsessions? Nothing is clearly defined. This makes for obscurantist work that is constantly striving for significance. Ultimately it is his concern for 'liberation' that most divides him from surrealism. Surrealism denies the very idea of liberation, as Breton made clear in the final scintillating pages of *Arcanum 17*, since it is founded in (and determined by) the very sickness against which it struggles. Liberty is to be found neither within nor without, but in the interstices of human relations. It does not inhere in things, but is found in the relations between them. Consequently, it is not something for which one can go looking; it rather comes unbidden when one is in a state of sufficient receptivity, able to recognise its signs and portents. In Breton's words: 'Humanity's aspirations for liberty must always be given the power to recreate themselves endlessly; that's why [liberty] must be thought of not as a state but as a *living force*...' (1994: 93).

Jodorowsky has, it is true, provided us with a key of sorts that can be applied to all of his films. This is the epigraph which opens *El Topo*: 'The mole is an animal that digs tunnels. In his quest for the sun, his path sometimes brings him to the surface. And when he sees the sun he is blinded.'

Marx, of course, saw the mole as a perfect example of subversion, turning away from the sun to dig away at the foundations of society. Georges Bataille, as we know, once used Marx's image to attack what he saw as Breton's Icarian idealism. Yet here we have Jodorowsky giving a transcendent, mystical meaning to the mole's digging, even making it the sign of an Icarian dreamer!

The assertion that the mole digs tunnels in a search for the sun is significant because it discloses Jodorowsky's inability either to think dialectically or to conceive of otherness (if he has an affinity with the abnormal, it is through its difference and the fact that it does not impinge upon, or bring into question, the stability of self-identity). The world is entirely contained within himself. This is not entirely solipsistic, since he does recognise another reality, but this exists only to be bound to his wishes. In a significant scene in *El Topo* the hero and Mara come upon a pool in the desert where Mara finds the water too bitter. El Topo therefore magically makes it sweet for her. No sense here, or elsewhere in his work, of any correspondence between the animate and inanimate worlds: Jodorowsky could hardly be further removed in this respect from the sensibility of Borowczyk or Švankmajer, or even Buñuel.

What is most surprising, however, is the extent to which Jodorowsky's films eschew both psychological and philosophical rigour. The former is strange in someone who has studied (and practices a form of) psychoanalysis. In the latter respect, Jodorowsky has stated that 'art doesn't need philosophy; it can be communicated from soul to soul'. Well, art in general may not need philosophy, but Jodorowsky's art certainly does since it is philosophy that holds his films together. Unfortunately it is a 'philosophy' drawn pell-mell from a range of different occult sources, none of which Jodorowsky appears to understand in anything more than a cursory way. The comment that art can be communicated from soul to soul reveals a naîvety that enables us to see the superficiality of Jodorowsky's worldview. He seeks enlightenment from within in a way that denies the existence of the world: there are only 'souls', whose 'reality' comes from within themselves and is transmitted across open space to that of another individual. The world, one imagines, exists only as an impediment to this communication. Society and cultural tradition thus mean nothing, and it is on this basis too that Jodorowsky can reject philosophy.

For all of these reasons we might conclude that Jodorowsky's distance from surrealism is complete. It is certainly the case that his vision is self-centred and inwardly focused, leaving no place for the collective exploration of consciousness that is at the heart of surrealism. He has no political or social awareness other than what emerges from a personal, messianic quest for an ill-defined justice, and there is a complete absence of dialectical tension in his work, which simply follows a trajectory of personal transcendence and growth. Furthermore, the human will in his films is dominant and reality must be brought under human control; 'real' and 'non-real' are different states whose mingling provides a heightened sense of reality rather than, as in genuine surrealism, a contradictory relation based upon an illusion which dissolves as one penetrates further into the sense of what reality is. What follows from this is an idealist determination to triumph against hurdles rather than to seek out the harmony of the correspondences of the world. Jodorowsky's engagement with the world is eclectic and self-satisfied, rather than rigorous and questioning. Within the framework of what he sets up, too much remains unexplored for us to be entirely satisfied with his films.

Nevertheless, divested of its New Ageist aura, Jodorowsky's work does still retain a surrealist affinity in its exuberance, and in his trust of the imagination and will to follow through his own obsessions wherever they may take him. To judge from his interviews, he appears to be a likeable and personable character and in the final analysis his films need to be experienced rather than critically dissected. He has stated:

I want to reach a mystical theatre characterised by the search for self; a kind of alchemist theatre where man changes, progresses and develops all his potentials... Return to the circus, where the artist risks his life and skin, make each performance a mortal danger, like the bullfighter with the bull. Then make each performance such that everyone is in a state of agony, in a state of mortal danger.

Considered in terms of enactment, his films certainly offer us a sense of visceral involvement in accord with this statement. This may be enough to satisfy us in a theatrical performance. Whether it is sufficient for a cinema audience is, on the other hand, open to question.

FERNANDO ARRABAL: FIGHTING WITH DEMONS

Born in 1932 in a Morocco under Spanish occupation (and of course the place where Franco's rebellions began), Fernando Arrabal has always lived under the shadow of the Civil War that raged around him as a child. His father was an anti-fascist who was apparently denounced by his mother and died after the war in mysterious circumstances, either in prison, or murdered after having escaped. What happened to his father haunted Arrabal's mind and provided him with one of the central themes of his work.

A precocious child, Arrabal was already writing plays and stories as a young boy. When he was 23, he left Spain for Paris, where he has mostly lived ever since. Yet although he generally writes in French, his work, like Buñuel's, can only be fully understood against the backdrop of his Spanish upbringing. His hatred of fascism and the repressive forms it used to control the Spain of his childhood is a perpetual theme of his work.

In the fifties, Arrabal soon established himself as a powerful figure in the theatre, writing a series of accomplished plays whose value was immediately recognised. In 1960 he met André Breton and joined the Surrealist Group, with which he seems to have maintained a harmonious relationship, although he ceased participating in it when he formed *Panique* with Jodorowsky and Topor. He has described his period in the Surrealist Group as 'utopian years' and his relationship with surrealism has none of the ambivalence of Jodorowsky's.

His prominence in the theatre has perhaps overshadowed his film work, which has not received the same attention as that of Jodorowsky, although he is probably a better film maker, even if he is rather less confident in his handling of film. Less thematically ambitious than Jodorowsky and with a greater social consciousness, Arrabal's cinema shares with Jodorowsky's the desire for liberation through violence and the direct confrontation of personal phantasms. Arrabal's violent and shocking images, however, seem never to be gratuitous or arbitrary but to be necessary responses to trauma.

Arrabal's first film, *Viva la muerte* (1970) is a powerful realisation of his novel *Baal Babylon*, published in 1959 and based on his childhood memories during the Civil War. The film begins with a credit sequence utilising scabrous images by Topor that are at the same time disturbing and charming, an impression emphasised by the child's song that accompanies them. The effect bears comparison with the opening of *Un Chien andalou*, inducing the audience both to want to look and not want to look at the same time.

The action opens in a desolate landscape as a loudspeaker from a lorry announces the end of the war and warns that 'traitors will be ruthlessly hunted down. If necessary we will kill half the country.' This is accompanied by the fascist battle cry: 'Long Live Death!' Hearing this, a young boy, Fando, has a vision of his father being garrotted, and rushes home to his mother for comfort. She explains death to him. He becomes aware of what it is to be an outcast when he is persecuted by the other kids at school because his father was a 'red'. This inflames his sense of rebellion. He burns down the school after the nun has reprimanded him for smoking, after which he climbs high above the city to a lighthouse, from which vantage point he urinates with such intensity as to inundate the whole city. When he discovers a letter indicating that it was his mother who betrayed his father in to the authorities, he embarks on a quest to discover the truth of his father's death. This is bound in with his own passage through puberty and his sexual and emotional awakening. He explores his father's suffering through his imagination, enacting his death in a toy theatre and through increasingly intense visions until the distinction between reality and dream blurs as his own sense of identity takes shape through his experience of his father's torments. Identifying with him to such an extent, he becomes tuberculoid (apparently from smoking his father's pipe) and almost dies. After an operation to save him, he is taken away from the hospital by his girlfriend in a cart in a scene which suggests the beginning of *Fando and Lis*, except that here it is Fando who is the disabled one in need of transportation.

Arrabal's next film, *I'll Walk like a Crazy Horse* (1973), is drawn from his play *The Architect and the Emperor of Assyria*. It is the story of Aden, a successful architect living in Paris who at the beginning of the film is driving into the desert. We learn that he is wanted by the police in connection with the death of his mother, with whom he had a claustrophobic relationship. It is not clear whether or not Aden has actually killed her, since his fantasies merge with reality so much that neither he nor we can be sure of what happened. We can say, nevertheless, that whether he really killed her or not, he feels responsible for her death and is overwhelmed with guilt. In the desert he encounters Marvel, a man living in perfect harmony with nature and imbued with the power to control the sun, the moon and all creatures. Aden persuades Marvel to go back to the city with him, but he finds it impossible to adapt to city life (or, more accurately, city life finds it impossible to adapt to him). Marvel is indifferent to all the charms that civilisation offers. Having murdered his girlfriend in a fit of rage when she refuses to make love with Marvel, Aden is the subject of an intensive police hunt, which ends when he dies following a gun battle with the police. Marvel recovers the body and carries it to the desert, crossing the sea in a cart. Finally, following his friend's instructions, he ceremoniously eats every part of Aden's body before undergoing the motions of childbirth and metamorphosing into Aden re-born.

Similar in structure to *Viva la muerte*, with graphic nightmares intermingling with the action of the story, *I'll Walk like a Crazy Horse* is a startling film of great power. Far more focused in the way he treats his themes than Jodorowsky, Arrabal nevertheless shares with him a denial of society and otherness. His world is a personal one, marked by a hatred of societal repression and the values of Western civilisation, but unable to offer any other solution than personal transcendence. That this seems to be almost completely achieved in *I'll Walk like a Crazy Horse* (although perhaps this is undermined by the fact that Marvel, for the cannibal ceremony, dresses, at Aden's request, in his mother's clothes, 'including her stockings and garters', suggesting that he is still under her spell) does not disguise the fact that it is achieved in a void. Aden 'liberates' himself through the intermediary of Marvel, but Marvel has no real existence: he is only an idealised version of Aden himself. In seeking the significance of the story, we have to say that the character of Marvel is problematic. Since he is too self-contained to need another person, why should he need to undergo the transformation ceremony at the end? Is this simply to 'save' Aden?

I'll Walk like a Crazy Horse could be considered a love story of two men, but it is hardly a kind of homosexual romance. The two men are really two aspects of the same person, and the story would more accurately be described as an ego confronting its alter ego. It is a story of the self seeking to complete itself. This is somewhat problematic, however, as Marvel seems already to be a complete person who has no need of Aden. Nothing that Aden offers him in civilisation makes the slightest impact on him. Its wonders are entirely lost on him to the extent that he simply transforms them, turning their luxury apartment into a garden or setting lions free from the circus. In addition, all that Marvel reveals to Aden is what he already knew: that civilisation is corrupting and that he needs to free himself from the spell his mother has cast over him. Otherwise one does not feel that Aden has actually learned anything from the experience other than the illusory sense that a person can live in an entirely self-contained and self-created way free from the corrupting influence of society.

Arrabal's films have a substance and coherence that is lacking in Jodorowsky's work, and the shock element in them is never gratuitous. His overall worldview is nevertheless similarly shallow. In addition, both men, having learned their art in the theatre, have not found it easy to think in a cinematic way. This is especially so in that where the starting point of the *Panique* experiments – a cathartic theatre in which audience and performers would undertake an intense journey into the soul – is ill-suited to a cinematic experience based upon an intimacy between film maker and audience. Too often in the films of both Jodorowsky and Arrabal one feels one is being assaulted by the film maker. This may be what they want. The fact is, however, that the nature of the cinema experience invariably dilutes such an assault. If we return to *Viva la muerte*, for instance, while acknowledging that it is a powerful film that viscerally calls up the trauma of the Spanish Civil War, one must say that both as a cinematic commentary on the pain of growing up and as a memoir of the war it cannot compare with Victor Erice's thematically similar *Spirit of the Beehive* (1975), a film which, quietly devastating rather than explosive, carries a far greater emotional charge because it does not engage in shock.

THE CYNICAL ENCOUNTERS OF ROLAND TOPOR

The third of the *Panique* triumvirate, Roland Topor, never directed a film, but he deserves a mention because he was at the heart of three very different but also very distinctive films that are worth considering in the light of surrealism: Roman Polanski's *The Tenant* (1976), René Laloux's *La Planète sauvage* (1973) and *Marquis* (Henri Xhonneux, 1989).

Roman Polanski is a director who claims surrealism as a formative influence:

I must acknowledge that that I owe my apprenticeship to surrealism. For ten years, and even when I made my first films, I viewed things solely by its light. There was something of the 'angry young man' about me as I opposed a society that really exasperated me. In the twilight days of Stalinism, to have a passion for surrealism was to be drawn to forbidden fruit ... ('Surréalisme et Cinéma', 1965: 171).

At the same time, however, he asserts that he had moved away from this influence by the time he began making films, retaining from it a sense of the importance of humour. From Polanski's comments in this essay, much as it inspired him, we can doubt whether he ever had any real understanding of surrealism, and it is certainly the case that in most of his films a marked psychologism distances his concerns from any genuinely surrealist sensibility. With *The Tenant*, however, though an involvement with Topor's novel, we can see a re-emergence of some of the themes that presumably attracted Polanski to surrealism in the fifties.

The Tenant concerns Trelkovsky, a Polish immigrant in Paris who finds a vacant flat in the apartment block owned by M. Zy. There is something disquieting about the flat, which seems associated with its previous tenant, Simone Choule, who committed suicide by throwing herself from the window. Gradually Trelkovsky perceives that the other tenants (and in fact the rest of the neighbourhood) are involved in a conspiracy: a conspiracy to turn him into Simone Choule.

Although Topor had no direct involvement in the making of the film, it is a remarkably faithful transposition of both the theme and the mood of the original story. The only substantial change the screenplay of Gérard Brach and Polanski made was the addition of a superfluous 'Ancient Egypt' link, which detracts from rather than enhancing the strange quality of the conspiracy against Trelkovsky.

The paranoid ordeal to which Trelkovsky is submitted contrasts in an interesting way with Švankmajer's equally nightmarish *The Flat*, except that whereas in Švankmajer's film it is the objects in the flat that malevolently conspire against the protagonist's will without affecting his sense of identity, in *The Tenant*, the conspiracy against Trelkovsky is on the part of the other tenants, if it isn't a construction of Trelkovsky's mind.

Perhaps the reason for the convergence between Topor's and Polanski's worlds is partly explained by the fact that both had a Polish background (Topor was born in Paris, but his parents were from Poland) and were living in an alien world. The film is a significant exploration of the sense of alienation that is especially felt by anyone living in a foreign environment of which they do not know the precise rules that should be followed. Trelkovsky is presented as a particularly timorous young man lacking in self-confidence, which prevents him from being able to respond to the pressures he perceives around him (we are never allowed to be sure whether these are real or a product of his fevered mind). His desperate need to assert his own identity paradoxically causes him to lose a sense of his identity so that he gradually identifies himself with the previous tenant in the flat. His surroundings thus increasingly come to consume him, causing him to collapse into them, unable to distinguish what he is from what is around him.

Questions of identity and otherness are themes in two other films which Topor wrote. *La Planète sauvage* is an animated science fiction fable set on the planet Ygam, inhabited by a blue-skinned race called the Draags. They keep as pets tiny humanoids, which they call Oms. The film begins as a Draag callously kills an Om mother whose child is taken by a young Draag girl Tiba as a pet, which she calls Ter. Ter is educated by osmosis as a result of Tiba holding him while she learns her lessons through a kind of distance learning. One day, Ter escapes, taking the education machine with him, and joins with wild Oms outside the Draag city. After some Draags are killed by a group of Oms, a mass extermination process is put in place by the Draggs, who see the Oms as pests. Having learned some of the secrets of the Draags through the education machine, however, the Oms rise up in rebellion.

La Planète sauvage is a powerful fable which shares many of the themes of *The Tenant*, even though its subject matter could hardly be more different. In some ways it might even be seen as a counterpart to it: where Trelkovsky loses his sense of identity as a result of persecution, the Oms discover theirs by rising up against oppression. A modern *Gulliver's Travels*, it is a film which conveys a genuine sense of otherness, with some strange and perplexing creatures which seem to defy any natural existence and yet are peculiarly compelling, such as the animals the Oms strap to their bodies as part of their ritual duels or the carnivorous plant that captures and devours passing flying creatures with a maniacal laugh. This is world in which the environment has an instability that marks it, as is suggested at the end of the film, as simultaneously at the beginning and end of human existence: we learn that the Oms are exiles, having destroyed their own world, as we perceive them as being in the process of forming a new human society. This suitably disquieting ending very much sums up the barbed mood of the whole film.

The other film upon which Topor collaborated was very different but equally eccentric. *Marquis* is set on the eve of the French Revolution and concerns a revolutionary aristocrat imprisoned for blasphemy. He shares his cell with Colin, his mischievous penis, whom he engages in lengthy philosophical discussions.

Obviously based on the life of the Marquis de Sade (although not exclusively so; that of the Comte de Mirabeau is also being invoked), *Marquis* is an audacious film as strange in its way as *La Planète sauvage*, not least because all of the characters are played as animals – the Marquis is a dog; Ambert, his guard, is a rat; the priest Dom Pompero (who has been responsible for the imprisonment of the Marquis, but is actually stealing his work and surreptitiously selling it) is a camel; the governor of the Bastille is a sado-masochistic cock whose lover, Juliette, is a mare who is plotting revolution and the release of the prisoners, among whom is Pigonou, a pork seller, Lupino, a wolf, and Justine, a heifer who has been raped by the king and unjustly imprisoned as part of the cover-up.

These characters are played by human actors wearing extraordinary masks, made by Jacques and Frédéric Gastineau but which Topor himself designed. This results in a powerful sense of equivocation between human and animal behaviour. *Marquis* is probably the only film that has so far been made which gives a fitting representation to Sade's ideas, although it is debatable how accurately it conveys them. It does not appear to have been intended as a strict transposition of Sade to the screen – Topor rather establishes a kind of complicity by which he seems to merge his own ideas with Sade's – so that the ambivalent context of the French Revolution becomes a marker for consideration of ideas about liberty and repression in contemporary society.

The three films Topor was associated with bear a consistency of theme and invention that suggests a comparable influence to that which Prévert cast on the films he collaborated with, and it is a pity that he did not have a greater involvement with film making. More cynical and imbued with a sense of humour that is far more subversive than that of either Jodorowsky or Arrabal (both of whom more often seen like naughty children in the way they use humour in their work to shock), Topor was also less in prey to his own personal obsessions than the others. Moreover, his work avoids being sucked into the shallowness of sixties counter-culture and thus appears to be more fully imbued with the spirit of surrealism. Topor's vision also seems to have been essentially tragic in a way that links him with Buñuel, Prévert, Borowczyk and Švankmajer more than it does with Jodorowsky and Arrabal, who both appear to have a belief that some form of liberation from the human condition is possible, something which, as we have seen, is ultimately inimical to surrealism.

CHAPTER 10

The Baroque Heresy of Raúl Ruiz

It is difficult to discuss Latin America in relation to surrealism since its influence is everywhere while being difficult to pinpoint in specific terms. This is especially so because of the way in which 'magic realism' (a phenomenon with which surrealism tends to be confused) has become a prominent – and hegemonic – form of representation in Latin America. Although they may at times be confused, the fundamental difference between magic realism and surrealism lies in the fact that the former is what surrealism is often mistaken for: a form of representation that acts on reality. For surrealism, 'magic' realism must be as doubtful as any other type of 'realism'. As we have already seen, surrealism rejects realism not as a form, but because of its claim to represent reality. Magic realism, on the other hand, accepts this claim and merely seeks to broaden reality's frame of reference, giving realism a wider frame of reference. In contrast, surrealism endeavours to shatter the bonds of realism, to discover and investigate an*other* reality. As a mode, therefore, magic realism should be seen as having no more link with surrealism than does socialist realism or naturalism.

We should consequently be wary of seeing surrealism in the work of Brazilian *cinema novo*, for instance, whose concerns ran in a quite different direction to surrealism, or in the work of those directors, like the Mexican Arturo Ripstein, who were influenced by Buñuel. The directors working in Latin America whose work seems to have the greatest real affinity with surrealism appear to be the Argentineans Leopoldo Torre Nilsson and Hugo Santiago, although in their case surrealism was but one influence among many.

We have looked at the work of Nelly Kaplan and Alejandro Jodorowsky, born respectively in Argentina and Chile, but neither director has maintained a real link with her or his home country: both left it when they were young and have never returned to work there. Kaplan largely regards herself as a French director while Jodorowsky considers himself to be thoroughly internationalist (although his films have been made in Mexico).

The director we shall consider whose work still seems to have its roots in a Latin American sensibility, even though he too, like Kaplan and Jodorowsky, is an exile, is another Chilean, Raúl Ruiz.[1] Although Ruiz has made most of his films abroad, he did not, like Kaplan and Jodorowsky, choose exile; it was forced upon him as a consequence of Pinochet's coup in 1973. Unlike the other film makers we have discussed, Ruiz never seems to have had any formal connection with surrealism, and indeed he disclaims any direct linkage with it. Nevertheless, despite this repudiation, he is an important director to consider in the light of surrealism since he is perhaps the only one (at least since Feuillade) who has made films in a way that links with the surrealist notion of automatism. His films (or some of them at least) are perhaps the only ones in cinema history to emerge from spontaneous, unconscious processes of creation. He explained this: 'I am interested in the idea of images generated by other images and the logic that's involved. I'm not a surrealist... But I am interested in surrealism on the level at which its technique can be used to examine different levels of consciousness' (in Ehrenstein, 1986: 6). This quotation tends to suggest an attitude closer to a genuinely surrealist one than Ruiz might believe. However, one would ultimately agree that his real source of inspiration is to be found more in a specifically Latin American form of the baroque than in surrealism.[2]

Ruiz is an enigmatic director, whose career itself assumes something of a mythical character. He is probably the world's most prolific contemporary film maker, apparently with more than a hundred films to his name, but also one of the most elusive: many of his films are very difficult - some are impossible - to get to see. He sometimes seems almost to be like a character in one of his films. How is it possible for one person, over less than forty years, to have made so many films, virtually all of which he has written himself, as well as having directed theatre performances and published several books, not to mention reputedly having written more than one hundred plays for the theatre between the ages of 16 and 20? Not content with this, he is also a significant theorist of cinema who has lectured at several US universities; he has also organised several exhibitions. He makes films in different languages and often several languages are used in the same film, including in one film, *On Top of the Whale* (1982), a language that he invented. This enigma of excess extends to any critique of his work. Given its inaccessibility, one is most often forced to rely upon one's memory of having seen the films years previously, with all the dangers this entails.

Since the pitfalls and uncertainties of memory are one of Ruiz's themes, it is perhaps appropriate that critical appreciation of his work should be based upon shifting sands. One would expect this situation to change as films become available on video and DVD, but even today few of Ruiz's best films have been made easily available in either medium. One also wonders, however, whether having greater access to viewings of his films would make it any easier to judge them. One critic, Luc Moulet, confesses to having seen one of Ruiz's films seven times but feeling that he knows less about it with each viewing. Faced with such profusion, one feels a little like Alice pursuing the White Rabbit in Švankmajer's film: 'Wait for me, sir!' The world into which Ruiz usually takes us is likely to be no less bewildering than the one into which the White Rabbit induces Alice to follow him into.

Everything about Ruiz seems to be paradoxical. He has a double reputation on the one hand as an uncompromising avant garde director and, on the other, as a director for hire, a mere journeyman (he says that he will make a film about anything, and never turns down a project that is offered to him). Moreover, these two reputations are intertwined. Many of his strangest films were made for television as programme fillers, and one has a vision of Portuguese housewives sitting down to enjoy an instalment of *City of Pirates* (1984) or *Manuel's Destinies* (1985) as others would consume soap operas. Ruiz appears to enjoy playing on such paradoxes, to the extent sometimes that one is not sure how to take his films. Are they serious explorations of the nature of existence, self-indulgent exercises in cinema techniques, or elaborate jokes played on the viewer? One may even wonder if there are not several Raúl Ruizes, working in collaboration to ever so slightly different agendas.

The Raúl Ruiz we know about, however, was born in Chile in 1941. He began working in the theatre in the early sixties but turned to the cinema after attending film school in Argentina. His first significant film, *Tres tristes tigres*, was made in 1968, and over the coming years he established himself as a director able to work quickly and effectively on a range of projects. Committed to developing film as part of the reform programme of Salvador Allende's Socialist government, he had already established a substantial body of work by 1973 when the US-sponsored overthrow of the government forced him into exile. Since then he has been something of an intellectual wanderer, making films principally in France, but also in Portugal, Italy, Germany, Britain and the United States.

In recent years, he has gained a higher public profile due to the commercial success of his acclaimed Proust adaptation, *Le Temps retrouvée* (1999) and the psychological thriller *Comédie de l'innocence* (2000). Neither of these films, however, gives much of a general sense of Ruiz's work. One would be tempted to say they are atypical, except that none of Ruiz's films are really 'typical'. However, *Le Temps retrouvée* seems curious in the setting of Ruiz's filmography for the respect it shows to its source. Although he has made many films that are ostensibly literary adaptations, he generally shows no respect for the source, using it simply as raw material to provide a framework for his own exploration. It is also curious in the fact that, although time is central to Ruiz's work, it is usually treated in a way that would seem to have little place for a Proustian recovery of lost time. *Le Temps retrouvée* is also atypical in that Ruiz has taken complex material and turned it into a relatively lucid narrative format; in most of his films he does the opposite. If this film succeeds in conventional terms, *Comédie de l'innocence* suffers from the fact that Ruiz's preoccupations are fitted into a conventional narrative format which cannot contain them. The film therefore comes over, like his previous 'commercial' efforts *Trois vies et une seule mort* (1996), *Généalogies d'un crime* (1997) and *Shattered Image* (1998), as somewhat forced and unconvincing. If we wish to see the points of linkage between Ruiz's work and surrealism we have to look elsewhere, especially to the films he made during the seventies and eighties.

It was in Chile that he honed his fast working method, making eleven films in five years. Of these, the only one to have been widely seen in Europe (and that only in a mutilated form) has been *The Penal Colony* (1971), a loose adaptation of

Kafka. Relocating to Europe in 1973, he disconcerted his fellow Chilean exiles by producing *Dialogue of Exiles* (1974), in which a story about the kidnapping of a Chilean singer is used to frame a discussion of the problem of exile. The negative reaction this film received was no doubt partly responsible for Ruiz retreating from addressing Chilean reality in his subsequent films. At least, even though the experience of exile is central to much of his work, he has not treated directly Chilean themes since that time until recently, when he returned to Chile to make *Cofralandes: Chilean Rhapsody* in 2002

In so far as it is possible to generalise about such a disparate range of work, the films Ruiz made during the seventies tended towards being puzzles of one sort or another. This includes some important films such as *The Suspended Vocation* (1977), supposedly adapted from the novel by Pierre Klossowski, which Ruiz used to explore the nature of institutions. This film led to Ruiz being commissioned to make a documentary about Klossowski. However, when Klossowski proved elusive, Ruiz – as he so often does – simply turned the project into something else. The result, *Hypothesis of a Stolen Painting* (1978), was a complex exploration of the links between painting and history, words and images, description and interpretation, and reality and appearance in a way that makes it a kind of companion piece to Orson Welles's *F for Fake* (1973).

In 1978 Ruiz had a commission to make another documentary, this one about the French elections, and came up with *Great Events and Ordinary People* (1979), which, once again, confounded expectations. Although in simple terms the film fulfils its brief, in as much as it consists of interviews with people in Ruiz's own neighbourhood about the elections, its real subject is the truth value of such documentaries and whether they really tell us anything at all.

In Ruiz's hands the documentary becomes a form of automatism, its content spiralling out of the control of its ostensible subject. Interviewing the inhabitants of his neighbourhood about their thoughts and feelings on the election, Ruiz soon loses patience with the fact that all he gets is what most television interviewers get – verbiage. Instead of trying to cover over the cracks as other interviewers would do, Ruiz brings our attention to them, in the process making us aware of the artificial nature of the television interview and the fact that it usually simply turns on itself and is lacking in real content. From this point, Ruiz systematically takes apart the standard documentary form, treating every one of its conventions in the most literal way so that their absurdity becomes apparent, most hilariously when he re-edits the entire film into shorter and shorter versions, showing how television can construct the 'truth' in whatever way suits it. Ruiz's film is so devastating that it is difficult to take the form seriously again after having seen it. The only 'reality' that television can show, Ruiz seems to imply, is the reality of television. The whole film could be seen as an application of Jean Baudrillard's contention that everything in modern society has become a simulation

This subversion of the documentary form was taken even further with *A Short Manual of French History* (1979), a collage film in which Ruiz splices together extracts from a vast range of films without making any apparent distinction as to their provenance (in the Revolution section, for instance, if my memory serves me well, Abel Gance's *Napoléon* is used alongside *Carry On Up the Revolution*) in order to tell the story of France's history as a process of representation in a way that fractures its continuity and coherence.

Equally curious from this period is *Colloque de chiens* (1977), in which Ruiz uses a pure surrealist technique of juxtaposition and transposition to re-tell a sensational tale based upon various stories he had read in the popular press. By cutting out phrases, transposing events from one story to another and mingling the details until he achieved some sort of narrative coherence, Ruiz again cuts the ground from under our feet. The commentary tells us a story of passion and murder that is just about plausible but so sensational that we would not take it seriously but for the deadpan voice in which the commentary is delivered, which never suggests that the narrator has any doubt about the accuracy of what is being reported and so we have to struggle to disbelieve it. Told against a set of still photographs in the manner of Chris Marker's *La Jetée*, *Colloque de chiens* does for newspaper reporting what *Great Events* did for television documentary: reduces it to absurdity. In its way I suppose it could also be called a 'documentary'.

All of these films are united by their playfulness, which never hides the serious intent behind them. The interest they have from a surrealist point of view should be clear. However, it is with the films Ruiz made during the eighties that we can see surrealist concerns coming still more clearly to the fore.

On Top of the Whale (1982) continues the subversion of form we see in the documentaries of the seventies, but here Ruiz's strategy is not so much to make a puzzle of what should have been a simple assignment as to play with language (both verbal and film) in order to take us nowhere (this is emphasised by the use of music which constantly builds up tension in such a way to suggest that something is about to happen which doesn't, a strategy Ruiz frequently used in subsequent films). The target here is another documentary form – the genre of ethnographic film – and the European taste for the exotic. Shot mostly near Amsterdam, it is supposedly set in Tierra del Fuego (no attempt at verisimilitude of milieu is made of course, so Tierra del Fuego becomes a Dutch seaside suburb) and concerns an anthropologist and his wife who seek out the last two surviving members of the most primitive Indian tribe. Five different languages are spoken in the film, including the one Ruiz apparently made up. One imagines that Ruiz based the film on the media coverage of the 'discovery' of the Tasaday (which at that time had not yet been revealed as a hoax), for it plays upon anthropological gullibility and condescension, unfortunately only sporadically hitting its targets. (An oblique, sceptical engagement with anthropology is a persistent background theme in Ruiz's films – in one of his guises, the Marcello Mastroianni character in his 1995 film *Trois vies et une seule* mort, for instance, is professor of 'Negative Anthropology', the only sort of anthropology one imagines Ruiz would find acceptable.) It is one of Ruiz's more infuriating films in so far as its intriguing premise is never worked out in a way that does justice to the theme, even though it contains some ingenious ideas, such as the anthropologists' son who changes sex while looking in a mirror and becomes pregnant: 'otherness', perhaps, has been attained.

If *On Top of the Whale* is not one of Ruiz's more successful efforts, he followed it with *Three Crowns of the Sailor* (1983), which appeared at the time to be a breakthrough film. One of his richest, most coherent and accessible films, it was quite widely shown and critically reviewed. It begins when a student commits a brutal murder and is then taken by a drunken sailor to a nearby dance hall, where the sailor tells his life story, as follows. Leaving his home town of Valparaiso aboard a strange ship, the sailor seems to be the only living member of the crew: 'We're all dead here, this is the other life,' he is told. Transported by this ghostly vessel, he has a series of adventures in the brothels and dives of the ports at which the ship embarks.

The film has a similar atmosphere as Orson Welles's *Immortal Story* (1968), a film with which it is often compared, and, like Welles, Ruiz plays with narrative structures in such a way as to challenge clear classifications of place and time and the effects of memory. The stories Ruiz tells appear indeed to be part of some 'immortal story'; they do not belong to the sailor himself but hang in the air, attaching themselves to whoever passes by. Ruiz creates a powerful effect of identity estrangement, not in the sense of a neurosis, but as a recognition of the fact that the self contains multiple selves. The *I* here is an other, in Rimbaud's sense: 'I saw myself through the eyes of another,' as the sailor himself says in the course of the film.

If any film could be said to sum up Ruiz's preoccupations, it would be *Three Crowns of the Sailor*. Certainly, it is one of his most personal films, in which the experience of exile is most apparent. With this film, he appeared to have found his own voice (rather than subverting other voices). Subsequent films, however, revealed that he has many voices, and this diversity of styles makes it difficult to come to terms with Ruiz's work as a whole. The films that immediately followed *Three Crowns of the Sailor* showed that the last thing on Ruiz's mind was the idea of developing a personal style or establishing a critical reputation.

City of Pirates (1984), for instance, takes up the narrative devices used in *Three Crowns* only to spin them so fast that (doubtless deliberately) they lose all coherence. The central character is Isidore, a young woman living by the sea with her parents, who are obsessed with what has happened to their vanished son. From this starting point, the film develops as a delirious dream, as intricate as it is outlandish, telling a tale of blood and thunder as sensational as that of *Colloque de chiens*. Reviewing it for *Monthly Film Bulletin* at the time, Paul Hammond (1985) saw it in exclusively surrealist terms, and we can certainly discern direct links with a kind of 'surrealist mythology', not least in the name of the heroine, surely named after the emblematic literary avatar of surrealism, the

Montevideo-born poet Isidore Ducasse. The film also maintains a clear affiliation with *L'Âge d'or* in its portrayal of the impact of a world violently adrift from its bearings. But its real surrealist provenance lies in the mode of storytelling and the faith it has in chance to imbue imaginative wanderings with meaning as Ruiz follows up the associations and possibilities of his different scenarios through a labyrinth of desire, cravings and blood lust in a way that could only be inspired by surrealist automatism.

Treasure Island (1985) is as delirious as *City of Pirates*, a genuinely cinematic evocation of the book, even if conventional admirers of Stevenson's novel might look askance at it. One of those books that enchanted the surrealists, *Treasure Island* plays on a sense of dialectic between adult and child worlds, which both merge at times and yet are retained as separate. Ruiz's version (one hesitates to call it an adaptation) draws out precisely those qualities the surrealists admired, as Jim Hawkins is gradually drawn into games played by adults, and what is especially impressive about the film is the way in which the activities of the adults are precisely games – deadly games, to be sure, but ones that show no greater maturity of sentiment than the ones children play – especially in the final showdown, an indescribable scene in which ideas about postmodernism become the weapons that determine the outcome of the fight.

Themes of childhood destiny, the importance of storytelling and the boundaries between adult and child's worlds are also present in *Manoel's Destinies*, another film made in 1985. Originally a series of four one-hour TV films, this was later edited down into two different feature films. I have only seen one of the versions which could have been among Ruiz's best had it been more carefully thought out. Unfortunately it collapses into incoherence in its latter parts, but its first half presents a finely textured set of accounts of the lives of Manoel, a boy living on the Portuguese coast who explores different life scenarios, each of which ends in tragedy.

The film begins at a house on the Portuguese coast. Manoel is a young boy who lives with his parents. One night they are burgled. Next day, on his way to school, Manoel is attracted by a wasteground, which he passes every day but has never explored. This time he gives into the temptation to enter, and he comes upon a strange fisherman who tells him wild stories of the sea. Manoel's teacher visits his home and tells his parents what a bad pupil he is for constantly missing school and that he will never amount to anything. In despair at the fact that her son is a wastrel, his mother eventually kills herself. The film returns us to the beginning. This time on his way to school Manoel meets his older self, who warns him against going into the wasteground. He goes to school, becomes a brilliant pupil. In the end his father, who has ruined himself paying for all the school fees needed to allow Manoel to fulfil his promise as a scholar, kills himself. In the third scenario, he strives to save both his parents and ends up dying himself.

The pattern is repeated in several different forms, emphasising the fragility of a life path and the mutability of destiny. In leading us through the various paths marked out by Manoel's different destinies, Ruiz encourages us to decipher the signs we encounter on the way as different configurations of a single truth, which nevertheless remains inscrutable. Thus, while no actions are without consequences, they are not measurable in such terms, since their wider implications are not contained by their immediate consequences. Ruiz puts his faith in images as generators of narrative, which thus veers off in various directions undetermined by causality. Events are linked rather by a kind of elective affinity, by crossovers, by transmission of signs through a process that may initially appear mystifying. Stories, art and science, the very fabric of language itself are means by which the cryptogram so formed may become comprehensible. In this respect, Ruiz here appears to be responding to Breton's demand that 'life has to be deciphered like a cryptogram' (1988: 716).

As extraordinary as *Manuel's Destinies* is *Mémoire des apparences* (1976). It takes as its starting point two plays by the Spanish Golden Age dramatist Calderón de la Barca, which Ruiz had directed on the stage; both of which were called *Life is a Dream* and tell the same story but in different ways. The original plays concern the son of the King of Poland, who has been imprisoned by his father because it is predicted that he will depose him. One day the king orders the sleeping son to be brought to the palace and given to believe that he is king for a day, causing his son to be confused about what is real and what is a dream.

In Ruiz's film, a literature teacher has learned by heart the names of 15,000 militants opposed to the military junta in Chile by memorising Calderón's play and using it as a mnemonic device. When he is captured, he has to forget everything so as not to betray his comrades, but ten years later he tries to recapture his memory by visiting a cinema showing a film based on *Life is a Dream*. Ruiz uses this setting to explore a complex set of relations dealing with memory and the layering of reality. The film is also about the experience of cinema, as the virtuality of the film is confounded with the materiality of the cinema auditorium, which becomes a place in which the story is enacted. For instance, characters on a train, whom we at first take to be part of the film the teacher is watching, are revealed to be on a model train set that runs around the cinema, in which other strange things occur: birds fly around the auditorium and a Western shoot-out takes place across the seats.

These are the films that are, I think, of most interest from a surrealist point of view, although, given the range and number of films Ruiz has made, this is necessarily a summary statement. It is tempting to divide his career into four periods: the Chilean era, when he devoted himself to the development of a film culture supporting a socialist agenda; the seventies films that deconstruct narrative and especially documentary traditions; those of the eighties (most of which were made for television) devoted to poetic exuberance and wild imaginings; and the films from the nineties, which try to apply what he has learned from his experiments to address a wider cinema audience. However, as with everything about Ruiz, this should not be taken as anything but a very rough schema: any attempt to reduce his work to a pattern should be regarded with caution.

Nevertheless, of the films he has made since 1990 which I have seen, the only one that can compare with the early ones is *Combat d'amour en songe* (2000), which might have been specially prepared for anyone who thought Ruiz was losing his touch. One of his richest and most allusive films, it seems partly marked by the sign of Raymond Roussel. We are told at the beginning of the film, which is set on an estate in Portugal, that nine stories will be told, all of which will be marked with letters of the alphabet. Each of these stories becomes intertwined with the others, crossing time, as though ghosts from different periods were making contact with one another.

Ruiz has provided us with a key of sorts to his films through his theoretical writings, most especially his *Poetics of Cinema* (1995), in which he explains his intentions with some clarity. One feature we can discern which is consistent throughout his work is its political intent. Even though this may not be manifest in the content of the films as such, it is clear that Ruiz has never left behind the concerns of his earliest work in Chile, especially the critique of cultural imperialism and the impact of Hollywood production methods.

The main focus in *Poetics of Cinema* is a critique of what Ruiz calls 'central conflict theory', which he claims underlies the vast majority of Hollywood film scenarios. Ruiz defines this in these terms: 'someone wants something and someone else doesn't want them to have it' (1995: 11). He objects to this because it 'forces us to eliminate all stories which do not include confrontation and to leave aside all events which require only indifference or detached curiosity, like a landscape, a distant storm, or dinner with friends – unless such scenes punctuate two fights' (1995: 11). This narrative strategy, according to Ruiz, underlies not simply Hollywood films, but also the political reality of the United States, and is the basis of a globalising attitude by which the American way of life is spread and accepted across the world. A homogeneity of affect is imposed so that politics are conducted as though they were part of a movie; thus 'politicians and actors have become interchangeable because they both use the same media, attempting to master the same logic of representation and the same narrative logic' (1995: 21).

Opposition to film making based upon central conflict theory is thus intensely political and is at the heart of what Ruiz is striving for in his own films. As an alternative to it, he offers a possible way of making a Western:

> The hero lays traps, never actually gets into a fight, but does all he can to submit to the will of God. One day, he finds himself face to face with the bad guy ... [who] says 'You held the bank up and you're going to pay for it.' The good guy's response is 'What exactly do you mean by held up a bank? How can you be sure I held up the bank? Anyway, what is new in what you've just said? And in what way do your comments bring us closer to God?' (1995: 20-1)

One can imagine just such a moment in a Ruiz film (in fact this largely describes what happens at the end of his *Treasure Island*). How does this translate into film making practice, and what, if any, relation does it have to surrealism?

While there seems little doubt that Ruiz's critique of American forms of representation is largely in accord with a surrealist view, we have seen that the surrealists have in fact been proponents of Hollywood cinema (or at least certain forms of Hollywood cinema). This was because, as we saw in chapter 4, many Hollywood films in their eyes transcended or otherwise evaded the strictures of Hollywood production practices.

There is no denying the fact that Hollywood does impose very restrictive codes on its film making, and this may have precisely the consequences Ruiz argues. A recent example to support his point is what has happened to the Chinese (Hong Kong) 'action' movie, which used often to deal with complex ideas embedded in Chinese tradition when it was aimed principally at a Chinese and South Asian audience and in which central conflict (which is incompatible with the traditional Chinese precepts based upon maintaining harmony between heaven and earth) was nowhere in evidence. It was introduced, however, through Ang Lee's *Crouching Tiger, Hidden Dragon* (2000), the success of which gave these films an international audience, which they have retained precisely by imposing central conflict and divesting the films of all of their resonances from Chinese tradition, a process reaching its apogee in Zhang Yimou's *Hero* (2002) and *House of Flying Daggers* (2004) by way of Tarantino's *Kill Bill* (2003–4). This mournful example might cause us to agree fully with Ruiz about the dangers posed to film making today by the cultural imperialism inherent in Hollywood production methods. Is the process, however, quite as monolithic as Ruiz believes, and, if it is, can it be confronted through the sorts of film making that he advocates and practises?

Ruiz argues for various strategies, some of which were already practised by the surrealists, such as viewers watching the films against the intentions of the makers (he speaks, for instance, of his fascination for biblical and classical Hollywood epics, which he would assiduously watch to locate the aeroplanes in the sky above, say, the chariot race in *Ben-Hur*). All of his suggestions, however, run up against a fundamental contradiction. If Hollywood production methods are quite as monolithic as he believes, how could it be possible to subvert them? If they are not so monolithic, then what purpose does subverting them serve?

Ruiz raises this problem in *Poetics of Cinema* without realising it. He relates that a teacher of film told him that Hitchcock's films are incomprehensible to some of his students. Ruiz uses this example to show how codes are always changing and that introducing new narrative modes does not necessarily mean losing the audience. But if this is so, if the codes are changing all the time and the films of such a classic maker of central conflict cinema as Hitchcock have lost their narrative hold on the audience in such a short time, doesn't this suggest that the mode is not as monolithic as Ruiz argues? Or at least that if it is monolithic, does it not also have protean qualities which enable it to adapt itself to changing circumstances, something which makes finding an alternative to it extremely problematic?

This difficulty is translated into Ruiz's own film making process, in which he rejects central conflict so totally that all motivation between the characters appears to vanish. In the films of the eighties, this works to give the films a freshness and originality that underlies their power of poetic resonance. With the films he made in the nineties, however, it tends to subside into self-parody, especially as he moves away from the confines of television production into commercial cinema. Avoidance of central conflict becomes an article of faith, almost a fetish, so that we may feel the characters' actions are simply arbitrary when they are not absurd, especially since many of the films are essentially murder mysteries, in which one would have thought that an element of conflict was an essential component. In *Ce jour-là* (2003), for instance, which Ruiz offers as a homage to film noir, we are presented with an artificial world wholly lacking in credibility (one which actually bears no relation to film noir other than as a pure denial of it). Rather than revealing the paucity of reality in Hollywood cinema by opening up other modes of representing reality, it takes us into a realm where reality is not so much brought into question as annulled. This alerts us to a fundamental problem of Ruiz's approach and I think explains the unsatisfactory nature of his later films. If you eliminate conflict, you are eliminating a fundamental aspect of the human experience, and this has the consequence that at the same time you also eliminate motivation and desire and the very foundation of the relation between people. In Ruiz's earlier films this was less apparent because they maintained vitality through being grounded in storytelling traditions and in his sheer joy at having the freedom to play with the possibilities of cinema. Having had to satisfy more commercial pressures in his later work, he appears to have become too self-conscious about his film practices and this has shorn his films of vigour. Too often, one might feel, Ruiz's films are perplexing rather than disturbing.

The point here, perhaps, is that one cannot address the problem of 'central conflict theory' by making films which eschew conflict, most especially because conflict is too elemental a part of the human experience. If Ruiz is right to see that the way in which Hollywood production models impose conflict as the *sine qua non* of film production functions as an arm of cultural imperialism, it does not follow that avoidance of central conflict can provide the basis for an alternative film practice.

If there may be a difficulty in applying Ruiz's theory to the practice of making films, there is no denying that he has given us films of great imaginative force and audacity. Through the eighties, working quickly on tiny budgets, he developed a unique and sometimes infuriating style that used outrageous camera angles and points of view to disorient a normal view of the world. Such working methods allow for a kind of film that is equivalent to automatic writing, and this reason alone is sufficient to make his work of interest in a surrealist context. Along with Borowczyk and Švankmajer, although each of them approaches the theme differently, Ruiz is also one of the great directors of objects, respecting their integrity as objects and giving them a life force that belongs to them and is not simply a reflection of human desires.

In Ruiz, however, there is no sense as there is in Švankmajer of a fluidity between the material and the immaterial world, nor are objects treated with the sort of force we see in Borowczyk. In Ruiz, objects are simply intractable, something emphasised by the weird angles from which he chooses to film them (one of his most notorious shots is from inside a person's mouth, with the image framed by the character's teeth), intervening in human action not to comment on it or bear witness to it, but simply to be there, and displacing human activity from centre stage simply by their very presence.

This reflects the extent to which Ruiz's cinema is situated in traditions of the baroque rather than surrealism. This distinction is not a qualitative one, as some commentators have sought to argue, but one of precision: there is no conflict between surrealism and baroque methods of representation and it is perfectly possible to be both surrealist and baroque. In Ruiz's cinema, however, it is clear that the baroque overshadows, but doesn't entirely displace, any surrealist intent. In this respect, he resembles the Polish director Wojciech Has, although the latter, more focused and disciplined in his approach, is founded in Eastern European rather than Latin American traditions of the baroque.

Ruiz leads us as viewers into a visual labyrinth from which we will never be able to find the way out. His baroque sensibility is allied with images so heavily textured that they overwhelm the viewer. In his cinema, representation always seems to be an excess of representation. That is, any representation is intended to reach beyond itself, so that it ceases to function as pure representation but becomes the signifier of multiple representations within a single image. As a viewer, one often feels that one is looking at a map which indicates that the same direction will lead us to different places. For Ruiz images never stand alone: one image is always linked to others but the linkage between images is spatial rather than situational. Therefore, one image does not lead necessarily to another in a causative way, but through its transformation or replacement. Stories are impressed upon stories and movement is lateral or oblique, not developmental: we should not expect images to follow one another in a logical manner if we are to appreciate the qualities of Ruiz's films. Ruiz disturbs the process of image recognition and signification: any image is intended to stand not for a set meaning but to invoke a multiplicity of relations. It is in this way of playing with images that he is closest to surrealism: in his films, to paraphrase Breton, 'images make love'. At the same time, however, he is distanced from surrealism by the intention behind this process, as we shall see in a moment.

The convergence between Ruiz and surrealism is nevertheless here largely in accordance with a surrealist phenomenology of the cinema experience, in which one is encouraged to experience the film obliquely, against its set meaning, in a way that disorients rather than comforts the senses. Within this framework, a further convergence with surrealism is revealed: a concern with communication.

A central aspect of Ruiz's work is exile. As much may be obvious to the extent that Ruiz is a man exiled from his own land and forced to confront the displacement involved in making films in foreign environments. However, his treatment of exile points to something more elemental – a fundamental sense of human exile from the sources of our being and from one another. For Ruiz, one imagines, everyone is in exile. At least, the impression given by almost all of his films is that direct communication in the here and now is impossible. His characters communicate only across time and space, never within it. If they connect at all, it is only obliquely, through a mutual recognition of signs that both have experienced once, although probably not within their current lives. One could say that in his films the present moment does not exist; his characters may be situated in a particular time and space but they are irrevocably apart from it. Their reality is elsewhere: simultaneously in the past and the future rather than the 'present'.

This enables Ruiz to traverse time and space as he incorporates different cultural traditions within his purview. The frame of his references is dazzling, taking in allusions from European culture (notably France, Spain and Portugal) but also revealing a more than passing acquaintance with other cultural traditions (Chinese, Arabic, Persian and North African in particular).

This might appear a similar sort of 'New Age' eclecticism to that which we encounter in the work of Jodorowsky. Nothing could be more inaccurate. Unlike Jodorowsky, Ruiz is always attentive to cultural difference. If he engages with different cultural traditions, it is always against the backdrop of his own Chilean formation, which provides the point from which his interest in these different traditions radiates. In fact, despite the similarities of background, no directors could be more different than Ruiz and Jodorowsky. Where Jodorowsky appears to have little recognition of otherness, in Ruiz it is everywhere. In fact his is a cinema of otherness: everything is other, and there is no stability of identity. The sort of 'enlightenment' or 'liberation' Jodorowsky seeks would no doubt be regarded by Ruiz as a huge joke, since for him when two people talk to one another they may not actually belong to the same time or place and any communication they manage to establish is oblique and opaque. Founded in recognition that time and space are not realms within which we exist but obstacles placed between us and others, any form of liberation must be a false solution. Furthermore, where Jodorowsky is possibly the most egocentric living film maker, Ruiz appears to have passed beyond the consciousness of ego.

From a surrealist perspective, we might in some ways see Jodorowsky and Ruiz as representing two halves of a whole, especially if they are seen in the light of Breton's assertion that 'the idea of surrealism tends simply towards the total recovery of our psychic strength by a means which is nothing other than the vertiginous descent into ourselves, the systematic illumination of hidden places and the progressive darkening of other places, perpetual promenading in the heart of forbidden zones' (1988: 791). In Jodorowsky, the first is at play, although the illumination of hidden places is somewhat superficial; in Ruiz, it is the darkening that is emphasised. In neither, however, is there really a suggestion of reconciliation between the two, and this ultimately is what distinguishes both directors from surrealism in a general sense.

Ruiz's films are layered like onions, and the difficulty is that as we unfold them, like onions, they may not uncover any mystery but simply reveal what is within. Ruiz even seems at times to be asking, isn't this enough?

As he takes us into his labyrinth, Ruiz at first follows the path that surrealism set, but he soon veers off. One has the feeling that he does not want to follow any kind of path but rather to tangle up the paths so that we get lost. Since this world contains all worlds, including heaven and hell (one of his less successful films, *A TV Dante*, envisions Hell in Santiago de Chile, without making any political point about Pinochet's regime), and since all reality is collapsed into one, clarity is the enemy. The dream and the everyday are either interchangeable or the everyday is infected by dream. Where Švankmajer worries about the destructiveness of communication, Ruiz appears not to recognise the possibility of direct communication at all. His characters are contained within themselves, and talk past one another. This may appear to be the ultimate disassociation, except that they do make some kind of contact, but only when they somehow recognise that the world does not obey a logical order.

As he takes us into the labyrinth, Ruiz, then, does not suggest any enlightenment. Dialectic there is, but without any resolution, or even any possibility of resolution. Everything has the status of an object; there are no subjects. Like Švankmajer or Borowczyk, Ruiz problematises our relationship with the material world, but where the former are both in different ways interested in the way we ignore objects at our peril, inviting their revenge, for the latter the animate world appears to be as passive as the inanimate one: human beings appear entirely at the mercy of their environment.

At their best, Ruiz's films offer genuine journeys of discovery. He is like Heraclitus' child at play, imbued with an ability to bestow significance upon the most banal things. Yet, while his technical virtuosity may be revelatory, it may also degenerate into a striving for effect that simply hides the lack of narrative coherence. And while he may still be a man of the left who recognises the necessity for social and cultural change, one has the impression that he would not see this in surrealist terms.

The injunction to see the ideas of 'changing life' and 'transforming the world' as one and the same would, it may be imagined, perhaps mean little to Ruiz precisely because he sees the world as already being in a process of constant transformation. There is in his films no 'reality' against which to measure any claim to 'realism', and one might be inclined to describe him as a 'postmodernist'. In fact, nothing could be less accurate. Ruiz does not reduce everything to the level of appearance. Rather, through his baroque sensibility, he amplifies everything to the level of reality. In Ruiz, nothing is appearance, nothing is a copy of a copy: everything is original. In every respect, he is really 'pre-modern'; his way of working does not eschew realism, but pre-dates it.

It is in this sense that we can, I think, see Ruiz as a kind of 'heretical' surrealist. Heretical not in the sense that he goes against its tenets or that he disavows them, but because he uses surrealist devices for purposes that are not against surrealism but outside of it, or rather that cross over it in the very act of veering away from it. His work is of value in a surrealist context as much for what separates him from it as for his affinity with it.

CHAPTER 11

Surrealism and Contemporary Cinema

In the course of this book we have sought to trace the extent to which surrealism retains a living core in its relation with cinema. The influence exerted by surrealism on film has been immense but elusive, and as time goes by it becomes ever more diffuse and nebulous, to the extent that one might wonder whether it retains sufficient specificity to make it possible to discuss it in a critically precise way. Having gained currency as an idea in the public domain frequently used to describe things that are non-surrealist or even distinctly anti-surrealist, surrealism might be considered to have become so diffuse that almost anything can be said about it.

In this book, by focusing on those film makers who have maintained a close link with surrealism, we have sought to instil some precision about the nature of surrealism and to show that it retains significance in relation to current debates in film.

As noted in the Introduction above, in his book *Le Surréalisme au cinéma*, first published in 1953, Ado Kyrou sought to show how the experience of cinema was 'essentially surrealist', and he demonstrated this by looking at the work of a vast number of films which, whether the film makers were conscious of it or not (most often they were not), could be said to have affinities with surrealism in one way or another. It would be difficult to write a comparable book today even were it desirable to do so, given the confusion that reigns over what might or might not be the influence of surrealism. To conclude, nevertheless, we will briefly look at some of those directors in whom the influence of surrealism seems clearly to coincide with an affinity with its ideas, as well as with those in whom such an affinity is apparent even if they may not appear to have been especially influenced by it.

The impact of surrealism on the generation of French directors who came to the cinema immediately after the Second World War, for instance, was immense, as we have seen in the chapter on documentary. It might in fact be argued that a chapter of the book should have been devoted to the work of Alain Resnais and Chris Marker, since their sensibilities are so close to surrealism that they might be as much 'surrealists' as Kaplan, Jodorowsky, Arrabal or Ruiz. According to Ado Kyrou, Resnais 'never makes anything without asking himself if it would please André Breton' (1985: 206), while Robert Benayoun suggests that the only reason

Resnais did not join the Surrealist Group was due to his own timidity, recounting that on the only occasion he ever saw Breton, Resnais was too shy to speak to him. Benayoun quotes Resnais in 1968 saying, 'I always hope to remain true to André Breton, who refused to consider imaginary life apart from reality' (Benayoun, 1980: 36). As close as he is to surrealism, however, it has always seemed to me that he runs along a slightly different path, albeit one that runs parallel to the one which the surrealists chart.

It is in his treatment of memory that Resnais is closest to surrealism, and in this respect his earliest features, especially *Hiroshima Mon Amour* (1959) and *Last Year at Marienbad* (1961), seem to have been made under a surrealist mandate. The exploration of the themes of memory and time is also what links Chris Marker most closely with surrealism, with which he shares the presumption that time is not given as a thing through which we pass but is rather a kind of mysterious presence that takes a concrete form through the activity taking place within a location. He is also close to a surrealist perspective in the way that he sees reality to consist of different layers which have to be excavated rather than assumed. This is especially seen in *La Jetée* (1962), his film that is closest to a 'pure' surrealist perspective. In this film life is revealed to be – as it was for the surrealists – simply one coil within a labyrinth of possible realities.

The influence of surrealism on French cinema had largely dissipated by the end of the fifties, however. From the early sixties, the ideology of the *nouvelle vague* cast a long shadow over French cinema from which it has still not fully emerged, and this largely appears to have eclipsed any interest that younger film makers may have had in surrealism.

Although the *nouvelle vague* critics never appear to have openly attacked surrealism, it was nevertheless deeply implicated in the focus of their critique. Neither the ideology of a *politique des auteurs*, nor the processes of film making advocated by the *nouvelle vague* would find favour with the surrealists (its inflection of a conservative – if not overtly right-wing – political orientation together with a temptation towards Catholicism naturally didn't help). Emphasising the role of the director as creator and the importance of realistic *mise en scène* (a cinema of representation and not of expression, as Godard put it), the *nouvelle vague* instituted a form of film making that virtually eliminated the qualities the surrealists were looking for in film. Robert Benayoun described this as a 'cinema of furnishing' and summed up the ideology of *nouvelle vague* as 'being secretly proud of having nothing to say, but of saying it well' (1962: 7). Two of the most acerbic critics of the *nouvelle vague* were in fact both surrealists who wrote for the journal *Positif*, Robert Benayoun and Raymond Borde (see in particular Benayoun, 1962; Borde, 1994). Jacques Brunius (1964), writing in *Sight and Sound*, was equally scathing. Responding to the *nouvelle vague*'s question 'who is the author?' he was trenchantly surrealist: 'I couldn't care less'.

Benayoun's critique remains of significance not so much in its specific terms as in its broader implications. He argued that the *nouvelle vague*'s attack on the supposed '*cinéma de qualité*' was not serious but was simply a pose designed to get its proponents noticed. Its morality – although founded in a Christian sense of 'spirituality' – was in fact amoral, a matter of 'saying whatever comes into your head'. Its directors were, in a sense, film critics who wanted to make films rather than film *makers*. That is, they lived through films and their starting point for making them was not lived experience but other films. What they instituted was a sensibility that exalted film above life. Ideas were elevated above content, but not in order to explore these ideas; they were simply hooks to hang the film on, but the idea could be anything at all just so long as it was an idea. In his critique, Benayoun was also anticipating Baudrillard in seeing the *nouvelle vague* as complicit with what the situationists called the society of the spectacle and reducing all reality to representation.

Furthermore, promoting cinema as a 'seventh art', a notion the surrealists have always ridiculed, the *nouvelle vague* had a lot in common as Brunius especially emphasised with the avant garde of the twenties, with whom the surrealists so vehemently clashed, and their difficulties with the *nouvelle vague* were comparable. The *nouvelle vague*, however, was far more significant than the avant garde and its influence has been more insidious.

I had the opportunity to discuss the *nouvelle vague* with Robert Benayoun when I met him in 1989. He insisted that his objections were still relevant then. Not only did the *nouvelle vague* institute a type of film making based upon an artificial sense of life rather than upon genuine experience so that its point of reference became other films, but more seriously the way it opened up film making encouraged complacency. It made it easier to make films, but in doing so an apprenticeship in film making was replaced with what we would call, in current parlance, 'networking'. This delivered cinema into the hands of the bourgeoisie. Whereas before it had been possible for people from the working class to enter the film industry and work their way up, film making after the sixties in France became the almost exclusive preserve of people who had the contacts, usually through family connections, and the entrepreneurial skills to convince producers they were capable of making films.

The hostility of the surrealists to the ideology of the *nouvelle vague* did not prevent them from recognising the value of some of the films made under its rubric. In fact, Gérard Legrand has strangely been one of Eric Rohmer's critical champions, even if the qualities he sees in his films seem a long way from surrealist ones. More particularly, the themes and approach of some of Jacques Rivette's films (especially *Céline and Julie Go Boating* [1974]) often seem close to a surrealist perspective.

Benayoun's critique in particular nevertheless reveals a certain prescience, if one bears in mind the emblematic position Godard has assumed in contemporary cinema, especially (via Tarantino) through his reductive influence on American directors. Whether *nouvelle vague* ideology is to blame for this or not, one does detect among many young film makers a mentality that is founded in film itself detached from the life process, which contributes – as much within commercial film as within 'art cinema' – to making film an increasingly sterile form of communication.

Irrespective of the influence of the *nouvelle vague*, surrealism seemed to have burned itself out as an influence on young French film makers by the sixties. Even in those directors most opposed to the *nouvelle vague* like Bertrand Tavernier and Alain Cavalier any cinematic affinity with surrealism seems slight (although we can see surrealist ideas penetrating into their work, notably in Tavernier's *Coup de Torchon* [1981]), while Cavalier's *Thérèse* (1986), his film of the life of Thérèse de Lisieux, is certainly indebted to the coruscating study that Pierre Mabille made of the saint.).

More recently, the films of Caro and Jeunet – *Delicatessen* (1991) and *The City of Lost Children* (1995) – have obvious stylistic links with surrealism, but they belong to the tradition of the grotesque and the fantastic rather than the marvellous (that is, they create an imagined world rather than look to transform this world) and are marked with a kind of sentimentality that doesn't seem at one with surrealism. A recent trend in French cinema (Catherine Breillat, Gasper Noë, for example) seems to have latched onto a certain 'black surrealism' – via Bataille and Lautréamont – to explore transgressive themes. This seems, however, to be little more than empty fashion – an example of the continuous transgression that Bataille himself expressly criticised.

In Italy, Antonioni, Fellini, Bertolucci and the Taviani brothers all have manifestly 'surrealist' sides, as in Germany, inflected through a common foundation in German romanticism, do Werner Herzog and Wim Wenders. Antonioni's *The Passenger* (1974) and Wenders's *Alice in the Cities* (1974) (a film that seems to appear more than any other on lists of favourite films drawn up by surrealists) seem especially close to surrealism in theme and sensibility.

In some countries surrealism has entered the cultural current so visibly that it has simply merged with the mainstream. In Belgium, for instance, the visual mark of René Magritte and Paul Delvaux has left such a striking impression that film directors cannot fail to be aware of it. Certainly, the influence of surrealism is stamped on the films of André Delvaux, especially in his early work like *The Man Who Had His Hair Cut Short* (1966) and *Un soir, un train* (1968). Some of his other films, *Rendezvous at Bray* (1971) and *Belle* (1973), for instance, treat themes that parallel the concerns of surrealist writers like Julien Gracq and André Pieyre de Mandiargues, although Delvaux's interest seems more to use the ambiguities of reality to construct visual tapestries than to seek out that point of the mind at which contradictions are resolved.

Less cerebral and with a more fevered imagination, Harry Kümel has struggled to bring his projects to fruition, but his most successful commercial film, *Daughters of Darkness* (1971), scripted by surrealist writer Jean Ferry, is a haunting and sensuous vampire story fully within the trajectory of surrealism.

In Spain, Buñuel's prestige has made it difficult for directors to escape his influence, sometimes perhaps to their detriment. At its best, surrealism enters the work of Carlos Saura or Victor Erice to enrich and deepen an already fertile exploration of the nature of reality and even in the work of Almodovar, a director whose sensibility generally seems removed from surrealism, one senses that his taste for provocation and the bizarre has been enhanced by its influence, especially in *Law of Desire* (1987), where a kind of surrealism *à rebours* seems to be at work. In lesser directors, however, the pervasive influence of surrealism may have proved more of a curse than a blessing.

We have considered the case of Poland in the chapter on Borowczyk but we should perhaps also here give a mention to Krzysztof Kieslowski for the way in which he treats themes of love and destiny, especially in *La Double vie de Véronique* (1991). More should also be said about Wojciech Has, whose work seems intimately linked with surrealism in thematic and ethical terms. On the basis of two of his early films, *Farewells* (1959) and *How to be Loved* (1963), Ado Kyrou declared in 1963 that he was 'the most surrealist director working today' (1985: 151). Soon after this, Has made the film for which he is best known: *The Saragossa Manuscript* (1964), very different in approach to his first two films, but certainly one that justified Kyrou's assessment. This was followed with three equally baroque extravaganzas, *Codes* (1966), *The Doll* (1968) and *The Sandglass* (1973), an adaptation of Bruno Schulz. His next film, *An Uneventful Story* (1982), was a return to the restraint of his early films, a marvellously crafted tale drawn from a story by Chekhov. His last film, *The Tribulations of Balthazar Kober* (1988), drawn from a novel by a Fredérick Tristan, a one-time surrealist fellow traveller, is as extravagant in conception and realisation as *The Saragossa Manuscript* or *The Sandglass*. It is frustrating that this not inconsiderable *oeuvre* is so overlooked in the West, making it difficult to judge the overall significance of Has's work. Even his most well-known film, *The Saragossa Manuscript,* tends only to be available in mutilated form, despite having been restored to its almost complete state due to the efforts of Grateful Dead guitarist Jerry Garcia. Has's work runs along parallel lines to surrealism but he belongs to traditions of Eastern European baroque rather than to surrealism strictly speaking, as we discussed in the chapter on Ruiz.

Looking outside the West, surrealism has been a pervasive influence in Japan from the twenties (for instance, Mizoguchi's films parallel the work of Borzage and Sternberg in their affinities with the surrealist understanding of love, especially in one of his more neglected films, *The Empress Yang Kwei-fei* [1955], as pure a tale of *amour fou* as the Hollywood films we earlier considered). The director who appears to have engaged, with surrealist ideas most explicitly here has been Hiroshi Teshingahara, especially in *The Woman of the Dunes* (1964) and *The Face of Another* (1966) the films he worked on with the novelist Kobo Abe, who himself drew upon surrealism to probe questions of identity. More recently, the animated features of Hayao Miyazaki bear a distinct kinship with surrealism in both theme and intent. The Japanese film most linked with a surrealist perspective, however, is probably Nagisa Oshima's notorious *Ai No Corrida* (1977) for the way its exploration of themes of love and death corresponds to the theories of Georges Bataille. This is only one aspect of the surrealist interest of the film, however, which was subject to a fascinating review by Robert Benayoun. He argued that it presents a challenge to Western ideas about the nature of reality and especially the divide between life and death. To understand the film fully, he argues, we need to see it in terms of an interplay between different realities that are beyond the divide between life and death, so that we may regard the film as illustrating the dialectical views of both Heraclitus ('Mortals are immortals and immortals are mortals, the one living the others' death and dying the others' life'), and Hegel ('The dialectic of reality is a bacchanal in which not a single participant is drunk') (Benayoun, 2002). Linking in with the Japanese tradition of the demon woman who comes from beyond death to bring the 'reality' of phenomenal existence into question, which also ties in with a surrealist interest in tales of succubi, *Ai No Corrida* is one of the few films which seek to engage in a dialogue of ideas between different cultural values and as such it raises the question the extent to which it is legitimate to see surrealist concerns in universal terms.

Such questions of correspondence across cultural traditions and whether we may see surrealism as a universal sensibility that transcends or elides cultural differences may be raised in relation to several African and Asian directors, as well as more generally in India or Hong Kong, where a genuinely popular cinema has been kept alive. In Africa, the work of the Malian director Souleymane Cissé immediately comes to mind, especially for *Yeelen* (1984), in which correspondences between surrealism and Bambara initiation rituals are clearly apparent.

Another film maker worth mentioning, as he seems in many ways to as close in spirit and intention of any director working today to a surrealist attitude, is the Iranian Mohsen Makhmalbaf.[1] It seems strange to see a surrealist sensibility at work in someone who began as an Islamic terrorist and has been condemned by Iranian exiles, at least in his earliest films, for being a stooge of the Islamist government. There is no sign whatever of such flunkeyism in the films that have reached the West, however. Even in the earliest film I have seen, *The Peddler* (1987), the idiosyncratic quality of everyday life and the undermining of rationalist common sense are delightfully at work. When we come to films such as *The Cyclist* (1989), which is probably the closest we have ever come to seeing a pataphysical film, *Once Upon a Time, Cinema* (1992) and *Gabbeh* (1996), we are in a realm which seems completely in accord with a surrealist perspective on the world.

Even if we can discern these affinities in such directors as Cissé and Makhmalbaf, however, we have to be wary about considering their work within the rubric of surrealism, since there is no indication that surrealism is even a partial source of their inspiration. It is apparent that both directors are principally situated within their own cultural traditions and have to be considered first within that context. That surrealist affinities are disclosed within such films, however, does lend support to the surrealist claim to having a universal application, at least to the extent that surrealism may be defined as striving to establish the site of convergence of different realities, which Breton defined as the 'supreme point', in addition to its double will to 'change life' and 'transform the world'.

Surrealism is not one thing, and there are as many manifestations of it as there are surrealists. Its protean nature, however, should not cause us to think that it can be anything, in the process causing us to lose sight of its specificity. The aim of this study has been to show the different ways in which film makers have responded to the demands that surrealism makes, but we should also remember that surrealism itself will always escape us. It will forever be *elsewhere*, that point on the horizon which, as Aragon pointed out, remains beyond our grasp. In the cinema it will be found wherever one has a sense of transparency in the dark.

Notes

INTRODUCTION
SURREALIST FILM THEORY AND PRACTICE

1. Roger Cardinal has collected a remarkable wealth of aphorisms by Novalis which anticipate in an uncanny way the surrealist response to cinema.

2. I recall talking some years ago with Pierre Naville when this founder member of the Surrealist Group told me he had been listening to a parliamentary debate during a week in which a politician had denounced another's proposition in these terms: 'Monsieur, ça c'est surréel!' This distorted use of the word, and the generalised devaluation of language that such a use of the word implied, imbued Naville with evident anger, even sixty years after he had left the Surrealist Group.

3. The most cited director was actually Cocteau! How long will it be, one wonders, before people finally realise what has been obvious to virtually every surrealist (as well as to Cocteau himself): that Cocteau's world view was at a total antipode from surrealism? See Thiber (1979) for a very clear account of the vast gulf that exists between surrealism and Cocteau. Another film included was Godard's *Weekend*, a film surely guaranteed to draw the ire of any surrealist. The most cited contemporary directors were David Cronenberg and Atom Egoyan. Fine film makers though they are, I am at a loss to see anything particular in their work that establishes any affinities with surrealism; could the compiler be Canadian, one wonders…

4. These debates surrounded two new film journals, *Cahiers de cinéma* and *Positif*, founded in an opposition which is still alive today. The surrealists have always been allied with *Positif*, with which several of them have collaborated over the years.

5. Bazin was one of the founders of *Cahiers de cinema*. His view of cinema was that it should both be realist and convey a sense of humanity's spiritual dimension (Bazin was a Catholic).

6. To describe them as definitive does not imply that they are above criticism, or that they unproblematically reflect a surrealist position in relation to cinema or art at the time they were written; it is as 'evidence' (the notion of surrealist evidence is something we will have occasion to consider later) that they are definitive, but evidence can always be challenged with other evidence.

7. These films (especially those of Zimbacca and Mariën) are nevertheless of
    great interest and would make a fascinating DVD if an enterprising producer
    ever has the astuteness to put them together.
8. Since writing this, I learned from Paul Hammond that *Paris n'existe pas* was
    screened in Madrid in May 2005, but this, so far as I know, has been the first
    sighting of it in many a year.

CHAPTER 2
LUIS BUÑUEL AND THE SNARES OF DESIRE

1. Despite this moral commitment, however, Buñuel made no secret of the fact
    that he remained friends with people the surrealists generally regarded as
    being beyond the pale, such as the Mexican painter and Stalinist thug David
    Alfaro Siquieros, not to mention Louis Aragon and Jean Cocteau. It would
    apparently irritate Breton that when Buñuel was in Paris he would visit the
    latter two after having seen him. Octavio Paz tells us that he saw *Los Olvidados*
    in 1951 'at a private showing with André Breton and other friends. A strange
    detail: the night of the showing, at the other end of the little projection room,
    Aragon, Sadoul and others were present. When I saw them I thought for a
    moment a pitched battle would ensue I think it was the first time Aragon
    and Breton had seen each other since their rift, twenty years earlier' (1986:
    163). This detail may seem to offer some support for Hammond's argument
    about Buñuel's political opportunism. Or does it simply show that he valued
    personal friendship and refrained from making moral judgements about
    others? Buñuel appears to have been infinitely fascinated by people of very
    different moral perspectives – his close friendships with priests being a good
    example. Buñuel's moral condemnation was generally reserved for society,
    not for individuals.
2. Love in surrealism is never simply an intensity of passion or attraction. More
    recent films that deal with overwhelming passion, such as Beineix's *Betty Blue*
    (1986), are not at all representations of mad love as the surrealists understood
    it. The concept of 'mad love' in surrealism does not signify an abandonment
    to passion, but a sense of encounter that brings into question the individual
    ego, allowing the individual to recognise and be transformed by what is other
    than itself. Transgressive and destructive it may be, but it is fundamentally
    transformative. As we will see in chapter 4, the finest expressions of mad
    love in cinema are to be found in some of the Hollywood films of the Golden
    Age. Another significant example is Clouzot's *Manon* (1949), scripted by a
    surrealist, Jean Ferry. In this film, drawn very loosely from the novel by Abbé
    Prévost, love overwhelms the protagonists in much the same way as in *L'Âge
    d'or*: Manon is without redeeming qualities except when she surrenders to
    this love, while Robert seems devoid of character except when he is roused

by it. Love acts on them to enable them to live beyond what they could otherwise experience, making them realise that the life offered to them is not the
life they want. In this often harrowing film the lovers pass through heaven
and hell before gaining a glimpse of paradise at the moment of their death.

CHAPTER 3
JACQUES PRÉVERT AND THE POETRY OF THE EVENTUAL

1. Even Breton had become involved seriously with film in 1930, working on
   scripts with Albert Valentin, a member of the Surrealist Group and aspiring film
   maker. Valentin didn't last long in the Surrealist Group (he was expelled at the
   instigation of Éluard and Crevel for working on a 'reactionary' film, René Clair's
   A nous la liberté [1931], but he did go on to become a productive film maker,
   if not a very illustrious one. He made fourteen films between 1934 and 1949,
   none of which seem to have made any impression on film history. Georges
   Bataille was another who unsuccessfully tried to hack it as a screenwriter during the forties.
2. In English we do have a study by Claire Blakeway (1990) dealing with Prévert's
   work both in film and in the theatre, which is informative but not especially
   insightful.
3. The ending of his relationship with Prévert did not end Carné's association
   with surrealists. For his next film, Carné turned to another former member
   of the Surrealist Group as his scriptwriter: Jacques Viot, adapted of a play
   by surrealist fellow traveller Georges Neveu, *Juliette ou la clef des temps*, a
   beautifully oneiric film which may lack the wit and subtlety of the films he
   made with Prévert, but which nevertheless has a continuity with them and is
   fully within a surrealist frame. Viot was a prolific scriptwriter, noted especially
   for *Macadam* (Jacques Feyder, 1946) and two films for Marcel Camus, *Black
   Orpheus* (1957) and *L'Oiseau de paradis* (1962), both of which look back to
   Viot's surrealist past when he was an anti-colonial critic.

CHAPTER 5
SURREALISM AND THE DOCUMENTARY

1. I have unfortunately been unable to view a sufficient number of Les Blank's
   films to include analysis of them here. He is principally concerned with
   charting the by-ways of American folk culture, especially its music (films
   about Clifton Chenier and Lightnin' Hopkins among many others) and food,
   for instance *Garlic is as Good as Ten Mothers* (1980), although he is probably
   best known for *Burden of Dreams* (1979), about the making of Werner
   Herzog's *Fitzcarraldo* and *Werner Herzog Eats his Shoe* (1980), which shows

what the title states. Herzog had vowed to eat his shoe when the film maker
Errol Morris told him that he was going to make his first film about pet
cemeteries. When the film, *Gates of Heaven*, was made, Blank's film reveals
that Herzog was as good as his word.

2. The film never rises above the anecdotal to elicit serious questions about
    the morality of ethnographic film making as Stoney did in *Man of Aran*. In a
    detail that shows an appalling lack of sensitivity that characterises the whole
    film, the film maker presents the bemused mayor of one village (who has
    already expressed his hostility to *Las Hurdes*) with a gift: a bust of Buñuel!
3. A mention should be made of the fact that Painlevé did not work alone.
    In virtually all of his films, he collaborated with his lifelong companion,
    Geneviève Hamon (when she died, Painlevé gave up film making).

CHAPTER 6
NELLY KAPLAN AND SEXUAL REVENGE

1. The interest feminists have shown in her work has also proved to be somewhat
    double-edged since most feminist critics are more concerned to appropriate
    the work to their own agendas rather than understand it in its own terms.
    Kaplan has responded in a purely surrealist way to the feminist interest in her
    work:'The feminists must be Kaplanian. I am not a feminist'. Interview with
    Nelly Kaplan by Anice Clément, France Culture radio, 4 April 2001.
2. This story can be found translated in a volume of surrealist stories I edited
    (Richardson, 1993).

CHAPTER 7
WALERIAN BOROWCZYK AND THE TOUCH OF DESIRE

1. Jan Lenica's work, too, has been too often neglected, though not for the same
    reasons. His *oeuvre* consists of some fourteen films, all but two of which are
    no more than ten or fifteen minutes long. His two features, *Adam 2* (1968)
    and *Ubu et la Grande Gidouille* (1979), are remarkably inventive animated
    films, the latter based on Jarry's Ubu plays.

CHAPTER 8
JAN ŠVANKMAJER AND THE LIFE OF OBJECTS

1. The other great tactile directors in contemporary cinema are the Brothers
    Quay, whose films bear a superficial resemblance to Švankmajer's. As

marvellous as they are (and of undoubted interest to surrealists), the films of the Brothers Quay are too singular, too resolutely personal, to be considered within the context of surrealism. This is ultimately where they differ from Švankmajer, whose films emerge from a collective engagement tied to a will of transformation which is the fundamental characteristic of surrealism. The Brothers Quay, on the other hand, create a hermetic world obeying its own logic and resistant to any external intrusion. Their sensibility appears to have been formed largely through an engagement with Central European culture, and any linkage which may be discerned between their work and surrealism is purely formal.

CHAPTER 9
PANIQUE: A CEREMONY BEYOND THE ABSURD

1. Most of the quotations from Jodorowsky in this chapter come from various lectures and interviews which can be found on the DVDs of his films.
2. Another anecdote he tells is of staying at Breton's home and one day opening a door to find Breton sitting on the toilet, at which Breton let out an anguished cry, which equally tends to suggest that Jodorowsky's relation with Breton was a kind of disappointed hero worship.
2. The DVD of *Fando and Lis* contains a fascinating commentary by Jodorowsky himself which reveals a lot about what he was thinking at the time. In particular it confirms the impression one has from watching not only this film but also his others that he simply does not think in terms of character motivation: his leading characters are merely extensions of himself, and the incidents and characters they encounter are phantoms conjured up by his imagination.

CHAPTER 10
THE BAROQUE HERESY OF RAÚL RUIZ

1. Although, like Kaplan, Ruiz has assumed French nationality and even sometimes uses the French form of his name (Raoul Ruiz) in the credits of his films, he nevertheless still shows an interest in his native culture that seems absent in the work of the other two directors.
2. Laleen Jayamanne tied herself in knots in an essay on Ruiz in trying to explicate the distance between him and surrealism. She was keen to separate Ruiz from an easy conceptualisation for, as she rightly says that, 'When surrealism is used as an exhaustive term it does not enable readings, except perhaps at a literal level' (1995: 161). The immediate context here was a festival at which Ruiz was unproblematically presented as a 'surrealist film maker'. Given her perception, however, it is extraordinary that Jayamanne takes

as her authorities on surrealism not a surrealist but Susan Sontag (whose misunderstanding of surrealism is notorious) and a film critic, Adrian Martin, based on this preposterous assertion: 'The medium of cinema was for the surrealists a privileged gateway to the realm of fantasy, the unconscious, dreams and desire' (1995: 165). Ruiz may not be a surrealist, but if he isn't it is for more complex reasons than these.

CHAPTER 11
SURREALISM AND CONTEMPORARY CINEMA

1. And this not only in Mohsen Makhmalbaf himself, but also in the work of his wife and his daughters. I would especially mention his wife Marziyeh Meshkini's delightful *The Day I Became a Woman* (2000), a film of female intractability and dark humour that seems fully to accord with a surrealist worldview.

Selected Filmography

It is not possible to establish a definitive filmography for some of these film makers (Painlevé, Ruiz and Rouch in particular). This list should therefore be regarded as provisional. For a filmography of other films made by surrealists see Paul Hammond *The Shadow and its Shadow* (2000).

FERNANDO ARRABAL:

Viva la muerte (1970); *I'll Walk like a Crazy Horse* (1973); *L'Arbre de Guernica* (1975); *L'Odyssée de la Pacific* (*The Emperor of Peru*) (1980); *Le Cimetière des voitures* (1981); *Adieu Babylone !* (1992); *Jorge Luis Borges - Une vita de poesia* (1998).

LES BLANK:

The Blues According to Lightnin' Hopkins (1968); *The Sun's Gonna Shine* (1968); *God Respects Us When We Work, But Loves Us When We Dance* (1968); *A Well-Spent Life* (1971); *Spend It All* (1971); *Chicken Real* (1971); *Dry Wood* (1973); *Hot Pepper* (1973); *Chulas Fronteras* (1976); *Always for Pleasure* (1978); *Burden of Dreams* (1979); *Del Mero Corazon* (1979); *Garlic is as Good as Ten Mothers* (1980); *Werner Herzog Eats His Shoe* (1980); *Sprout Wings and Fly* (1983); *In Heaven There Is No Beer?* (1984); *Sworn to the Drum: A Tribute to Francisco Aguabella* (1985); *Ziveli! Medicine for the Heart* (1987); *Gap-Toothed Women* (1987); *J'ai été au bal / I Went to the Dance* (1989); *Yum, Yum, Yum!* (1990); *Innocents Abroad* (1991); *The Maestro: King of the Cowboy Artists* (1994).

WALERIAN BOROWCZYK:

Feature films:

Le Théâtre de M. et Mme Kabal (1967); *Goto, Île D'amour* (1968); *Blanche* (1971); *Immoral Tales* (1974); *Story of Sin* (1974); *The Beast* (1975); *La Marge*

(1976); *Behind Convent Walls* (1977); *Heroines du mal* (1978); *LuLu* (1980); *The Art of Love* (1983); *Dr Jekyll and Miss Osborne* (1984); *Emmanuelle 5* (1986); *Love Rites* (1987); *The Almanac* (1990); *Halima the Expert* (1991); *Golden Lotus* (1993).

Shorts:

Glowa (1953); *Living Photographs* (1954); *The Workshop of Fernand Léger* (1954); *Autumn* (1954); *The Modest Photographer* (1955); *Striptease* (with Jan Lenica, 1957); *Standard of Youth* (1957); *Once Upon a Time* (with Jan Lenica, 1957); *Sentiment Rewarded; Education Days* (1957); *Dom* (with Jan Lenica, 1958); *School* (1958); *Terra Incognita* (1959); *The Magician* (1959); *Les Astronauts* (with Chris Marker, 1959); *Head* (1939); *Solitude* (with Jan Lenica, 1959); *The Music Box* (with Jan Lenica, 1959); *Le Concert de M. et Mme. Kabal* (1962); *Grandma's Encyclopedia (1963); Holy Smoke* (1963); *Renaissance* (1963); *Stroboscopes* (1963); *19ᵗʰ-Century Stores* (1963); *Writing* (1963); *Libraries* (1963); *Schools* (1963); *A Well-Behaved Girl* (1963); *Tom Thumb* (1963); *The Museum* (1964); *Jeux des anges* (1964); *Joachim's Dictionary* (1965); *Rosalie* (1966); *Gavotte* (1969); *Diptych* (1969); *The Phonograph* (1971); *A Special Collection* (1973); *Brief von Paris* (1975); *Venus's Snail* (1975); *Scherzo Infernal* (1988).

LUIS BUÑUEL:

Un Chien andalou (1928); *L'Âge d'or* (1930); *Las Hurdes* (1932); *Don Quintin el amargeo* (1935 – credited as producer); *España leal en armas* (1937); *Gran Casino* (1947); *El Gran Calavera* (1949); *Los Olvidados* (1950); *Susana* (1951); *La Hija de Engaño* (1951); *Una Mujer sin amor* (1951); *Subida al cielo* (1951); *El Bruto* (1952); *El* (1952); *La Ilusion Viaja en Tranvia* (1953); *Cumbres Borrascosas (Wuthering Heights)* (1953); *Robinson Crusoe* (1954); *El Rio y la muerte* (1954); *The Criminal Life of Archibaldo de la Cruz* (1955); *Cela s'appelle l'Aurore* (1955); *La Mort en ce Jardin* (1955); *Nazarin* (1958); *La Fièvre Monte à El Paso* (1959); *The Young One* (1960); *Viridiana* (1961); *The Exterminating Angel* (1962); *Diary of a Chambermaid* (1964); *Simon of the Desert* (1965); *Belle de jour* (1966); *The Milky Way* (1969); *Tristana* (1970); *The Discreet Charm of the Bourgeoisie* (1972); *The Phantom of Liberty* (1974); *That Obscure Object of Desire* (1977).

HUMPHREY JENNINGS:

Spare Time (1939); *London Can Take It* (1940); *Listen To Britain* (1941); *Fires Were Started* (1943); *The True Story of Lili Marlene* (1944); *Silent Village* (1944); *Diary for Timothy* (1945); *The Cumberland Story* (1949); *A Family Portrait* (1950).

ALEJANDRO JODOROWSKY:

Fando and Lis (1967); *El Topo* (1971); *The Holy Mountain* (1973); *Tusk* (1979); *Santa Sangre* (1989); *The Rainbow Thief* (1990); *Journey to Tulún* (1994).

NELLY KAPLAN:

Feature films:

La Fiancée du pirate (1969); Papa, les petits bateaux (1971); Néa (1976); Charles et Lucie (1979); Abel Gance et son Napoléon (1983); Pattes de Velours (1985); Plaisir d'amour (1991).

Shorts:

Gustave Moreau (1961); *Rodolphe Bresdin* (1962); *Abel Gance, hier et demain* (1962); *Á la source, la femme aimée* (1964); *Dessins et merveilles* (1965); *La Nouvelle Orangerie* (1966); *Les Années 25* (1966); *Le Regard Picasso* (1967).

JEAN PAINLEVÉ:

Mathusalem (1926); *Hyas and Stenorhynchus* (1929); *The Normet Serum* (1930); *Dr Claoué's Corrective and Reconstructive Surgery* (1930); *The Sea Horse* (1934); *The Fourth Dimension* (1937); *Bluebeard* (1938); *The Vampire* (1939-45); *Freshwater Assassins* (1947); *A Notation for Movement* (1949); *Sea Urchins* (1954); *Dancers of the Sea* (1956); *How Jellyfish Are Born* (1960); *Shrimp Stories* (1964); *Love Life of the Octopus* (1965); *Acera or The Witches' Dance* (1972); *Liquid Crystals* (1976).

JACQUES PRÉVERT:

Ciboulette (Claude Autant-Lara, 1933); *L'Hôtel du libre échange* (Marc Allégret, 1934); *Si j'étais le patron* (Richard Pottier, 1934); *Un oiseau rare* (Richard Pottier, 1935); *Le Crime de Monsieur Lange* (Jean Renoir, 1935); *Jenny* (Marcel Carné, 1936); *Moutonnet* (René Sti, 1936) ; *Drôle de drame* (Marcel Carné, 1937); *Quai des brumes* (Marcel Carné, 1938); *Ernest le Rebelle* (Christian-Jaque, 1938); *Le Jour se lève* (Marcel Carné, 1939); *Remorques* (Jean Grémillon, 1941); *Le Soleil a toujours raison* (Pierre Billon, 1941); *Les Visiteurs du soir* (Marcel Carné, 1942); *Lumière d'été* (Jean Grémillon, 1943); *Les Enfants du Paradis* (Marcel Carné, 1945); *Sortilèges* (Christian-Jaque, 1945); *Aubervilliers* (Eli Lotar, 1945); *Les Portes de la nuit* (Marcel Carné, 1946); *L'Arche de Noé* (Henry Jacques, 1946); *Les Amants de Vérone* (André Cayatte, 1949); *Souvenirs Perdus* (Christian-Jaque, 1950); *Notre-Dame de Paris* (Jean Delannoy 1956); *La Seine a rencontré Paris* (Joris Ivens, 1957); *Le Roi et l'oiseau* (Paul Grimaut, 1980).

Films written by Jacques Prévert and directed by Pierre Prévert:
Souvenirs de Paris ou Paris-Express (1928); L'Affaire est dans le sac (1932); Adieu Léonard (1943); Voyage-Surprise (1946); Paris Mange Son Pain (1958); Paris La Belle (1958); Little Claus and Big Claus (1964); La Maison du Passeur (1965); À la belle étoile (1966).

JEAN ROUCH:

(This is an abbreviated filmography. A complete [or as complete as can be] list of Rouch's film can be found in Jean Rouch, *Ciné-Ethnography* (2003).

Features :

Moi, un noir (1958); *La pyramide humaine* (1959); *Chronique d'un été* (with Edgar Morin, 1960); *La chasse au lion à l'arc* (1964); *Jaguar* (1969); *Sigui 68: les danseurs de Tyogou*; *Yenendi de Ganghel* (1968); *Sigui 69 : la caverne de Bongo*; *Petit à petit* (1969); *Horendi* (1972); *Tanda Singui* (1973); *Corcorico! Monsieur Poulet* (1974); *Babatu, les trois conseils* (1975); *Sigui synthese : Les cérémonies soixantenaires de Sigui*; *Le renard pâle* (Germaine Dieterlen, 1981); *Dionysos* (1984); *Enigma* (1986); *Folie ordinaire d'une fille de Cham* (1987); *Madam L'Eau* (1992); *Moi fatigué debout, moi couché* (1997); *La vache merveilleuse* (2002).

Shorts :

Au pays des mages moires (1947); Initiation à la danse des possédés (1948); Les Magiciens de Wanzerbé (1948); Cimetière dans la falaise (1950); Les gens du mil (1951); Bataille sur le grand fleuve (1952); Les maîtres fous (1955); Sigui 66: année zero (1966); Sigui 67: l'enclume de Yougo ; Yenendi de Boukoki (1967); Sigui 70: les clameurs d'Amani; Yenendi de Yantala; Yenendi de Simiri (1970); Sigui 71: la dune d'Idyeli' Tourou et Bitti: Les tambours d'avant (1971); Sigui 72: les pagnes de Iamé; Bongo, les funérailles du vieil Anaï (all 1972); Sigui 73: l'auvent de la circoncision (1974); Faba Tondi (1976); Liberté égalité, fraternité, et puis apres... (1990).

RAUL RUIZ:

Feature films:

Tres tristes tigres (1968); *The Penal Colony* (1971); *No One Said Anything* (1971); *The Expropriation* (1972); *Socialist Realism Considered as one of the Fine Arts* (1973); *Palomita blanca* (1973): *Dialogue of Exiles* (1974); *The Scattered Body and the World Upside Down* (1975); *The Suspended Vocation* (1977); *Hypothesis of a Stolen Painting* (1978) ; *Great Events and Ordinary People* (1979); *A Short Manual of French History* (1979) ; *The Territory* (1981); *On Top of the Whale* (1982); *Bérénice* (1983); *Three Crowns of the Sailor* (1983); *City of Pirates* (1984); *Régime sans pain* (1984); *Treasure Island* (1985) ; *Manoel's Destinies* (1985); *Aventure au Madeira* (1986); *Richard III* (1986); *Mémoire des apparences* (1986); *Dans un miroir* (1986); *Point de fuite* (1987); *Le Professeur Taranne* (1987); *The Blind Owl* (1987); *Tous les nuages sont des horloges* (1988); *The Golden Boat* (1990); *L'Oeil qui ment* (1992); *Fado majeur et mineur* (1995); *Trois viees et une seule mort* (1996); *Généalogies d'un crime* (1997); *Shattered Image* (1998); *Le Temps retrouvé* (1999); *Combat d'amour en songe* (2000); *Comédie de l'innocence* (2000); *Les Âmes fortes* (2001); *Ce jour-là* (2003); *A Place among the Living* (2003); *Vertigo of the Blank Page* (2003); *Livre à vendre* (2004); *Días de Campo* (2004).

Shorts:

Militarismo y Tortura (1969); *Now We'll Call You Brother* (1971); *Poesia popular* (1972) ; *Los Minuteros* (1972); *New Chilean Song* (1973); *Popular Chilean Poetry: Theory and Practice* (1973); *Palomita Blanca* (1973); *Palomita brava* (1973); *Abastecimiento* (1973); Sotelo (1976); *Colloque de chiens* (1977); *Les*

Divisions de la nature (1978); *Snakes and Ladders* (1980); *La Ville nouvelle* (1980); *Le Borgne* (1980); *Images de sable* (1981); *Querelle des jardins* (1982); *Le Petit théâtre* (1982); *Ombres chinoises* (1982); *La Ville de Paris* (1983); *Dans un miroir* (1984); *Voyage autour d'une main* (1984); *L'Eveillé du pont de l'Alma* (1985); *La Présence réelle* (1985); *Mammame* (1986); *Le Professeur Taranne* (1987); *Brise-glace* (1987); *Tous les nuages sont des horloges* (1988); *Allegoria* (1988); *Il Pozzo dei pazzi* (1989); *Hub* (1989); *The Well of Fools* (1989); *Palla y Talla* (1989); *L'Autel de l'amitié* (1989); *Derrière le mur* (1989); *La Novela errante* (1990); *Le Livre de Christophe Colombe* (1990); *Lexot* (1991); *Basta la palabra* (1991); *Visione e meraviglia della religione cristiana* (1992); *Les Solidades* (1992); *Miroirs de Tunisie* (1993); *Capitolo 66* (1993); *Viaggio clandestino - Vite di santi e di peccatori* (1994) ; *La Notte Oscura dell'Inquisitore* (1994); *Promenade* (episode of *À propos de Nice, la suite* (1995); *Wind Water/Feng Shui* (1996); *Le Film à venir* (1996); *Miotte vu par Ruiz* (2001); *Cofralandes : Chilean Rhapsody* (2002); *Médée* (2003).

HENRI STORCK:

History of the Unknown Soldier (1932); *Misère au Borinage* (with Joris Ivens, 1933); *Three Lives and One Rope* (1933); *The Three Masts Mercator* (1935); *Southern Cape* (1935); *Easter Island* (1935); *Cotton* (1935); *A Look at Old Belgium* (1936); *On Summer Roads* (1936); *Houses of Poverty* (1937); *The Earth of Flanders* (1938); *The Boss is Dead* (1938); *Peasant Symphony* (1942-4); *The World of Paul Delvaux* (1944); *Rubens* (1948); *At the Crossroads of Life* (1949); *The Open Window* (1952); *Herman Teiorlinck* (1953); *The Gestures of Silence* (1960); *The Gods of Fire* (1961); *The Happiness to be Loved* (1962); *The Misfortunes of War* (1962); *New Materials* (1964); *Paul Delvaux or the Forbidden Women* (1969-70); *Permeke* (with Patrick Conrad, 1985).

JAN ŠVANKMAJER:

Feature films:

Alice (1987); *Faust* (1994); *Conspirators of Pleasure* (1996); *Little Otik* (2001); Sílení (2005).

Shorts:

The Last Trick of Mr Schwarzwald and Mr Edgar (1964); *J.S. Bach: Fantasy in G minor* (1965); *A Game With Stones* (1965); *Punch and Judy* (*Rakvickárna*)

(1966); *Et Cetera* (1966); *Historia Naturae* (1967); *The Garden* (1968); *The Flat* (1968); *Picnic with Weissmann* (1968); *A Quiet Week in the House* (1969); *The Ossuary* (1970); *Don Juan* (1970); *Jabberwocky* (1971); *Leonardo's Diary* (1972); *Castle of Otranto* (1973-9); *The Fall of the House of Usher* (1980); *Dimensions of Dialogue* (1982); *Down to the Cellar* (1982); *The Pit, the Pendulum And Hope* (1983); *Virile Games* (1988); *Another Kind of Love* (1988); *Meat Love* (1989); *Darkness-Light-Darkness* (1989); *Flora* (1989); *The Death of Stalinism in Bohemia* (1990); *Food* (1992).

ROLAND TOPOR:

La Planète sauvage (René Laloux, 1973); *The Tenant* (Roman Polanski, 1976); *Marquis* (Henri Xhonneux, 1989).

Bibliography

Adorno, Theodor (1974) *Minima Moralia: Reflections from Damaged Life*, translated by E.F.N. Jephcott. London: Verso.

—— (1981) *Prisms*, translated by Samuel and Shierry Weber. Cambridge, Mass: MIT.

—— (1991) *The Culture Industry: Selected Essays on Mass Culture*. London: Routledge.

Afterimage 13 (1987) 'Animating the Fantastic', Special issue on Švankmajer.

Agamben, Giorgio (1998) *Homo Sacer: Sovereign Power and Bare Life*. Stanford: Stanford University Press.

—— (2002) 'Difference and Repetition: On Guy Debord's Films' in Tom McDonough, (ed.) *Guy Debord and the Situationist International* Cambridge, Mass.: MIT Press.

Andrew, Dudley (1995) *Mists of Regret: Culture and Sensibility in Classic French Film* Princeton: Princeton University Press.

Anon. (1970) *Lexique succinct de l'erotisme*. Paris: Eric Losfeld.

Aranda, Francisco J. (1975) *Luis Buñuel: A Critical Biography*, translated by David Robinson. London: Secker & Warburg.

Artaud, Antonin (1972) *Collected Works*, Vol. 3. London: Calder & Boyars.

Bataille, Georges (1986) *Eroticism: Death and Sensuality*, translated by Mary Dalwood. San Francisco: City Lights; London: Marion Boyars.

Baxter, John (1995) *Buñuel*. London: Fourth Estate.

Bellows, Andy Masaki, Marina McDougall and Brigitte Berg (eds) (2000) *Science Is Fiction: The Films of Jean Painlevé*. Cambridge, Mass.: MIT Press.

Benayoun, Robert (1951) 'Détruisez cet enfant' in *L'Âge du cinéma* nos 4/5.

—— (1961) *Le dessin animé après Walt Disney*. Paris: Jean-Jacques Pauvert.

—— (1962) 'Le roi est nu', *Positif*, no. 42. (Translated as 'The King is Naked' in Peter Graham

—— (1968) *The New Wave*. London: Secker & Warburg.

—— (1964a) 'Les Indes a l'attaque!', *Positif*, nos 64/5.

—— (1964b) 'The Phoenix of Animation' in *Film Quarterly* (Spring).

—— (1964c) *Erotique du surréalisme*. Paris: Jean-Jacques Pauvert.

—— (1969) 'Les volets de fer de Boro-Boro', *Positif*, no. 105.

—— (1970a) 'Trois tempéraments à leur parfaite extrémité: *Zabriskie Point, Tristana, The Arrangement*', *Positif*, no. 117.

—— (1970b) 'Les Enfants du Paradigme', *Positif*, no. 122.

—— (1971) 'Un Victorien de l'an 2000', *Positif*, no. 125.

—— (1972) *Bonjour, Monsieur Lewis*. Paris: Losfeld.

—— (1973) 'Dîner en ville avec le commandeur: *Le Charme discret de la bourgeoisie*', *Positif*, no. 146.

—— (1974) 'Un plaisantin de l'innommable', *Positif*, no. 162.

—— (1976) 'Histoire d'un péché' *Positif*, no. 181.

—— (1977) 'Forêt d'indices délicate balance', *Positif*, no. 198.

—— (1980) *Les Marx Brothers*. Paris: Seghers.

—— (1981) *Alain Resnais, arpenteur de l'imaginaire*. Paris: Stock.

—— (1983) *The Look of Buster Keaton*, translated by Russell Conrad. New York: St Martin's Press.

—— (1987) *Woody Allen Beyond Words*. London: Pavilion.

—— (1989) 'Jan Švankmajer et ses paliers: *Alice*', *Positif*, no. 346.

—— (2002) 'The Spiral of the Absolute' in Ciment Michel and Laurence Kardish (eds) *Positif: 50 Years*. New York: The Museum of Modern Art

Benjamin, Walter (1970) *Illuminations*, translated by Harry Zohn. London: Jonathan Cape.

Blakeway, Claire (1990) *Jacques Prévert: Popular French Theatre and Cinema*. London & Toronto: Associated University Presses.

Borde, Raymond (1994) *La Nouvelle vague*. Paris : Première Plan.

Borde, Raymond and Ètienne Chaumeton (2002) *Panorama of the American Film Noir 1941–1953*, translated by Paul Hammond. San Francisco: City Lights.

Borde, Raymond, Freddy Buache and Jean Curtelin (1962) *Nouvelle vague* (privately published).

Breton, André (1965) *Surrealism and Painting*, translated by Simon Watson Taylor. New York: Harper & Row.

—— (1987) *Mad Love*, translated by Mary Ann Caws. Lincoln: University of Nebraska Press.

—— (1988) *Oeuvres complètes* Vol. 1. Paris: Gallimard.

—— (1993) *Conversations: The Autobiography of Surrealism* translated by Mark Polizzotti. New York: Marlow & Company.

—— (1994) *Arcanum 17*, translated by Zack Rogow. Los Angeles: Sun & Moon Press.

—— (1997) *Anthology of Black Humour*, translated by Mark Polizzotti. San Francisco: City Lights.

Brunius, Jacques-Bertrand (1954) *En marge du cinéma français* Paris: Arcanes.

—— (1964) 'Cinema Eye, Cinema Ear', *Sight and Sound*, vol. 33, no. 4.

Buñuel, Luis (1982) *Mon dernier soupir.* Paris: Robert Laffont.

—— (1993) *L'Âge d'or: correspondance Luis Buñuel–Charles de Noailles, lettres et documents (1929–1976)*, edited by Jean-Michel Bouhours and Nathalie Schoeller. Paris: Centre Georges Pompidou.

—— (1995) *An Unspeakable Betrayal: Selected Writings of Luis Buñuel*, translated by Garrett White. Berkeley: California University Press.

Calle-Gruber, Mireille and Pascale Risterucci (2004) *Nelly Kaplan: le verbe et la lumière*. Paris: L'Harmattan.

Cardinal, Roger (1979) 'Metaphysical Cinema', *The Moment*, no. 3, 15 December.

Casaus, Victor 'Las Hurdes: Land Without Bread' in Joan Mellen (ed.), *The World of Luis Buñuel: Essays in Criticism*. Oxford: Oxford University Press.

Christie, Ian (1981) 'Exile and Cunning: Raúl Ruiz', *Afterimage*, no. 10.

Ciment, Michel and Lorenzo Codelli (1989) 'Entretien avec Jan Švankmajer', *Positif*, no. 345.

Ciment, Michel and Laurence Kardish (eds) (2002) *Positif: 50 Years*. New York: The Museum of Modern Art.

Colaux, Denys-Louis (2002) *Nelly Kaplan: Portrait d'une Flibustière.* Paris: Dreamland.

Colina, José de la and Thomas Perez-Turrent (1981) 'Entretien avec Luis Buñuel', *Positif*, no. 238.

Cortazár, Julio (1986) *Around the Day in Eighty Worlds*, translated by Thomas Christensen. San Franciso: North Point Press.

Debord, Guy (1983) *The Society of the Spectacle*. Detroit: Red & Black.

Desnos, Robert (1966) *Cinéma*. Paris: Gallimard.

—— (1992) *Les rayons et les ombres : cinéma*. Paris: Gallimard.

Dryje, František (1998) 'Formative Meetings' in Jan Švankmajer and Eva Švankmajerová, *Animus Anima Animation*. Prague: Slovart Publishers Ltd and Arbor Vitae – Foundation for Literature and Visual Arts.

Durgnat, Raymond (1967) *Luis Buñuel*. London: Studio Vista.

Effenberger, Vratislav (1994) 'Another Sight' in Simeona Hosková and Kveta Otcovská (eds) *Jan Švankmajer: Transmutation of the Senses.* Prague: Edice Detail.

Ehrenstein, David (1986) 'Raul Rúiz at the Holiday Inn', *Film Quarterly*, Fall.

Eisner, Lotte (1973) *The Haunted Screen*. London: Secker & Warburg.

Elsaesser, Thomas (1987) 'Dada/Cinema' in Rudolf E. Kuenzli (ed), *Dada and Surrealist Film*. New York: Willis, Locker & Owens.

—— (2001) 'Six Degrees of *Nosferatu*', *Sight & Sound*, vol. 11, no. 2.

Evans, Peter William and Isabel Santaolalla (eds) (2004) *Luis Buñuel: New Readings*. London: British Film Institute.

Eyles, Allen (1992) *The Complete Films of the Marx Brothers*. Carol Publishing Group.

Fijalkowski, Krzysztof and Michael Richardson (eds) (2001) *Surrealism against the Current: Tracts and Declarations*. London: Pluto Press.

Freud, Sigmund (1984) 'The Pleasure Principle' in *On Metapsychology: The Theory of Psychoanalysis*, translated by James Strachey. Harmondsworth: Penguin.

Giukin, Lenuta (2003) 'Demystification and Webtopia in the Films of Nelly Kaplan', *Cinema Journal*, vol. 42. no. 3.

Gould, Michael (1976) *Surrealism and the Cinema*. London: Tantivy Press.

Green, Malcolm (ed.) (1989) *Black Letters Unleashed*. London: Atlas Press.

Hames, Peter (ed) (1995) *Dark Alchemy: The Films of Jan Švankmajer*. London: Flick Books.

Hammond, Paul (1974) *Marvellous Méliès*. London: Gordon Fraser.

—— (1978a) 'Off at a Tangent', introduction to the first edition of *The Shadow and its Shadow* London: BFI.

—— (1978b) 'Poetic Justice', *Sight & Sound*, vol. 47, no. 3.

—— (1979a) '"Rrose Hobart", or The Wealth of Innuendo', *The Moment*, no. 3, 15 December.

—— (1979b) 'Melmoth in Norman Rockwell Land ... On *The Night of the Hunter,' Sight & Sound*, vol. 48, no. 2.

—— (1985) '*City of Pirates*', *Monthly Film Bulletin*, January.

—— (1997) *L'Âge d'or*. London: BFI.

—— (1999) 'To the Paradise of Pitfalls' in Mercè Ibarz (ed.) *Tierra sin pan. Luis Buñuel y los nuevos caminos de la vanguardia*. Valencia: IVAM.

—— (ed.) (2000) *The Shadow and its Shadow*, 3rd edition. San Francisco: City Lights.

and Román Gubern (2001) 'Buñuel de "l'Union libre" au "Front rouge"', *Positif*, no. 482.

—— (2004) 'Lost and Found: Buñuel, *L'Âge d'Or* and Surrealism' in Peter Evans and Isabel Santaolala (eds) *Luis Buñuel: New Readings*. London: BFI.

Higginbotham, Virginia (1979) *Luis Buñuel*. Boston: Twayne.

Hodgkinson, Anthony W. and Rodney E. Sheratsky (1982) *Humphrey Jennings: More than a Maker of Films*. Hanover, NE: University Press of New England.

Holmlund, Chris (1996) 'The Eyes of Nelly Kaplan', in *Screen*, vol. 37, no. 4.

Hosková, Simeona and Kveta Otcovská (eds) (1994) *Jan Švankmajer: Transmutation of the Senses*. Prague: Edice Detail.

Jackson, Kevin (ed.) (1993) *The Humphrey Jennings Film Reader*. Manchester: Carcanet.

Jennings, Mary-Lou (ed.) (1982) *Humphrey Jennings: Film Maker, Painter, Poet* London: BFI and Riverside Studios.

Jayamanne, Laleen (1995) '*Life is a Dream* – Raúl Ruiz was a Surrealist in Sydney: A Capillary Memory of a Cultural Event' in her *Kiss Me Deadly: Feminism and Cinema for the Moment*. Sydney: Power Publications.

Jodorowsky, Alejandro (1990) '*Santa Sangre*', *Monthly Film Bulletin*, April.

Joubert, Alain (1979) 'The Perpignan Question', *The Moment*, no. 3, 15 December.

—— (1999) 'Le Cinéma des surréalistes' unrealised project for a film programme.

Kaplan, Nelly (1964) 'Au repas des guerrières'. *Positif*, no. 61–3.

—— (1971) *Le Collier de Ptyx*. Paris: Jean-Jacques Pauvert.

Kinder, Marsha (1975) 'The Tyranny of Convention in *The Phantom of Liberty*', *Film Quarterly*, Summer.

Kovacs, Steven (1980) *From Enchantment to Rage: The Story of Surrealist Cinema*. Rutherford, NJ: Fairleigh Dickinson; London: Associated University Presses.

Král, Petr (1979) 'Cinema, Reality and Imagination', *The Moment*, no. 3, 15 December.

—— (1984a) *Le Burlesque ou Morale de la tarte à la crème*. Paris: Stock.

—— (1984b) *Les Burlesques ou Parade de somnabules*. Paris: Stock.

—— (1981a) 'La chair des images', *Positif*, no. 243.

—— (1981b) '*L'Âge d'or* aujourd'hui', *Positif*, no. 247.

—— (1985b) 'Questions to Svankmajer', *Positif*, no. 297.

—— (1985a) *Private Screening*, translated by Paul Hammond. London: Frisson.

—— (2002) 'American Detour: On the Trail of Wim Wenders' in Michel Ciment and Laurence Kardish (eds) *Positif: 50 Years*. New York: The Museum of Modern Art.

Kuenzli, Rudolf E. (ed.) (1987) *Dada and Surrealist Film*. New York: Willis, Locker & Owens.

Kyrou, Ado (1962) *Luis Buñuel*. Paris: Seghers.

—— (1967) *Amour, Érotisme au cinéma*. Paris: Le Terrain Vague.

—— (1985) *Le Surréalisme au cinéma*, 3rd edition. Paris: Le Terrain Vague.

Lacassin, François (1986) *Feuillade*. Paris: Henri Veyrier.

Legrand, Gérard (1969) 'Cité pleine de rêves: *Paris n'existe pas*', *Positif*, no. 105.

—— (1979) *Cinémanie*. Paris: Stock.

—— (1981) 'Le Cinéma et nous', *Positif*, no. 242.

Levin, Thomas Y. (2002) 'Dismantling the Spectacle: The Cinema of Guy Debord' in Tom McDonough (ed.) *Guy Debord and the Situationist International*. Cambridge, Mass.: MIT Press.

Mabille, Pierre (1998) *The Mirror of the Marvellous*, translated by Jody Gladding. Rochester, VT: Inner Traditions.

Masson, Alain (1977) 'Le Plaisir de la confusion', *Positif*, no. 198.

Matthews, J. H. (1971) *Surrealism and Film*. Ann Arbor: University of Michigan Press.

—— (1979) *Surrealism and American Feature Films*. Boston: Twayne.

Mellen, Joan (ed.) (1978) *The World of Luis Buñuel: Essays in Criticism*. Oxford: Oxford University Press.

Michelet, Jules (1966) *La Sorcière*. Paris : Garnier-Flammarion.

Naremore, James (1998) *More than Night: Film Noir and its Contexts*. Berkeley: University of California Press.

Novalis (1979) 'Aphorisms on the Cinema', collected by Roger Cardinal, *The Moment*, no. 3, 15 December.

O'Pray, Michael (1986) 'Jan Švankmajer – Militant Surrealist', *Monthly Film Bulletin*, July.

—— (1989) 'Surrealism, Fantasy and the Grotesque: The Cinema of Jan Švankmajer' in James Donald (ed.) *Fantasy Cinema*, London: BFI.

Pagliano, Jean-Pierre (1987) *Brunius*. Paris: L'Âge d'Homme

Paranagua, Paulo Antonio (1979a) 'Manifesto for a Violent Cinema', *Cultural Correspondence* nos 10/11.

—— (1979b) 'Hommage à Jan Švankmajer, surrealiste tchèque', *Positif*, no. 224.

—— (1981) 'Le Cinéma et nous', *Positif*, no. 246.

Paz, Octavio (1961) *The Labyrinth of Solitude: Life and Thought in Mexico*, translated by Lysander Kemp. New York: Grove Press.

—— (1973) 'The Image' in his *The Bow and the Lyre*, translated by Ruth L. C. Simms. Austin: University of Texas Press.

—— (1986) 'Luis Buñuel: Three Perspectives', in his *On Poets and Others*, translated by Michael Schmidt. New York: Arcade Publishing

—— (1996) *The Double Flame: Essays on Love and Eroticism*, translated by Helen Lane. London: Harvill.

Péret, Benjamin (1992) 'L'œuvre cruelle et révoltée de Luis Buñuel' in his *Oeuvres complètes*, vol. 6. Paris: José Corti.

Peters, Nancy Joyce (1979) 'Nelly Kaplan's *Néa* – Women and Eroticism in Film', in *Cultural Correspondence* , nos 10/11.

Pick, Zuzana M. (1993) *The New Latin American Cinema: A Continental Project*. Austin: University of Texas Press.

Pieyre de Mandiargues, André (1976) 'L'Amour sublime', *Positif*, no. 181.

Prévert, Jacques (1995) *Attention au fakir*. Paris: Gallimard.

Richardson, Michael (ed.) (1993) *The Identity of Things: The Dedalus Book of Surrealism*. Sawtry, Cambridge : Dedalus.

Rimbaud, Arthur (1966) 'A Season in Hell', *Complete Works, Selected Letters*, translated by Wallace Fowlie. Chicago: University of Chicago Press.

Rojo, José Manuel (1997) 'Tim Burton y el mito de la rebelion', *Salamandra*, nos 8/9.

Rosemont, Franklin (ed.) (1979) 'Surrealism and its Popular Accomplices'. Special issue of *Cultural Correspondence* nos 10/11.

Rothman, William (1997) 'Land without Bread' in his *Documentary Film Classics* Cambridge: Cambridge University Press.

Rouch, Jean (2003) *Ciné-Ethnography*, edited and translated by Steven Feld. Minneapolis: Minnesota University Press.

Ruiz, Raúl (1981) 'Object Relations in the Cinema', *Afterimage*, no. 10.

—— (1995) *Poetics of Cinema*. Paris: Éditions Dis Voir.

Ruoff, Jeffrey (1998) 'An Ethnographic Surrealist Film: Luis Buñuel's *Land without Bread*', *Visual Anthropology Review*, vol. 14, no. 1 (Spring/Summer).

Salles Gomez, P. E. (1972) *Jean Vigo*. London : Secker & Warburg.

Short, Robert (2003) *The Age of Gold: Surrealist Cinema*. London: Creation Books.

Sitney, P. Adams (1979) *Visionary Film: the American Avant-Garde 1943-1978*. Oxford: Oxford University Press.

Smith, John M. (1972) *Jean Vigo*. New York: Praeger Publishers Inc.

Sobchack, Vivian (1998) 'Synthetic Vision: The Dialectic Imperative of Luis Buñuel's *Las Hurdes*' in Barry Keith Grant and Jeanette Sloniowski (eds) *Documenting the Documentary: Close Readings of Documentary Film and Video*. Detroit: Wayne State University Press.

Solarik, Bruno (2004) 'The Walking Abyss: Perspectives on Contemporary Czech and Slovak Surrealism' conference paper, 'Platform to Prague: An International Conference on Czech Surrealism, University of Essex.

Stoller Paul (1992) *The Cinematic Griot: The Ethnography of Jean Rouch* Chicago University of Chicago Press.

Storck, Henri (1981) *La court échelle et autres scénarios*. La Louvière: Le Daily-Bul.

Suleiman, Susan (1978) 'Freedom and Necessity: Narrative Structure in *The Phantom of Liberty*', *Quarterly Review of Film Studies*, Summer.

'Surréalisme et Cinéma' (1965) Special issue of *Études Cinématographiques*, nos 41/42.

Švankmajer, Jan and Eva Švankmajerová (1998) *Animus Anima Animation*. Prague: Slovart Publishers Ltd and Arbor Vitae – Foundation for Literature and Visual Arts.

Talens, Jenaro (1993) *The Branded Eye: Buñuel's Un Chien andalou*, translated by Giulia Colaizzi. Minneapolis: University of Minnesota Press.

Tavernier, Bertrand and Jean-Paul Torok (1969) 'Entretien avec Robert Benayoun', *Positif*, no. 105.

Teige, Karel (1972) 'Le nouvel art prolétarien' and 'Photo Cinéma Film', *Change*, no. 10.

Thiber, Alain (1979) *The Cinematic Muse: Critical Studies in the History of French Cinema*. Columbia: University of Missouri Press.

Thirard, Paul Louis (2000) 'Colloque à Pordenone', *Positif*, no. 471.

Thomas, Nicholas (1994) 'Colonial Surrealism: Luis Buñuel's *Las Hurdes*', *Third Text*, no. 26, Spring.

Virmaux, Alain (1976) *Les Surréalistes et le Cinéma*. Paris: Seghers.

Walker, Ian (1978) 'Once Upon a Time ...' *Sight & Sound*, vol. 47, no. 1.

—— (2002) *City Gorged with Dreams: Surrealism and Documentary Photography in Postwar Paris*. Manchester: Manchester University Press.

Walz, Robin (2000) *Pulp Surrealism: Insolent Popular Culture in Early Twentieth-Century Paris*. Berkeley: University of California Press.

Warner, Marina (1993) *L'Atalante*. London: BFI.

Williams, Linda (1981) *Figures of Desire: A Theory and Analysis of Surrealist Film*. Berkeley: University of California Press.

Williams, Linda Ruth (1994) 'An Eye for an Eye', *Sight & Sound*, vol. 4, no. 4.

Wood, Michael (1999) *Belle de Jour*. London: BFI.

General Index

Abe, Kobo, 169
Adorno, Theodor, 9, 15-17, 18, 20-1, 26, 61, 74, 125
Agamben, Giorgio, 37
Age of Gold: Surrealist Cinema (Short), 13
Alain, Marcel, 22
Aldrich, Robert, 73
Allen, Woody, 71
Allende, Salvador, 151
Almodovar, Pedro, 169
Altman, Robert, 73
Anderson, Hans, 59
Andrew, Dudley, 46, 49
Antonioni, Michaelangelo, 168
Aragon, Louis, 30, 33, 36, 47, 52, 77, 171, 174 n. 1
Arbuckle, Fatty, 62
Arcanum 17 (Breton), 141
Arnim, Achim von, 15
Arrabal, Fernando, 11, 135, 137, 143-6, 165
Arsan, Emmanuelle, 98-9
Artaud, Antonin, 8, 11-12, 78, 135
Attenborough, David, 84
Aub, Max, 29
Aurenche, Jean, 29
Aux Orchidées sauvages (1998), 106
Avery, Tex, 97, 128

Baratier, Jacques, 87
Bataille, Georges, 77, 141, 168, 170, 175 n. 1
Batcheff, Pierre, 28
Baudrillard, Jean, 152, 167
Bazin, André, 6, 48, 173 n. 5
Bédouin, Jean-Louis, 87
Beineix, Jean-Jacques, 174 n. 2
Benayoun, Robert, 11, 13, 27, 37, 45, 62, 73, 107, 165-8, 176
Benjamin, Walter, 18, 53, 88
Benoît, Jean 136
Bergerac, Cyrano de, 98
Berry, Jules, 52

Bertolucci, Bernardo, 116-17, 168
Blakeway, Claire, 175, n. 2
Blank, Les, 77, 155 n. 1
Bloody Countess, The (Penrose), 114
Boiffard, Jacques-André, 84
Bonnot gang, 22
Boorman, John, 73
Borde, Raymond, 12, 166
Borgia, Lucrezia, 114
Borowczyk, Walerian, 11, 41, 107-22, 129, 142, 148, 160, 162, 169
Borzage, Frank, 56, 66, 68, 169
Brach, Gérard, 146
Brando, Marlon, 105
Branice, Ligia, 109, 111
Brecht, Bertolt, 70
Bresson, Robert, 6
Breton, André, 1, 4-10, 20, 27, 30-1, 33, 39, 56, 64, 73, 77, 95, 136-7, 141, 143, 156, 160, 165, 171, 174 n. 1, 175 n. 1, 177 n. 2
Breton, Eliza, 137
Browning, Tod, 67-8
Brunelleschi, Filippo, 26
Brunius, Jacques-Bertrand, 45, 47, 77, 166
Buñuel, Luis, 2, 10-11, 26-43, 47, 50, 53, 55, 68, 74-5, 77-83, 86, 88, 93, 103, 121, 126, 142-3, 148-9, 169, 174 n. 1, 176 n. 2
Burton, Tim, 75

Cahun, Claude, 104
Caillois, Roger, 84
Calderón de la Barca, Pédro, 156
Camus, Marcel, 175 n. 3
Cardinal, Roger, 173 n. 1
Carmilla (Le Fanu), 116
Carné, Marcel, 46, 48-9, 175 n. 3
Caro, Marc, 168
Carpenter, John, 72
Carrey, Jim, 97

Carroll, Lewis, 127
Cavalcanti, Alberto, 86
Cavalier, Alain, 168
Cayatte, André, 59
Chaney, Lon, 66
Les Chants de Maldoror (Lautréamont), 68
Chaplin, Charles, 28, 62
Chapot, Jean, 94
Chenier, Clifton, 175 n. 1
Christian-Jaque, 45
Cisse, Souleymané, 170
Clair, René, 11, 175 n. 1
Clouzot, Henri-Georges, 174 n. 2
Cocteau, Jean, 6, 73, 173 n. 3
Collier de Ptyx (Kaplan), 100
Coppola, Francis, 22, 73
Cornell, Joseph, 11, 69–70
Craven, Wes, 72
Crevel, René, 30, 175 n. 1
Croenenberg, David, 173 n. 3
Cuisses de grenouille (Kaplan), 106

Dalí, Salvador, 2, 28, 33, 137
Daumal, René, 140
Debord, Guy, 12
Delannoy, Jean, 45, 59
Delvaux, André, 168
Delvaux, Paul, 168
Depp, Johnny, 105
Deren, Maya, 11
Déshonneur des poètes, Le (Péret), 52
Desnos, Robert, 12, 47, 78
Dieterle, William, 65
Dietrich, Marlene, 66
Disney, Walt, 6
Dryje, František, 122, 126
Ducasse, Isidore, 17, 155
Duchamp, Marcel, 11, 18, 104
Dulac, Germaine, 11
Durgnat, Raymond, 42

Edwards, Blake, 73
Effenberger, Vratislav, 4, 128, 132, 134
Egoyan, Atom, 173 n 3
Einstein, Albert, 103
Elsaesser, Thomas, 12
Eluard, Paul, 30–1, 33, 52, 175 n. 1
En Rade (Huysmans), 95
Erice, Victor, 146, 169
Ernst, Max, 13, 29

Fautrier, Jean, 109
Fellini, Federico, 168
Ferry, Jean, 45, 168, 174 n. 2

Feuillade, Louis, 17, 21–6, 150
Fields, W.C., 48, 62, 67
Figures of Desire (Williams), 13
Flaherty, Robert, 80–1
Fleischer, Max, 97, 128
Fondane, Benjamin, 12, 78
Forshage, Mattias, 43
Fort, Charles, 85
Fourier, Charles, 98, 101, 104
Franju, Georges, 68, 77, 87
Freddie, Wilhelm, 12
Freud, Sigmund, 9, 12, 15, 63
Frey, Sami, 100

Gabin, Jean, 50–1
Gance, Abel, 93–4
Garcia, Jerry, 169
Garnett, Tay, 55, 65
Géricault, Théodore, 36
Gieling, Raymond, 82
Gilliam, Terry, 73
Godard, Jean-Luc, 166, 173 n. 3
Goldfayn, Georges, 12, 45
Goll, Ivan, 84
Gould, Michael, 13
Gracq, Julien, 168
Gréco, Juliette, 45
Grémillon, Jean, 45, 51
Griaule, Marcel, 89
Grierson, John, 86
Griffith, D.W., 6, 25–6, 76
Grimault, Paul, 59
Grimm Bros, 15

Hames, Peter, 121, 124
Hammond, Paul, 7, 28–9, 31, 33–5, 42, 61–2, 64, 68–70, 154, 174 n. 8
Hamon, Geneviève, 176 n. 3
Has, Wojciech, 107, 160, 169
Hathaway, Henry, 64
Hegel, G.W.F., 36, 38–40, 58, 133, 170
Heraclitus, 162, 170
Herriman, George, 17
Herzog, Werner, 168, 175 n. 1
Heusch, Luc de, 77
Hitchcock, Alfred, 70–1, 158
Hooper, Tobe, 72
Hopkins Lightnin', 175 n. 1
Huston, John, 73
Huysmans, Joris Karl, 95
Ils furent une étrange comète (Kaplan), 106

Ivens, Joris, 45, 77

Jarmusch, Jim, 75-6
Jarry, Alfred, 109, 176 n. 1
Jayamanne, Laleen, 177 n. 2
Jennings, Humphrey, 77, 86
Jeunet, Jean-Pierre, 168
Jireš, Jaromil, 121-2
Jodorowsky, Alejandro, 11, 135-43, 145, 149, 161, 165, 177 n. 1-3
Joubert, Alain, 2, 27

Kafka, Franz, 20, 111
Kaplan, Nelly, 11, 93-106, 119-20, 149, 165
Kaufman, Boris, 79
Keaton, Buster, 28, 48, 62
Kiarostami, Abbas, 81
Kieslowski, Krzysztof, 169
Klossowski, Pierre, 152
Král, Petr, 10, 28, 30-2, 62
Kubrick, Stanley, 73
Kuhn, Thomas, 25
Kümel, Harry, 168
Kyrou, Ado, 5-6, 12-13, 18-21, 24, 27, 39, 45, 64-5, 69-70, 72, 89, 93, 165-6, 169

Lane, Lupino, 62
Lang, Fritz, 59, 64
Langdon, Harry, 28, 48, 62
Last Nights of Paris (Soupault), 47
Laughton, Charles, 70-1
Lautréamont, 68
Le Fanu, Sheridan, 116
Lee, Ang, 158
Legendre, Maurice, 80
Legrand, Gérard, 45, 167
Lenica, Jan, 109, 176 n. 1
Lennon, John, 139
Lewin, Albert, 65
Lewis, Jerry, 71
Liberty or Love! (Desnos), 47
Lloyd, Frank, 65
Lloyd, Harold, 62
Lotar, Eli, 78
Lugosi, Bela, 66
Lumière, Louis, 19-20, 77
Lynch, David, 72-3, 75

Mabille, Pierre, 63
Mac Orlan, Pierre, 50
Mad Love (Breton), 64
Madot, Gaston, 29
Magritte, René, 2, 168
Makhmalbaf, Mohsen, 170, 178 n. 1
Makovski, Claude, 94
Malick, Terrence, 73

Manifeste d'un Art Nouveau, Le (Kaplan),
Manifestoes of Surrealism (Breton), 4-5, 9
Mann, Michael, 73
Marceau, Marcel, 155
Mariën, Marcel, 12, 147 n. 7
Marker, Chris, 77, 87-8, 109, 153, 165-6
Marx Brothers, 47-8, 62, 67
Marx, Groucho, 62
Marx, Harpo, 113
Marx, Karl, 5, 22, 141
Masson, André, 94
Mastroianni, Marcello, 153
Mathews, J.H., 12-13, 70
Maurier, George du, 64
McKay, Windsor, 17
Mead, Margaret, 82
Melford, George, 69
Méliès, Georges, 19-21, 23, 77, 126
Mémoires d'une liseuse de draps (Kaplan), 101-2, 106
Meshkini, Marziyeh, 178
Métraux, Alfred, 83
Michelet, Jules, 98
Mists of Regret (Andrew), 46
Miyazaki, Hayao, 59, 170
Mizoguchi, Kenji, 169
Molinier, Pierre, 104
Montand, Yves, 45
Moreau, Gustave, 104
Morgan, Michèle, 51
Morris, Errol, 176 n. 1
Moulet, Luc, 150
Mount Analogue (Daumal) 140
Musidora, 23

Nadja (Breton), 77
Naville, Pierre, 174 n. 3
Neveu, Georges, 175 n. 3
Nezval, Vítezslav, 122
Noailles, Charles de, 29, 33
Noailles, Marie-Laure, 29
Novalis, 1, 173 n. 1

O'Pray, Michael, 123-4
Ophuls, Max, 115
Oshima Nagisa, 116-17, 170
Ovid, 118

Painlevé, Jean, 77, 83-6, 88, 176 n. 3
Paranagua, Paulo de, 8
Parent, Mimi, 114
Paris Peasant (Aragon), 77
Pasolini, Pier Paolo, 116
Paz, Octavio, 9, 27, 64, 83, 174 n. 1

Peckinpah, Sam, 73
Penrose, Valentine, 114
Péret, Benjamin, 27, 52, 87
Pieyre de Mandiargues, André, 101, 107,
  114, 117-19, 168
Piscator, Erwin, 47
Poetics of Cinema (Ruiz), 157-9
Polanski, Roman, 107, 146
Pottier, Richard, 47
Prévert, Jacques, 11, 29, 41, 45-59, 71, 78,
  175 n. 2
Prévert, Pierre, 45-9, 77-8, 84, 148
Proust, Marcel, 151

Quay, The Brothers, 176-7 n. 1
Queneau, Raymond, 97

Ray, Man, 11, 47
Reggiani, Serge, 45
Renoir, Jean, 45, 47-50
Réservoir des sens (Kaplan), 150-1
Resnais, Alain, 26, 77, 87-8, 165-6
Richter, Hans, 11
Rimbaud, Arthur, 5, 15, 64, 97, 154
Ripstein, Arturo, 150
Rivette, Jacques, 167
Rocha, Glauber, 139
Roger, Bernard, 69
Rohmer, Eric, 167
Romero, George, 72
Rosemont, Franklin, 16
Rouch, Jean, 77, 88-90
Rouff, Jeffrey, 80-2
Rousseau, Henri, 21, 103
Roussel, Raymond, 157
Ruiz, Raúl, 11, 149-63, 165, 169, 177 n. 1

Sade, D.A.F., 148
Santiago, Hugo, 149
Saura, Carlos, 168
Schelling, Friedrich von, 108
Schoedsack, Ernest, 103
Schulz, Bruno, 169
Schuster, Jean, 4
Scott, Ridley, 74
Semon, Larry, 62
Shadow and its Shadow, The (Hammond),
  13
Short, Robert, 13
Simon, Michel, 112
Sobchak, Vivian, 80-1
Solarik, Bruno, 3

Sontag, Susan, 178 n. 1
Sorcière, La (Michelet), 98
Soupault, Philippe, 12, 47, 78
Souvestre, Pierre, 22
Stejskal, Martin, 132
Stendhal, 117
Sternberg, Josef, 66-8, 169
Stevenson, Robert Louis, 155
Stoller, Paul, 90
Stoney, George, 82, 176 n. 2
Storck, Henri, 77-80
Sunlight d'Austerlitz, Le (Kaplan), 93
Surrealism and Painting (Breton), 4, 9
Surréalisme au Cinéma, Le (Kyrou),
  5, 6
Švankmajer, Jan, 11, 41, 68, 108, 121-34,
  142, 147-8, 150, 160, 162, 177 n. 1
Švankmajerová, Eva, 122
Swift, Jonathan, 4

Tarantino, Quentin, 158, 167
Tavernier, Bertrand, 168
Taviani brothers, 168
Teshingahara, Hiroshi, 169
Thiber, Alain, 173 n. 3
Thirion, André, 30
Thomas, Nicholas, 81-2
Topor, Roland, 11, 135, 143, 146-8
Torre Nilsson, Leopoldo, 149
Tourneur, Jacques, 130
Tristan, Fredérick, 169
Trouille, Clovis, 96
Tual, Denise, 45
Tual, Roland, 45

Unik, Pierre, 28, 33, 80

Vaché, Jacques, 7
Valentin, Albert, 175 n. 1
Verhoeven, Paul, 73-5
Vertov, Dziga, 79, 89
Vigo, Jean, 45, 77-9, 83, 85, 88
Viot, Jacques, 45-6, 51, 175 n. 3

Walz, Robin, 19
Welles, Orson, 73, 151, 154
Wenders, Wim, 168
Williams, Linda, 7, 13, 30-1, 38-40

Zeromski, Stefan, 114
Zhang Yimou, 158
Zimbacca, Michel, 12, 45, 87, 174 n. 7

Film Index

A la Source, la femme aimée (Kaplan), 94
A Propos de Nice (Vigo), 78-9
ABC Africa (Kiarostami), 81
Abel Gance, Hier et Demain (Kaplan), 93
Abel Gance et son Napoléon (Kaplan), 93
Adam 2 (Lenica), 176 n. 1
Affaire est dans le sac, L' (Prévert), 47-8
Age d'or, L' (Buñuel/Dalí), 7, 28, 33, 35, 38, 42, 47, 57, 64, 114, 137, 155, 174
Ai No Corrida (Oshima), 116, 170
Alice (Švankmajer), 124
Alice in the Cities (Wenders), 168
Amants de Vérone, Les (Cayatte), 56, 59
Anemic Cinema (Duchamp), 11
Années 25, Les (Kaplan), 94
Antonio das Mortes (Rocha), 139
Art of Love, The (Borowczyk), 118
Astronauts, Les (Borowczyk/Marker), 108
Aubervilliers (Lotar), 78
Austerlitz (Gance), 93

Barrabas (Feuillade), 22
Basic Instinct (Verhoeven), 74
Beast, The (Borowczyk), 114, 116-17
Belle (Delvaux), 168
Bergère et le Ramoneur, La (Grimaut), 59
Berkeley Square (Lloyd), 65
Beyond Convent Walls (Borowczyk), 117-18
Birth of a Nation (Griffith), 25
Black Cat, The (Ulmer), 63
Black Orpheus (Camus), 175 n. 3
Blackbird, The (Browning), 67
Bladerunner (Scott), 74
Blanche (Borowczyk), 110-16, 118
Bloko (Kyrou), 12
Blue Velvet (Lynch), 72
Bride of Frankenstein, The (Whale), 63
Burden of Dreams (Blank), 175 n. 1

Ce Jour-là (Ruiz), 159
Céline and Julie Go Boating (Rivette), 167

Chant de styrène (Resnais), 87
Charles et Lucie (Kaplan), 101-3
Chien andalou, Un (Buñuel/Dalí), 2, 7, 9, 28-31, 40, 42, 47-8, 73, 78, 144
City of Pirates (Ruiz), 151, 154-5
Codes (Has), 169
Cofralandes: Chilean Rhapsody (Ruiz), 152
Colloque des chiens (Ruiz), 153-4
Combat d'amour en songe (Ruiz), 157
Comédie de l'innocence (Ruiz), 151
Conspirators of Pleasure (Švankmajer), 125, 134
Coup de Torchon (Tavernier), 168
Crime de Monsieur Lange, Le (Renoir), 47-9, 52, 56-7
Cyclist, The (Makhmalbaf), 170
Cyrano et d'Artagnon (Gance), 93

Daughters of Darkness (Kümel), 168
Day I Became a Woman, The (Meshkini), 178 n. 1
Dead Man (Jarmusch), 75
Dead of Night (Cavalcanti/Deardon/ Hamer), 37
Dessins et Merveilles (Kaplan), 94
Devil Doll, The (Browning), 67
Devil is a Woman, The (Sternberg), 66
Dialogue of Exiles (Ruiz), 152
Diary of a Chambermaid (Buñuel), 41
Dimensions of Dialogue (Švankmajer), 125
Discreet Charm of Bourgeoisie (Buñuel), 37-8, 50
Dishonoured (Sternberg), 66
Doll, The (Has), 169
Double Vie de Véronique, La (Kieslowski), 169
Down by Law (Jarmusch), 75
Down to the Cellar (Švankmajer), 130
Dr Jekyll and Miss Osborne (Borowczyk), 118

Dracula (Browning), 66
Drôle de Drame (Carné), 49

East of Borneo (Melford), 69–70
Easter Island (Storck), 78–9
Edward Scissorhands (Burton), 75
El (Buñuel), 105
El Topo (Jodorowsky), 138–9
Emmanuelle 5 (Borowczyk), 117–18
Empress Yang Kwei-fei, The (Mizoguchi), 169
En Passant par la Lorraine (Franju), 88
Enfants du paradis, Les (Carné), 52–3, 56–7, 71
Eraserhead (Lynch), 72
Et Cetera (Švankmajer), 133
Exterminating Angel, The (Buñuel), 36–7, 50

F for Fake (Welles), 152
Face of Another, The (Teshingahara), 169
Fando and Lis (Jodorowsky), 137–8, 144
Fantômas (Feuillade), 22–3
Farewell to Arms, A (Borzage), 65
Farewells (Has), 169
Faust (Švankmajer), 125, 129, 133
Fiancée du pirate La, (Kaplan), 94–6, 98–100, 103
Flat, The (Švankmajer), 129, 147
Food (Švankmajer), 128
Freaks (Browning), 67

Gabbeh (Makhmalbaf), 170
Garden, The (Švankmajer), 125
Garlic is as Good as Ten Mothers (Blank), 175 n. 1
Gavotte (Borowczyk), 109, 111
Généalogies d'un crime (Ruiz), 151
Ghost Dog (Jarmusch), 75
Godfather, The (Coppola), 22
Goto, Ile d'amour (Borowczyk), 110–12
Great Events and Ordinary People (Ruiz), 152–3
Gustave Moreau (Kaplan), 94

Hiroshima Mon Amour (Resnais), 88, 166
History of the Unknown Solider (Storck), 78
Holy Mountain, The (Jodorowsky), 139–40
Hôtel des invalides (Franju), 88
Hôtel du Nord (Carné), 49
How to be Loved (Has), 169
Hurdes, Las (Buñuel), 28–9, 78–81, 90
Hypothesis of a Stolen Painting (Ruiz), 151

I'll Walk Like a Crazy Horse (Arrabal), 144
Immoral Tales (Borowczyk), 114
Immortal Story (Welles), 154

Jabberwocky (Švankmajer), 130
Jack's Dream (Cornell), 11
Jenny (Carné), 49
Jetée, La (Marker), 153, 166
Jeu des anges (Borowczyk), 109
Jodorowsky Constellation, The (Mouchet), 141
Jour se lève, Le (Carné), 50–2, 57
Judex (Feuillade), 22, 24
Juliette ou la clé des champs (Carné), 175 n. 3

King Kong (Cooper/Schoedsack), 63

Last Tango in Paris (Bertolucci), 116
Last Trick of Mr Schwarzwald and Mr Edgar, The (Švankmajer), 124
Last Year at Marienbad (Resnais), 166
Law of Desire (Almodovar), 169
Leopard Man, The (Tourneur), 130
Letter from an Unknown Woman (Ophuls), 115
Long Pants (Capra), 62
Love Rites (Borowczyk), 119
Lucky Star (Borzage), 29
Lumière d'été (Grémillon), 56

Magirama (Gance), 93
Maître des Forges, Le (Gance), 94
Maîtres fous, Les (Rouch), 88–90
Malombra (Soldati), 69–70
Man of Aran: How the Myth was Made (Stoney), 82
Man who had his Hair Cut Short, The (Delvaux), 168
Manoel's Destinies (Ruiz), 151, 155–6
Marge, La (Borowczyk), 117–18
Marie du port, La (Carné), 59
Marquis (Xhonneux), 146, 148
Mars Attacks! (Burton), 75
Mémoire des apparences (Ruiz), 156
Misère au Borinage (Storck/Ivens), 78
Moi, un noir (Rouch), 90
Monk, The (Kyrou), 13
Moonrise (Borzage), 66
Morocco (Sternberg), 66
Most Dangerous Game, The (Schoedsack/ Pichel), 63, 103
Mulholland Drive (Lynch), 73

Napoleón (Gance), 94
Nazarin (Buñuel), 39
Néa (Kaplan), 98-100
Night of Hunter, The (Laughton), 70-1
North by Northwest (Hitchcock), 71
Notre Dame de Paris (Delannoy), 59
Nouvelle Orangerie, La (Kaplan), 94
Nuit et Brouillard (Resnais), 87

Oiseau de Paradis, L' (Camus), 175 n.3
Oiseau rare, Un (Pottier), 47
Olvidados, Los (Buñuel), 83, 174 n.1
On Top of the Whale (Ruiz), 153-4
Once Upon a Time Cinema (Makhmalbaf), 170
One Way Passage (Garnett), 55, 65
Ossuary, The (Švankmajer), 126-7
Otesánek (Švankmajer), 126

Pandora and the Flying Dutchmen (Lewin), 65
Papa, les petits bateaux (Kaplan), 96-8, 102
Paris n'existe pas (Benayoun), 13
Passenger, The (Antonioni), 168
Peddler, The (Makhmalbaf), 170
Peter Ibbetson (Hathaway), 64-5
Phantom of Liberty, The (Buñuel), 38, 43
Pit, the Pendulum and Hope, The (Švankmajer), 129
Plaisir d'amour (Kaplan), 103-5, 119
Planète sauvage, Le (Laloux), 146-7
Portes de la nuit, Les (Carné), 52-7
Portrait of Jenny (Dieterle), 65

Quai des Brumes (Carné), 50-1

Regard Picasso, Le (Kaplan), 94
Règle du jeu, La (Renoir), 49
Remembrance of Things to Come (Marker), 88
Remorques (Grémillon), 51, 56-7
Renaissance (Borowczyk), 109
Rendezvous at Bray (Delvaux), 168
River, The (Borzage), 66
Robinson Crusoe (Buñuel), 42
Robocop (Verhoeven), 74
Rodolphe Bresdin (Kaplan), 94
Roi et le oiseau, Le (Grimault), 56-7
Rosalie (Borowczyk), 109
Rose Hobart (Cornell), 11, 69-70

Saga of Anatahan, The (Sternberg), 66
Sandglass, The (Has), 169

Sang des bêtes (Franju), 88
Sans Soleil (Marker), 88
Santa Sangre (Jodorowsky), 140
Saragossa Manuscript, The (Has), 169
Scarlet Empress, The (Sternberg), 66
Seashell and Clergyman, The (Dulac), 11
Seine à rencontré Paris, La (Ivens), 78
Sérieux comme le plaisir (Benayoun), 13
Seventh Heaven (Borzage), 66
Shanghai Gesture, The (Sternberg), 53, 66, 68-70
Shattered Image (Ruiz), 151
Si j'étais le patron (Pottier), 47
Sigui (Rouch), 88
Simon of the Desert (Buñuel), 39, 53
Souvenirs de Paris ou Paris-Express (Prévert), 46, 77
Spare Time (Jennings), 86
Spellbound (Hitchcock), 71
Spirit of the Beehive, The (Erice), 146
Starship Troopers (Verhoeven), 74
Statues meurent aussi, Les (Marker/ Resnais), 87-8
Story of Sin, The (Borowczyk), 114-16, 122
Story of the Wind (Ivens), 78
Street Angel (Borzage), 66
Susana (Buñuel), 53
Suspended Vocation The (Ruiz), 152

Tenant, The (Polanski), 146-7
Texas Chain Saw Massacre (Hooper), 72
That Obscure Object of Desire (Buñuel), 40, 103, 105, 116-17
Theatre of Mr and Mrs Kabal, The (Borowczyk), 109
Thérèse (Cavalier), 168
Three Crowns of a Sailor (Ruiz), 154-5
Tih Minh (Feuillade), 22
Time Regained (Ruiz), 151
Total Recall (Verhoeven), 74
Treasure Island (Ruiz), 155, 158
Tres tristes tigres (Ruiz), 151
Tribulations of Balthazar Kober, The (Has), 169
Tristana (Buñuel), 41
Trois vies & une seule mort (Ruiz), 151, 153
Trouble with Harry, The (Hitchcock), 70

Ubu et la Grande Gidouille (Lenica), 176 n.1
Un soir un train (Delvaux), 168
Uneventful Story, An (Has), 169

Unholy Three, The (Browning), 67
Unknown, The (Browning), 67

Valerie and her week of wonders (Jiriš), 122
Vampires, Les (Feuillade), 22, 24-5
Vertigo (Hitchcock), 70-1
Viridiana (Buñuel), 39, 41, 53, 116
Visiteurs du soir, Les (Carné), 52, 54, 56-7
Viva la muerte (Arrabal), 144-6

West of Zanzibar (Browning), 67
What's Buzzin' Buzzard (Avery), 128
White Zombie (Halperin), 63
Witch's Cradle (Deren), 11
Woman of Dunes, The (Teshingahara), 169
Wuthering Heights (Buñuel) 33, 38

Yeelen (Cisse), 170
Yeux sans visage, Les (Franju), 88
You Only Live Once (Lang), 64